JOHN TERRY
CAPTAIN MARVEL
THE BIOGRAPHY

OLIVER
DERBYSHIRE

JOHN BLAKE

Published by John Blake Publishing Ltd,
3 Bramber Court, 2 Bramber Road,
London W14 9PB, England

www.blake.co.uk

First published in paperback in 2007

ISBN: 978 1 84454 364 9

British Library Cataloguing-in-Publication Data:

A catalogue record for this book is available from the British Library.

Design by www.envydesign.co.uk

Printed in the UK by CPI Bookmarque, Croydon, CR0 4TD

1 3 5 7 9 10 8 6 4 2

Papers used by John Blake Publishing are natural, recyclable products made from wood grown
in sustainable forests. The manufacturing processes conform to the environmental regulations
of the country of origin.

Photographs courtesy of Clevamedia, Empics, Rex Features and John Ingledew (prints of John
Ingledew's photographs are available from www.chelseabluesinblackandwhite.com).

Every attempt has been made to contact the relevant copyright-holders, but some were
unobtainable. We would be grateful if the appropriate people could contact us.

CONTENTS

PROLOGUE
WHO?

'I certainly hope we can dominate English football. We have got the squad, a young side that wants to win and do things together. It feels very emotional. I just want to break down and I probably will when I get back to my hotel room on my own, when I sit back and watch it on TV. It will mean an awful lot to my family and friends, but more importantly, it will mean a lot to my players, to the people I train and work with every day and every week. We have made a lot of sacrifices and it's paid off on the pitch.'

After a long, hard season, his team had just won the Premiership. As captain, he was about to have another big trophy to lift after holding aloft the League Cup earlier in the year and, to cap a wonderful season, he had recently been named the Professional Footballers' Association Player of the Year. But who is he?

The answer is simple. He is the rock on which Chelsea

is built: it is his defensive solidity that allows Frank Lampard, Shaun Wright-Phillips, Didier Drogba, Michael Essien, Florent Malouda and Joe Cole to dazzle. He is the foundation for the footballing dynasty which Roman Abramovich and Jose Mourinho are constructing at Stamford Bridge. He is Chelsea through and through.

Known simply to his team-mates as 'JT', he is John Terry.

CHAPTER ONE
BARKING LAD

'I was a United fan, and so were my dad and grandad, so going up there and having my picture taken with all the trophies, and with Alex Ferguson, was just brilliant. They wanted me to sign schoolboy forms on my fourteenth birthday, and I can't fault the way they handled it. There was no pressure at all; they just said the choice was up to me. The fact was that I was so happy at Chelsea at the time that I didn't want to leave. I enjoyed the training here, and the club made me and my family feel welcome and wanted.'

John George Terry made history when he lifted the Premiership trophy in May 2005. As the first Chelsea captain to win the league in fifty years, he claimed his place among the Stamford Bridge legends but it could all have been so different. The Blues weren't the only team looking to recruit the talented teenager and, if he had signed for Manchester United back in 1994, then who knows how things might have turned out.

On 18 December 1980, Ted and Sue Terry celebrated the birth of their second child in Barking. It was another boy to follow the arrival of Paul eighteen months earlier. John forged a close relationship with his big brother as the two lads helped each other on their way to achieving their dreams as professional footballers.

Ted Terry had had trials with West Ham in his youth and, when the young Terrys were growing up, they would watch their father organising his Sunday team from defence and it clearly made a big impression on them.

'I remember watching my Dad as a kid and he was always screaming and shouting,' recalled John recently on Chelsea TV. 'I'd see him come off the pitch and people would say how he never stopped talking, so it was something I learnt from him. He was a leader and a centre-half as well.

'He just played pub football really. He had trials at West Ham but didn't want to follow it up. He is quite small, but everyone said he was renowned for his heading and being dangerous at set-plays just like I am now. That's why people compared us.'

Maybe it was a good comparison when John Terry was growing up but to compare the two now wouldn't be fair on either of them. The elder Mr Terry may not have been as talented a player as his boys but his commitment to their future would certainly be hard to beat.

Working as a forklift operator at a wood yard he would

turn in twelve-hour shifts, unloading boats and loading up lorries to keep food on the table and new boots on his boys' feet. During a typical weekend Ted Terry would get up early in the morning – no lie-in for him after working a sixty-hour week – to make sure John and Paul got to their games. Then he would join all the other proud dads on the touchline watching the boys do what they did best.

Their talent was obvious from an early age and he wasn't going to let anything come between them and their football. And when the opportunity arose for John and Paul to join one of the best boys clubs in the country, they grabbed it with open arms.

John Terry had been playing for a team called Comet when his best friend and team-mate moved to Senrab FC, a name now famous across England for producing Premiership players year after year. Echo League side Senrab has a fine tradition as *the* breeding ground for the South-east's finest players since the club was founded in 1961. The capital's most talented schoolboys have found themselves drawn to the east London club since Chelsea signed Ray Wilkins from Senrab in 1973 and, before John Terry arrived at the club in the early 1990s, Sol Campbell, Lee Bowyer, Muzzy Izzett and Ade Akinbiyi had recently graduated from what may be regarded as the cradle of London's footballing youth.

Crewe Alexandra's long-serving manager Dario Gradi cut his coaching teeth on Wanstead Flats with his charges running out in Senrab colours and Charlton Athletic's Alan Curbishley also had a spell coaching the schoolboys before taking on his higher-profile position as manager at The Valley. The standards of instruction were very high and the players were exceptional. John Terry ran out in the same team as Ledley King, Paul Konchesky, Jlloyd Samuel and Bobby Zamora and this was back in the distant days when Ian Porterfield was the manager of Chelsea.

It is hard to believe that one schoolboy team could produce so many Premiership players: any club in the world would consider themselves exceptionally lucky to produce five top-class players from the same youth team, so what was the Senrab secret? Club secretary Tony Carroll put it down to a combination of top coaching and instilling a professional attitude in the players from a young age.

'Our predecessors set such a high standard that we have to follow on the tradition,' Carroll told BBC Sport. 'Some of our coaches here are top class. Alan Curbishley used to play for Senrab and Dario Gradi was a coach here – those sorts of people leave their mark. All of the staff give their time freely. We get paid by seeing the boys enjoying themselves, improving and, if they join a club, then you know you've done a good job.

'Players also have a code of conduct. We've thrown people out of the club for misbehaving, for causing aggravation at games and in training. But if people want their boys to play football then they come to us.

4

'There are thousands of kids that have got the talent but haven't got the right temperament. You can send a player to a professional club and think he's the best thing since sliced bread but then they send him back two weeks later because his time-keeping is poor and he's not disciplined. The players have to be 100 per cent committed and, if they're not, then they're wasting the club's time.'

The attitude of Terry and King impressed everyone even from a young age, but it was still a special day when the two Senrab boys took to the pitch in the white shirts of England with the Three Lions on their chests many years later. The pair happily recalled those days on Wanstead Flats.

'I used to play Sunday football with him [Ledley King] at Senrab. Even then people would rant and rave about him,' Terry said to a press conference. 'Well, he's in the Premiership now, up against some of the best players in the world and still he looks brilliant. He's two-footed, great in the air, he's quick. Ledley's got everything – he's brilliant to play alongside. He's talkative, helps you out; if the ball goes over you, you know he'll be there to mop up. He's an all-rounder and he's got everything, he really has. He's very modest, a cool, calm customer and a lovely lad off the pitch as well. On the pitch, he's letting his feet do the talking.'

King was just as complimentary when asked about his old team-mate. 'We were just East End lads coming together and making a good team,' said the Tottenham defender to the *Daily Telegraph*. 'I was with Senrab from nine until fourteen and they were good times. I played in the same team as John. He was in midfield and I was centre-half. But when we played together in the England Under-21s, I was in midfield and John was at the back. It's funny to see the way our positions have changed.

'John used to be a midfield player because he wasn't that big in those days. He had a growth spurt and shot up, so now he's an obvious choice for centre-back because he was really good in the air even when he was quite short.'

Unsurprised that his team-mate became a defender, the Tottenham stopper could see a captain in the making right from the start. 'Even then, you could see he had leadership qualities.'

Terry didn't lead the all-conquering Senrab side very often though as one of the other lads had a closer relationship with the gaffer. Terry recalls: 'Paul Nicholls was captain... his dad was coach... but I did get to captain a few times.'

Today he is still in touch with his old skipper. 'He has been my best mate throughout. When we were eleven, we were both playing for Comet and then he went to Senrab and got me to go there as well. We have just stayed together throughout. He was always there for me and he still is now.

'We had a good bunch of lads that made it easier. The standard we had was really good: Ledley King, Paul Konchesky, Jlloyd Samuel, Bobby Zamora and myself. The best was Muzzy Izzett's brother Kemi but Bobby Zamora was getting all the headlines and scoring all the goals.'

It was quite a team and scouts came from far and wide to watch Terry and his young team-mates. Unable to sign schoolboy forms with any club before their fourteenth birthday, the boys had the opportunity to 'try before you buy' from the best clubs around. As well as playing for Senrab, the young prodigies went on trial with teams all across London and occasionally further afield.

As a Barking lad, Terry spent a long time with West Ham and took advantage of the coaching at the 'academy' during the school holidays. But the training became tedious after a while and he had a spell with Arsenal. He even had trials up at Manchester United's famous old training ground, the Cliff.

The young midfielder had impressed Alex Ferguson and, in turn, the Old Trafford supremo tried his best to impress Terry. During one school holiday, Ferguson sent Malcolm Fidgeon, the scout who had spotted Terry, to drive him up to Manchester for a trial. And after he picked up the youngster from his house in Barking, he drove a couple more miles to pick up David Beckham from his parents' home.

'Beckham lived just a few miles away in Leytonstone. I'd met him before when I was playing for Essex,' Terry recalls. 'I was thirteen, David was three or four years older and already in digs in Manchester. He sat in the front with me in the back. We did get to know each other a bit on the journey, although I was quite nervous about the trial and didn't say a lot.'

Once in Manchester, Terry performed brilliantly during the trial and, off the pitch, he even had his photograph taken with Eric Cantona and Ryan Giggs while holding the Premiership trophy for the first, but fortunately not the last, time.

On another occasion, when Manchester United played at Upton Park, Ferguson called on Terry and his parents to join up with the squad at their hotel. As a Manchester United fan from a family of United fans, it was almost too good to be true and Terry remembers it well.

'Like my dad, I was a United fan at the time and had the chance to go up there. United made an effort to sign me, and that was a great experience,' Terry remembered at a press conference. 'They were playing at West Ham one day and invited me and my family to have the pre-match meal with them at the Swallow Hotel in Waltham Abbey. I was sitting at the same table as my heroes Paul Ince and Eric Cantona and had my photograph taken with them. I had beans on toast but I was too scared to eat it in case I dropped it on the floor. It was a great experience – a real dream come true.'

The Manchester United manager has a first-class pedigree when it comes to producing exceptional players from his youth team and Giggs, Beckham, Paul Scholes and the Neville brothers all received similar treatment before joining Salford's finest. However, Terry had already been won over by the boys from the Bridge.

'As a boy, I supported United and people were always saying to me: "You've got to sign for United, the team you support." United were champions at the time, and I went up to the Cliff and trained there in the summer holidays and had my picture done with Cantona, Giggs and all the trophies,' recalls Terry. 'It was a dream come true but when I came here I loved it so much that I decided to sign for the club. While I got on with the players there, I just enjoyed it so much more at Chelsea. I felt it was right as soon as I came here. It's one of those things that will always live with me. They wanted to sign me but I ended up signing for Chelsea.

Terry told the *Daily Telegraph*: 'I just love Chelsea. When I first started coming here, Gwyn Williams [who became assistant manager under Gianluca Vialli and Claudio Ranieri] used to make my family happy and take us out for meals. He was a big influence on why I signed for them.

'My parents couldn't take me to training all the time, and so Gwyn would arrange for someone to pick me up and take me back home. He would also phone to see how I was and little things like that meant a lot.

'If I needed boots, they were on the doorstep the next morning, and they gave me training kit to play in. They might seem silly things but they made all the difference to me. This is a family club and they made me feel so welcome. All the boys I talk to say the same thing. United's interest was a dream come true but when I came here I loved it so much I decided to sign for the club. Being looked after like that was enough for me to choose Chelsea. It upset my dad as a United fan but he could see Chelsea were going places. It was the right decision.'

Signing for the Blues meant Terry had to turn his back on Senrab – who are unable to field players once they have signed schoolboy terms with a professional club – as well as the talented players with whom he had shared his early years. He would soon be seeing them again in the Premiership. Konchesky headed for Charlton Athletic before joining West Ham; King joined Tottenham Hotspur; Samuel joined Aston Villa and Zamora worked his way up the football ladder, joining Tottenham and then West Ham after showing what he could do at Brighton.

Paul Terry found more than just football at Senrab and started seeing Paul Konchesky's sister Sarah, whom he married in June 2001. But even with the backing of a good woman, Paul couldn't emulate his younger brother. The elder of the Terry boys didn't make it straight into the top flight but did break into the team at non-League Dagenham & Redbridge following unsuccessful spells with Charlton and Millwall. After five good seasons with the Daggers, Paul joined Yeovil Town and helped them into League One in 2005.

Senrab's conveyor belt of talent didn't stop after Terry and his mates left though, and Jermain Defoe joined West

Ham from the year below. All of the players still show their loyalty to the old club and Terry, like the other players who have 'made it', has even been back to hand out trophies at the end-of-season presentation to the next generation of Senrab graduates.

CHAPTER TWO
CHELSEA BOY

'At fourteen, I signed a two-year schoolboy form for Chelsea, and then it was a case of would I make it? I was playing in midfield and was really small. I was small and fat, basically. I think Chelsea were umming and aahing about my size, until all of a sudden, with perfect timing, I started shooting up. Then one day in the youth team we were struggling for centre-halves. So I played there and we won 3–0 and I've never looked back.'

John Terry left the dodgy pitches of Wanstead Flats behind and started his quest to find a place in the Chelsea starting XI, but first he needed to find his best position. A midfielder all his life, the teenage Terry had great touch and combined composure on the ball with a fine range of passing plus an ability to read and control a game. Too short to play at the back, he also lacked pace, but that wasn't too big a problem at that age.

One of his early coaches at Chelsea was Mick McGiven.

'He was a central midfield player then with a velvety touch on the ball,' said McGiven in the *Daily Telegraph*. 'You always got a good rhythm to your team from John, although sometimes he would try to force the pace a bit too much. His mobility was often called into question, but you can work on that with a young player.'

For two years, the diminutive Terry combined his schoolwork at Eastbury Comprehensive School in Barking with training and coaching at Chelsea, and it's not too tough to work out which aspects he preferred. 'I wasn't great at school. It was only in the last year that I really knuckled down because my parents had really drummed it into me,' Terry told Chelsea TV. 'I got eight GCSEs but not great grades, and up until then I didn't really concentrate on my work because all I wanted to do was play football.

'I didn't want to do my homework. When I got home from school, I'd be straight over the field with my mates. I was always with the in crowd, maybe it was because of my football that I was with them. But I was always with them walking about. I didn't get into a lot of trouble to be fair.'

Off the pitch, Terry was just one of the crowd but on the other side of the white line he was a natural leader. 'I was captain at school district with Essex and a little bit with the Chelsea youth team as well,' he said. 'All through growing up I have been a leader and a captain really. When I was younger, the role was just all about encouraging on the pitch. I remember watching my dad play as a kid and he was always screaming and shouting. My brother is different. He is quiet on and off the pitch. He tends to just think about his own game.'

Terry was always thinking about the team and the game as a whole, and his constant encouragement to those around him drew obvious comparisons with one of his heroes, Tony Adams. Adams was captain of Arsenal throughout the 1990s and led his side to four league titles, and five cups, including the European Cup Winners' Cup, as well as skippering England and making more appearances at Wembley Stadium than any other player.

Terry said on Chelsea TV: 'I spoke to Tony Adams's dad when I was younger and he came up to me after a game and said: "One day you will be a good leader and a good player." I was about thirteen then, and I remember him grabbing my hand and he's a real big guy. That was where Tony Adams had got it from and my dad had a bit of a powerful presence whenever he went on the field, so I guess that is where I got it from.'

Even as a schoolboy, Terry had presence but a little too much of it was concentrated on his waistline in his early days on the Chelsea books. From the day he signed schoolboy forms with the Blues on his fourteenth birthday, Terry had growing up to do on and off the pitch. He was worried about his stature but the Chelsea coaches were impressed enough with his performances to give him a YTS apprenticeship when he was sixteen. 'I was short and fat when I was younger. When I first signed, I was fourteen and still had a bit of puppy fat,' Terry said. 'I did my two years schoolboys and then in my first year at YTS I just shot up. I got taller and it took me a year to adjust to it. By about eighteen or nineteen, I was fully developed. My mum is tall and I think that's where I get it from.

'The leadership came with growing up and understanding the game a bit more. When I first went full time at YTS, I was learning and training all the time, learning how to organise different things… it took a few years to understand it properly, but then it was there.'

In his first few years at the club, Terry changed both physically and as a player but that was put into the shade by the changes going on at Chelsea. The Blues had a great history of fine players such as Peter Osgood and Charlie Cooke putting the flair, and flared trousers, into the club in the 1960s and 1970s. Looking back on the Chelsea team of that time, it is clear to see that it wasn't just how well they played but how well they dressed and looked that mattered.

With such a carefree attitude, the only way was down until Ken Bates stepped in to rescue the debt-ridden Blues, buying the club for £1 in 1982. He saw them safely out of the old Division Two and, although they slipped down again briefly in 1988, they returned to the top flight at the first time of asking. When Terry agreed to join Chelsea in 1994, they were on the up and up. Dissatisfied with the work of John Hollins, Bobby Campbell, Ian Porterfield and David Webb, Bates decided to hire a big-name manager in 1993 and that man was Glenn Hoddle.

As a player Hoddle was known throughout Europe after his visionary passing from midfield took him from Tottenham to Monaco, and as a player-manager he had guided lowly Swindon Town into the Premiership.

The decision proved fundamental in the progress of the west London club. With millions of pounds of television money pouring into the Premiership and the Blues receiving further investment from Matthew Harding in 1994, the biggest names in world football were now viewing England with interest. Suddenly Chelsea had a manager top players had heard of which made them a very attractive proposition indeed. Besides, who wouldn't want to live in a sophisticated capital city like London?

As Terry worked his way through his apprenticeship in the youth and reserve teams, the stars were pouring in to Stamford Bridge. The summer of 1995 saw Ruud Gullit and Mark Hughes sign from Sampdoria and Manchester United respectively. Gullit was voted European and World Footballer of the Year in 1987, and in 1988 he captained Holland to victory in the European Championships in Germany. Available on a free transfer, the Dutch striker chose Chelsea out of respect for Hoddle.

Hughes was an exceptional leader of the line who made his name at Manchester United and had spells at Barcelona and Bayern Munich before returning to Old Trafford. And even though the champions were willing to let him go, he still had plenty to offer. Terry learned a lot from the experienced striker.

'It was great at the time,' Terry said on the FA website. 'When I first signed and was a young YTS, Hughes was a legend to us and all the YTS boys were fighting for his autograph. I was a Man United fan when I was growing up and he was my hero. So to get a chance to play against him in training and to play with him was fantastic for me.

'Yeah, I got his autograph. He was brilliant. He was a great professional on and off the pitch. He was very good around the dressing room and he was good with the young lads. He always had five minutes if you wanted to talk to him and took time out to do that. I had a couple of battles with him. He used to bully me really. I was only a young lad and fairly small at the time. But I think it helped me playing against players like that, so he helped me along the way really.

'He never gave me any advice verbally, but when we were playing in little games, I learned exactly what I needed to learn. He was one of those players who likes to hold the ball up and, when you play against a great player like that, you need to respect that. You can't always win it and you have to let him have the first touch and wait for your midfielders to come and help. It was little things like that during his few years at Chelsea that I learned off him.'

There's always a lot to learn from great players and they just kept coming at the Bridge. Hoddle was lined up to take over from Terry Venables as England manager after Euro 96, but Gullit slipped seamlessly into Hoddle's shoes and the big names continued to make their way to

Chelsea. Gianluca Vialli, Frank Leboeuf, Roberto Di Matteo and Gianfranco Zola all arrived in 1996 and played a key part in securing some silverware for the Blues as they won the FA Cup in 1997, beating Middlesbrough 2–0.

Players continued to flow in from all around the footballing world as Chelsea developed a cosmopolitan dressing room to match England's cosmopolitan capital. The Uruguayan Gustavo Poyet joined Nigeria's Celestine Babayaro, Norway's Tore Andre Flo, Holland's Ed De Goey, Bernard Lambourde from France and the Channel Islander with the French surname, Graeme Le Saux from Jersey, as Chelsea fans brushed up on their geography in the summer of 1997.

Edging closer and closer to the first-team squad and on his way to a professional contract, Terry needed to find himself an agent but fortunately he didn't have to look too far. 'Aaron has been great for me,' Terry said to Chelsea TV, talking about Aaron Lincoln, his agent. 'I first met him when I was a kit boy and he came in as a kit man. The thing I liked about him was that he was the same with everybody, whereas some people would be different if the manager or someone else was around.

'He would sometimes watch a youth game I was in and would tell me if I was crap, which is the sort of thing you need to hear. At other times, he would do the opposite and tell me if I was good. We are probably best mates.'

Chelsea continued to grow on the pitch and Terry watched on enviously as his older club-mates picked up more silverware in 1998. As the business end of the season approached, Gullit was sacked and replaced by Vialli, ironically his first signing when he arrived at the club less than two years previously. But the managerial upheaval failed to knock the team off course as they won a cup Double, first beating Middlesbrough, again, to win the League Cup at Wembley, and then by defeating VfB Stuttgart 1–0 in the Cup Winners' Cup Final at the Rasunda Stadium in Stockholm.

Terry was getting well used to seeing the players he trained with picking up silverware and, on the eve of the 1998 World Cup, Chelsea signed AC Milan's colossal defender Marcel Desailly, who was to be an integral part of the French team that won football's biggest prize on home turf.

Playing regularly as a centre-back, Terry now found two World Cup-winning defenders blocking his way to the first team at Chelsea. But the young Englishman, still only seventeen, was just excited at the prospect of training alongside such great players. Nicknamed The Rock, a tribute to his muscular and uncompromising approach, Desailly was an immediate hit with Terry.

'When I used to finish training with the youth team, I would go over and watch the first team for an hour,' Terry recalled in the *Daily Telegraph*. 'I was in digs at the time so I never, ever had anything to rush home for. So I would watch Marcel Desailly and Frank Leboeuf, and then go and try the things they were doing. That improved my game. I watched them in the World Cup final and they were both superb. Frank has such quality on the ball and his tackling is brilliant. Marcel's defending is different class. The first couple of times I trained with the first team, I asked Marcel and Frank loads of questions. They were looking at me and thinking: "Little kid, give it a rest."

'But it paid off. They would spend ten minutes with me, advising me on how to position myself when the attacker came in. They told me always to stay on my feet as long as possible, always to watch the ball rather than the attacker's legs. To learn off two World Cup-winners is brilliant.'

Terry was coming along splendidly and his attitude was first class. He was always looking to learn, to pick up any little thing that would help to improve him as a player. 'I used to go and watch all of the first team if we finished training before them,' he said. 'I used to watch how they would go in the gym and do exercises. I learned how careful they are about what they eat and how they look after their bodies.'

His work ethic and natural ability quickly got him noticed by the new manager. Vialli hadn't seen much of Terry in action, as Gullit liked to keep the first team separate from the youth team and the reserves. But with the Italian in charge, things changed. 'Vialli had a lot of time for me,' Terry said in the *Sunday Times*. 'If the first team weren't working, he'd come and watch the youth team training. He'd stand there and afterwards he'd come over and say a few things. He always made a point of saying hello to the young lads and spending a bit of time with us, which was great for a young player.'

The previous manager had been rather aloof and the youth team welcomed the change in management. 'I didn't enjoy it under Ruud. He was distant towards the young lads. You'd say hello and he would just ignore you. The young players didn't respect him, as he was only interested in the first team,' Terry said in the *Daily Star*. 'He didn't bother with the young lads, and a few of us didn't like that. When Luca took over, it was totally different. He was brilliant from the word go. He'd say hello and have a laugh. He knew all our names and that meant a lot to us.'

The first time Terry trained with the big boys he made a memorable impression on his new boss – clattering the shaven-headed striker to the ground with all the enthusiasm of youth. Under many managers such actions may have brought a punishment, but Vialli was more impressed than anything: here was a player with no fear, no respect for reputation.

'The other lads said: "You can't do that,"' Terry remembers. 'But he came over and shook my hand and said: "That's what I want to see," and that, no matter who a player is, they are to be kicked on a match day. But that's just the way I am: if a tackle is there to be made I'll make it.'

Terry continued to train with the first team and turn in solid performances for the reserves. It was only a matter of time before his chance came. 'I was training with the first team as a centre-back when Luca said he was short of a right-back, and asked if I would play there. He told me: "Go and do the best you can. Just enjoy it." I played a couple of games at right-back, but my preferred position is centre-half.'

It wasn't in his favourite position but Terry finally got his chance to pull on the blue shirt of Chelsea on Wednesday, 28 October 1998. Playing against Aston Villa in the third round of the League Cup at Stamford Bridge Terry received a mixed reception.

The crowd all roared their approval when they saw that a young Englishman was about to make his debut in his now famous number 26 shirt. The hardcore fans had heard speculation that the reserve team captain had real ability and they were looking forward to seeing him for themselves, but one of his team-mates wasn't so happy. Terry came on after 86 minutes for Dan Petrescu, and the Romanian full-back was in a full-on strop.

Having joined Chelsea from Sheffield Wednesday in November 1995, Petrescu spent two-and-a-half years as the first-choice right-back and hadn't enjoyed the transition to the substitutes' bench, so he was a little frustrated at being replaced in what was a rare start. So upset, in fact, that he refused to shake hands with his replacement, normally a common courtesy among players, and then he slapped away the water bottle that was offered his way, before throwing down his track-suit top and kicking the dugout.

This was little more than a passing irritation for Terry though as he strode out across the Stamford Bridge turf to officially become a Chelsea player. He had played alongside a number of the other men wearing the blue shirt that day, since Vialli was using the League Cup as an opportunity to give game time to the less frequently played members of his squad. As such Terry, at right-back, completed a back four with Bernard Lambourde, Michael Duberry and Celestine Babayaro, who all lined up in front of Ed De Goey's Russian understudy, Dmitri Kharine.

The game became safe in the 85th minute after Vialli completed his hat-trick, making it 4–1 and sending the Premiership leaders on their way to a first defeat in sixteen matches. But there was still life left in the game as Dennis Wise was sent off for a rash two-footed lunge on Villa's Darren Byfield. Terry kept his cool in the ensuing fracas, and stayed clear when Vialli got involved in an argument with the Villa bench.

Everybody was pleased to hear the final whistle after such a fraught end to proceedings, especially Petrescu who had calmed down and sought out the teenage debutant to make an apology for his display of petulance. The Romanian said in the *Daily Mail*: 'Straight away after the game I did say sorry to the kid because it was his first game. I regret what I did for the fans and for John Terry – I was waiting a long time just to play one game. I thought it was a good performance and I didn't deserve to be substituted.'

The press welcomed Terry's debut as a sign that, despite

all the big-name, big-money signings at the Bridge, the Chelsea youth team was still producing. The assembled media were amazed that he was one of six home-grown players involved in the match against Villa: Duberry was an established first-team player, midfielders Mark Nicholls and Jody Morris made their first starts of the season, and the versatile duo Neil Clement and Jon Harley came off the bench for their first action of 1998/99.

The backroom staff were understandably delighted to see youth given a chance. Coach Graham Rix said in the *Guardian*: 'The young lads who came on did exceptionally well and it was a good chance for them to show what they are made of. They don't get many chances for first-team football and it was a credit to the club that we could field five good young home-grown players.'

But the media were obsessed with writing off the future of Terry and his fellow youth-team products, pointing to the examples of Nick Crittenden loaned to Plymouth, Danny Granville signed from Cambridge but then sold on to Leeds, and Muzzy Izzett at Leicester City, who had been joined by Frank Sinclair at Filbert Street. Another product of Chelsea's youth set-up, Sinclair said in the *Guardian*: 'It is difficult for home-grown players at Chelsea because the squad is so big – there are sixteen or seventeen internationals. It is especially difficult for the youngsters because they are going to be the last to be looked at. There is a lot of good young talent at Chelsea but I wouldn't be surprised if people move on.'

Having just made his first appearance for the Blues, people were already talking of when John Terry would move on. With Desailly, Leboeuf, Lambourde and Duberry ahead of him in the pecking order, what hope was there for a youth-team centre-back?

Ken Bates insisted that having world-class internationals helped to attract and improve the youngsters, not drive them away. 'We are totally committed to our youth policy,' the chairman stressed to the *Guardian*. 'Young kids want to come here because of the quality of our senior professionals. Look at how much they learn. And they are also able to see how a good professional should work.

'Given a choice between a Gascoigne or a Zola, who would a talented youngster rather be around? The only way a youngster improves is by being around players who are professional both on and off the pitch.'

Terry was learning but, still only seventeen, he was far from the finished article. Vialli kept him involved with the squad, and he was on the bench as Pierluigi Casiraghi's career came to a sickening end at Upton Park. The £5.4m Italian striker suffered catastrophic damage to his knee ligaments in a collision with Rio Ferdinand and Shaka Hislop of West Ham.

He was on the bench again the day after his eighteenth birthday, as Chelsea went to the top of the league for the first time since November 1989. A 2–0 win over Tottenham at Stamford Bridge, with late goals from Gustavo Poyet and Tore Andre Flo, put the Blues on top after a nine-year absence: Terry was part of a squad with genuine title aspirations.

Vialli gave Terry another chance against Southampton, bringing him on in central midfield for the last 20 minutes of a 2–0 win. In a Boxing Day fixture at the Dell, the young Brit got his Christmas wish when he replaced the injured Poyet alongside Morris in the middle of the park. The three points re-established Chelsea at the top of the league and Graham Rix was sure of the reasons for the good form.

'We have come to places like this in years gone by and struggled,' the coach said to assembled media after the game. 'Today, we more or less controlled it. World Cup-winner Leboeuf or seventeen-year-old boy Terry, they're all pulling in the same direction.' He may have got the age wrong but Rix was right when he talked about the unity in the squad, and Terry was just happy to be involved. He stepped up his involvement a week later as he made his first start in the FA Cup clash at Boundary Park fresh into the New Year.

Playing Oldham in the third round, Terry showed further versatility following his midfield cameo by completing 90 minutes at right-back. Vialli struck two more Cup goals to ensure a 2–0 win, but the game was overshadowed by an Oldham fan launching a hot dog at referee Paul Durkin, who was hit but fortunately not injured.

Up against a Division Two side in a typical cup-tie, Terry

was as composed as ever and did a fine job in what was a pretty scrappy affair. 'We didn't play at our best but we did a difficult job well,' Vialli said. 'Oldham did very well and battled and fought for everything. They made us work very hard, but in the end we deserved to win. We know what the FA Cup is about, it's about spirit.'

That spirit was evident as the Blues held on to top spot with a couple of hard-fought wins over Newcastle, then managed by Ruud Gullit, and Coventry City before the next round of the FA Cup. After seeing his worth against Oldham, Vialli selected Terry at right-back again in the fourth-round match at Oxford United's Manor Ground.

Sitting pretty at the top of the Premiership and unbeaten in the league since an opening-day defeat to Coventry, Chelsea were undisputed favourites against an Oxford side struggling against relegation from the First Division. Perhaps the Blues were starting to believe their own hype, but whatever the reason for their complacency, they were very fortunate to head back down the M40 still in the Cup after salvaging a draw with a controversial injury-time penalty.

Following this lucky escape, the manager recalled some more experienced heads for a Premiership game at Highbury, so Terry was again confined to the bench as Arsenal ended Chelsea's twenty-one game unbeaten streak in the league. He was then named among the substitutes the following Wednesday as Oxford came to west London.

The Blues fought back from a goal down to go 4–1

ahead, two goals coming from another young player given a chance by Vialli. Mikael Forssell had only recently been signed from HJK Helsinki and was just seventeen, but the Finn had put the result beyond doubt and the gaffer decided it was time to give Terry a chance to play in his preferred position. After 59 minutes Leboeuf made way and Terry played the final half an hour alongside Desailly at the heart of the Blues defence. The match finished 4–2 but there was little the young centre-back could have done about the goal, as Wise foolishly handled in the area and Dean Windass converted the resulting penalty.

Despite another commendable display from the bench, first-team action was sparse for the remainder of the season and, barring a couple of appearances, Terry had to make do with games in the reserves and occasionally the youth team, as the first-choice defenders returned from injury and suspension. He was often handed the captain's armband and was happy to play for either side. 'I didn't play much for the youth team,' he said. 'Even though I was still young enough, I was mostly in the reserves and on the fringes of the first team.'

Before the season was out, Terry did get his first taste of European action as he started another game at full-back, this time against Valerenga. Defending the European Cup Winners' Cup, Chelsea travelled to Oslo with a 3–0 lead from a comfortable first leg and soon destroyed any faint hopes of revival the Norwegians may have been harbouring, scoring twice in the opening quarter of an hour.

Terry made the first goal for his manager, as he whipped a low cross to the far post, which Vialli lashed into the roof of the net at the second attempt. The Blues were in control throughout a game which ended 3–2 to the visitors, despite the home side's valiant attempts to rescue an equaliser right up until the final whistle.

Real Mallorca proved too good in the semi-finals, and Chelsea added their names to the many sides that never successfully retained Europe's third competition. Manchester United had beaten Vialli's side 2–0 in an FA Cup quarter-final replay; Wimbledon had stopped the Blues in the League Cup and both Arsenal and United had raced ahead in the Premiership. A season which had promised so much drew to a close with only the European Super Cup as testament to the supremely talented squad assembled in SW6.

Assured of third place in the league, Vialli rotated his squad for the last game of the season and Terry appeared as a substitute when Chelsea finished the campaign with a 2–1 win over Derby County. He replaced Duberry after 57 minutes and played the last half hour alongside Lambourde. After a long season on the edge of the first team, it was Vialli's way of thanking the youngster for all his hard work, and a tribute to his professionalism.

There was more reward for Terry, though, when he was named as Chelsea's Young Player of the Year. An award from the fans, they recognised the huge potential in the young stopper and, despite only three first-team starts and four substitute appearances in a season of fifty-six matches, the Stamford Bridge faithful liked what they saw.

Speaking after the Derby game about his first full term in charge, Vialli said: 'It was the best way to finish the season. We got three points even though we knew there was nothing on the game. We showed good professionalism and enthusiasm and we made our supporters happy.'

The fans were happy with the team. Chelsea finished third with 75 points, eight points ahead of Leeds but more importantly three points behind Arsenal and four behind Manchester United. It was the Blues' highest league finish since 1977 and secured them a place in the Champions League qualifying round, as well as the promise of riches associated with mixing with Europe's big boys. Beyond that, it was a definite improvement on the 63 points picked up in 1997/98.

'We have improved a lot. We've improved our consistency since last season and also our determination,' Vialli continued. 'My main concern now is to become a better manager. If this means I've got to hang up my boots, it's something quite sad, but that's what will happen.'

So Stamford Bridge waved goodbye to Vialli as a player, but the season had seen the arrival of a young player who would prove to be very important to Chelsea's future.

CHAPTER THREE
LOAN STAR

'Obviously it was a bit worrying when the club kept going out and buying players, but at the time I wasn't really expecting to be ready for the first team until I was twenty-two,' Terry said in the *Sunday Times*. 'Maybe if I hadn't got into the first team by then I'd have looked elsewhere, but until I was twenty-one or twenty-two I was prepared to be patient.'

Chelsea have much to thank John Terry for, not least his patience. After proving himself a more than capable deputy in his few appearances the season before, the 1999/2000 campaign provided only baby steps forward for a man already showing maturity far beyond his tender years.

On his way to winning the award as Chelsea's Young Player of the Year, Terry made a handful of first-team starts as well as a few appearances from the bench; he played in every competition Chelsea were involved in and he never let anyone down. With a solid foundation in place, his career was now ready to develop. But blocking his way to the first team was the French triumvirate of Desailly, Leboeuf and Lambourde. Now this fearsome threesome was to be supplemented by a Dane.

The summer of 1999 was another busy one for Chelsea in the transfer market, with mixed results for Terry. The good news was that Michael Duberry had been sold to Leeds United for £4.5m; the bad news was that Vialli had signed another centre-back, Jes Hogh from Fenerbahce. Unhappy at playing understudy to the French World Cup-winning duo, Duberry, twenty-four, had moved to pastures new, and Chelsea had received a good price. The signing of Hogh, thirty-three, placed a fresh cloud on Terry's horizon but the obvious silver lining was the age of his new team-mate.

Vialli had faith in Terry, but as a young manager in a high-profile job he needed experienced performers with an impending campaign in club football's premier competition – the Champions League – and, as a veteran of more than forty internationals available for £333,000, Hogh was a perfect short-term signing.

Whoever played in the Chelsea defence would have been happy to see the signing of another World Cup-winning Frenchman, Didier Deschamps. The man once cruelly described by Eric Cantona as a 'water carrier' provided exceptional cover for those lucky enough to play behind him, and as a two-time European Cup winner and captain of France he brought valuable experience to his new club.

The other new recruits were a younger bunch as Mario Melchiot, Chris Sutton, Carlo Cudicini and Gabriele Ambrosetti all made their way to the Bridge. The signings of Sutton, £10m from Blackburn Rovers, and Ambrosetti, £3.5m from Vicenza, made all the headlines, but Melchiot, a free from Ajax Amsterdam, and Cudicini proved much better business in the long run. The Italian goalkeeper was signed initially on loan from Castel Di Sangro but Chelsea later forked out the bargain-basement fee of £160,000 to make the move permanent.

Chelsea went through their pre-season friendlies unbeaten with their new improved squad, and Terry was involved in most of the games until he picked up an injury, which put him out of action for the whole of August. Other members of the Blues squad enjoyed much better fortunes though as they carried their good form into the season and opened with an impressive demolition of Sunderland at Stamford Bridge. The Black Cats received a rude awakening to life in the Premiership as they were comprehensively beaten 4–0.

Everything was rosy for the Blues that month as they successfully overcame Skonto Riga in the Champions League third qualifying round and were placed in Group H with Hertha Berlin, Galatasaray and AC Milan. In September a couple of away defeats against Watford and Hertha Berlin again revealed the inconsistency that had so often proved their undoing in the past. But that was nothing compared to October.

The month started brilliantly. Chelsea destroyed Manchester United at the Bridge, scoring five unanswered goals in a game that will live long in the memory of all those lucky enough to be there. But then the season fell apart as the squad began to show two distinctly different faces.

After the slaughter of Fergie's lambs in SW6, the next visitors were some Division One Terriers. Just days after signing a new four-year contract at Chelsea, Terry made his first appearance of the season as Vialli continued his policy of resting his top players in the League Cup. The manager even went so far as to make ten changes from the team that had beaten United 5–0.

Huddersfield Town were deserved 1–0 winners courtesy of Kenny Irons' long-distance strike thirteen minutes from time, the first goal the Blues had conceded at home in any competition that season. But Vialli refused to accept that he had underestimated his opposition – Steve Bruce's side had led Division One until the previous weekend – insisting: 'We had five or six internationals playing. All the players are good enough to be in our squad otherwise they wouldn't be here.'

But the Blues weren't good enough to win the game, and they were out of the League Cup – the one competition in which Terry was sure to be picked. Things got even worse for Chelsea as they lost a second league game, 1–0 against Liverpool at Anfield, and although the players lifted themselves for a 5–0 win against Galatasaray in Istanbul that just made the results either side of it look worse.

After returning from Turkey, Chelsea faced Arsenal at Stamford Bridge. Everything was going smoothly and the season appeared to be back on track as goals from Tore Andre Flo and Dan Petrescu had put the Blues 2–0 up after 52 minutes. The game looked safe. Arsenal's Kanu then turned the game on its head in the final quarter of an hour with a performance he has never looked like producing since. The Nigerian striker scored a fifteen-minute hat-trick of incredible skill to win the game for the Gunners.

It wasn't just three points that Chelsea lost that day, the confidence went from the whole squad as they picked up just five points from the next six games. Even more incredibly, the players continued to deliver in Europe, where the cosmopolitan veterans helped them to the top of Group H and into the second group stage.

It was obvious to all and sundry that Chelsea's big-money imports could continue to perform effortlessly on the European stage simply because they were European. But in the blood and thunder of the Premiership you need more than just skill to survive – you need a certain combative quality, the British 'bulldog spirit' that the tabloids harp on about. And against Sunderland Vialli finally realised this. Unfortunately for Chelsea it took a 4–1 defeat at the Stadium of Light to bring about his epiphany but some lessons are better learned the hard way.

'In many ways, playing in the Champions League is much easier for us. And in Europe my players have never let me down,' Vialli said at a press conference. 'But when you believe that mentally, physically and tactically you are prepared to come to a place like this, and then something goes wrong, it makes you think. What I have discovered now is that ability alone in the Premiership is not enough. You need a better spirit for the Premiership, better organisation and I am the one who has to learn this and to teach it to my players.'

Against Sunderland, Terry brought some of the 'bulldog spirit' back to the Blues in the second half as Desailly made way for him due to a thigh injury. Having conceded four without reply in the first 45 minutes, the young Brit took some solace in defeat after keeping the Wearsiders out on his watch. And he came off the bench again the following Saturday in what proved a much easier match. Terry replaced Hogh after an hour as Chelsea proved they had fire in their bellies, beating Hull City 6–1 at Boothferry Park. The manager was delighted to prove his doubters wrong.

'People think we are soft, but we are not soft,' said Vialli. 'We were expecting an enthusiastic and strong team in Hull. They gave everything they had. Unfortunately for them, we were in the right frame of mind. We knew we were a better team than them, but we had to prove it on the pitch.

'We showed we have learned a lesson. It's been a hard

one, but we have time to get better and improve. It is up to me to put it right. We want to be successful and now we need to get into the position we should be in the Premiership. Against Hull, we showed we have the desire to do that.'

Chelsea's Premiership aspirations took another dent the following weekend as Leeds maintained their top spot with a 2–0 win in west London. This was further complicated by injuries to Desailly, shoulder, and Hogh, torn hamstring, along with a red card shown to Leboeuf for fouling Harry Kewell.

With three centre-backs out of action, things seemed to be looking up for Terry as Santa came riding into town. But rather than bringing more time on the pitch for the Englishman, St Nick brought Vialli a present in the form of a new defender.

Emerson Thome joined Chelsea for £2.7m from Sheffield Wednesday and the Brazilian made his debut on Boxing Day as Chelsea made more history. Against Southampton at the Dell, Terry watched from the substitutes' bench as Chelsea fielded the first-ever all-foreign starting XI in English football: De Goey; Ferrer, Thome, Leboeuf, Babayaro; Petrescu, Deschamps, Di Matteo, Poyet, Ambrosetti; Flo. But far more important for Chelsea were the three points picked up away from home, the first away win in the league for three months.

Terry was joined on the bench by three other young English players – Jon Harley, Jody Morris and Mark

Nicholls – and, after the game, all the talk was of the nationality of the players and the seemingly inevitable death of English football. But Vialli was unapologetic.

'Nationality is not important,' he said. 'I've never really thought about it. We are an English side of English and foreign players. We had four home-grown players on the bench in Jon Harley, Mark Nicholls, Jody Morris and John Terry. We're not just full of foreign superstars; we have a lot of British talent coming through here. As long as we talk the same language on the pitch, that's all that matters.'

Even with the signing of Thome, Chelsea were still short of players at the back and, at Valley Parade on Saturday, 8 January 2000, John Terry made his full Premiership debut. Starting for the first time in the league, Terry didn't enjoy a great beginning as Bradford City went 1–0 up inside a minute. But he came close to his first Chelsea goal two minutes later as he shinned a Wise corner against the bar.

Matthew Clarke was in inspired form in the Bradford goal, and he made countless fine saves as Chelsea continued to carve out chances. The pick of them was a remarkable stop at full stretch when Terry met a Wise free-kick with a firm header. But there was no debut goal for Terry and it took a cool finish from Dan Petrescu to beat the seemingly superhuman Bantams keeper.

Despite such heavy one-way traffic, the match finished 1–1 and everybody was amazed by the performance of Clarke. 'After a while I didn't think we were going to score; it looked like it was going to be one of those days,'

Terry said. 'It was a crazy game, although the first goal was down to some rubbish defending.'

His manager refused to criticise anyone though. 'I can't complain about the effort our lads made. We didn't have the luck we deserved,' Vialli said. 'Watching something like that was difficult to take. But that's football.

'It's the first time in my career I've seen anything like that. But when it's not your day there is nothing you can do about it. I thought their goalkeeper was outstanding. He stopped everything we threw at him.'

It seemed the Bradford keeper had also put an end to Chelsea's fading title aspirations. As Vialli added: 'The gap is now too big for us to think about winning the title. We are too far behind the leaders. We will still play every game like a Cup Final and try to pick up three points and see what happens at the end of the season. But, realistically, the gap is too big for us to think about the title.'

With Chelsea seventh in the table, a massive twelve points behind Leeds, things looked black for the Blues but one man who refused to discount them was Andy Myers. 'Chelsea are different class, a world-class unit, it would be foolish to write them off,' said the former Chelsea defender. 'There's still more than four months to go and you never know what's going to happen. People say their minds are on other things like the Champions League but Luca will want a domestic title, I know.'

The Bradford full-back had left Chelsea the previous summer to pursue first-team football and was sure he'd made the right decision. 'I've no regrets about leaving, I'm just pleased to see players such as John Terry get their chance,' Myers continued. 'They have a good youth set-up at Chelsea now and he will do well.'

With Desailly out injured, Terry had another chance four days later as Chelsea entertained Tottenham in the Premiership. A win was a must after two away draws, and the Blues took all three points at the Bridge thanks to a fine debut from George Weah. The Liberian former World, European and African Footballer of the Year had signed from AC Milan only days before, and he came off the bench to score the only goal of the game three minutes from time.

The press again jumped on Vialli's preference for signing a big name in an emergency rather than trusting in his reserves. 'I suppose that all the young players have realised it's going to be difficult to break through,' the manager said, 'but the younger players can learn from George, enjoy watching him in training and try to nick some secrets.'

So Terry had another fine teacher to help his game improve, but he was already showing considerable ability whenever called upon. He again belied his years with a composed and mature performance, as he helped his side to a win and a clean sheet in a fierce London derby, as the Blues beat Tottenham 1–0, but he was left out for the next game as Vialli again shuffled his pack. Terry missed the dour 1–1 draw with Leicester but returned to the starting XI for the visit of Nottingham Forest in the FA Cup.

In his programme notes for the fourth-round cup-tie, Ken Bates described the game against the Foxes as 'the worst display I've seen from a Chelsea team for many a year', before pointing an accusing finger at his big-money squad. 'I don't blame Vialli. There is a lesson here for our star-studded international team. It doesn't matter how much talent a player has if he doesn't use it.'

With that tirade to motivate them, the players dared not lose and put in a decent performance against the Division One strugglers to win 2–0. Goals from Leboeuf and Wise secured victory for Vialli against his old Juventus team-mate David Platt, and in spite of Forest keeper Dave Beasant's impressive return to Stamford Bridge.

Terry's first-team appearances were confined to the FA Cup as Thome was cup-tied after playing in the competition for Sheffield Wednesday earlier in the season, and this gave the manager an opportunity to blood the youngster, which he took pleasure in. 'It's good to be able to introduce some youngsters,' Vialli said, 'not just to the squad but to the team itself.'

Against Leicester City in the fifth round Terry slipped into the team at half-time, as Chelsea battled their way into the quarter-finals at the expense of Martin O'Neill's combative side. Terry again came close to scoring, but his header cannoned off the bar from another Wise corner. Perhaps most notable was the way he dealt with the physical presence of Emile Heskey and Matt Elliott, playing up front. Oliver Holt was moved to write in *The*

43

Times, 'John Terry, a home-grown rarity, looked assured beyond his years at centre-half.'

Vialli was impressed by the way all of his players stood up to the challenge. 'It was physical but I think that's the way you like it in England,' the Italian said. 'We wanted to make sure if it was a battle we were going to win it and if it was a good football match we would win it as well. Sometimes we try to be too pretty and then the opposition take advantage of that. That was not the case today.'

Chelsea were showing no signs of weakness in the FA Cup and, in the quarter-final, they made quick work of Gillingham, winning comfortably 5–0. The second came from the head of Terry as he registered his first senior Chelsea goal.

Having come close to scoring a couple of times in the previous rounds of the Cup, it was a great moment for the young defender as he met Gianfranco Zola's corner forcefully from six yards out and powered the ball past Vince Bartram, the man between the sticks for the visitors.

The goal was well taken and thoroughly deserved but it was all too much for one of the men inside Stamford Bridge that Sunday afternoon: Ted Terry sat weeping tears of joy. 'My parents try to go to every game when they are not working. My mum wasn't at the game against Gillingham but my dad was. He told me he was in tears when I scored,' the younger Terry said in the *Evening Standard*. 'He was so proud that he started crying in the East Upper stand when everyone was celebrating. My mum cried too when I spoke to her on the phone later. My dad is not an emotional guy and I was quite surprised when he told me. His mate, who was there with him, said he'd never seen my dad cry until then.

'I want to prove they don't need to buy another big-name centre-half,' he went on, outlining his aims. 'When I signed my contract last summer, they said I was part of the future of the club, and so I had no hesitation in deciding to stay.'

But some of Chelsea's youth products did feel the need for a change of scenery. Mark Nicholls' patience had grown thin and, three years older than Terry, he felt the need to go out on loan to Reading to get more competitive game time. 'I basically hit a brick wall at Chelsea and wasn't progressing as a player,' confessed the twenty-two year-old striker in the *Daily Mail*. 'It was great to be around so many world-class foreigners but it ultimately worked against me. I wasn't playing, I was getting really down and had to move to get my career going in the right direction again.'

He took a step down to the Second Division but he was happy. 'I love it at Reading and want to stay here. I'm playing in front of a crowd every week, for three points in games that really matter to people. More than that, I've got my confidence back.

'There are young players in the same position as I was, the likes of Jon Harley and John Terry. They're playing in the first team now, but when the established players are back from injury and fit again, they'll almost certainly be out again,' he predicted, ruefully spelling out the possible problems ahead for Terry at Chelsea. 'I never wanted to leave but I've got to think of my future. I didn't want to get to twenty-four or twenty-five and still be playing in the reserves – I've got too much to offer for that to happen.'

Not everybody is as patient as Terry, and who knows what would have happened if he had got itchy feet. But fortunately for the Blues, Terry was in no hurry and he was happy to bide his time in the reserves until his next opportunity arose. Even after his goal against the Gills, he returned to the reserve team, as predicted by Nicholls, since the manager was able to choose two from Desailly, Leboeuf and Thome.

When Hogh returned from injury in March to complete a full house of centre-backs for the Blues, Vialli decided to help out an old friend and he sent Terry to Nottingham Forest on loan until the end of the season. David Platt's side were struggling in Division One following their relegation from the Premiership at the end of 1998/99. And their defence desperately needed shoring up.

On transfer deadline day, Platt swooped for Manchester City's Tony Vaughan and Terry in a bid to stop a second consecutive drop. Before his arrival in Nottingham, Terry's new team-mates had picked up two points from four games and were just two places off relegation. Things got worse for Platt's side when Blackburn left the City

Ground with three points, as Terry watched from the stands just days after joining the battle for survival.

Terry had impressed Platt when he played in the side that dumped Forest out of the FA Cup, and the former England captain was quick to strike a deal when he realised how many defenders Vialli had at his disposal. The Chelsea boss realised how valuable the experience of a relegation battle could be for the youngster and was happy to do a favour for his former team-mate.

That Division One experience started when Terry played the last half hour against the champions elect. Charlton Athletic travelled north knowing that they were only four points away from promotion to the Premiership but, thanks to Terry, they returned south only one point better off.

When Terry came off the bench, the Addicks were 1–0 up, and things got more difficult for the youngster when his fellow centre-back Colin Calderwood received his marching orders ten minutes later. With only 20 minutes to play, Charlton should have been home and dry, but the red card only proved to inspire Forest and they snatched a point thanks to a Chris Bart-Williams penalty in the 81st minute.

In his next match Terry helped his new side to an away win, only their fourth of the season, as Platt's side left St Andrews with three points, after beating Birmingham City 1–0 thanks to a Darren Purse own goal. There was a perfect blend of youth and experience in the Forest defence as Terry forged a resolute partnership with the Scottish veteran Calderwood.

The double-act came to an unfortunate end early in the second half as the former Tottenham centre-back broke his ankle in a collision with one of the Birmingham midfielders. But Terry held firm alongside Jon-Olav Hjelde for the rest of the match and the whole of the next match against Sheffield United, which finished 0–0 as Forest maintained their unbeaten run. Things weren't going so smoothly for the Blues, however, and, while Terry was guiding his adopted club to safety, Chelsea had reached the FA Cup Final by beating Newcastle 2–1 at Wembley, but had crashed out of Europe after losing 5–1 to Barcelona in the Nou Camp.

The Blues were just seven minutes away from the semi-finals, thanks to a 3–1 win in the first leg a fortnight before, but they conceded a late third and lost their way in extra-time. This rang out like a bell mourning the dead as far as the press were concerned and they began a post-mortem on Vialli's team. Fortunately for Terry, Morris and Harley, the media were in agreement – Chelsea were too old.

Leboeuf, Desailly, Deschamps, Zola, Wise and De Goey were said to be over the hill having left their twenties behind. Roberto Di Matteo and Albert Ferrer weren't much better off at twenty-nine, and Gus Poyet and Dan Petrescu should have been heading for the retirement home since they were thirty-two. According to the press, the 2000/01 season would be the one for Terry and the other youngsters to shine at Stamford Bridge.

Terry stayed focused on the present though, and on maintaining Forest's Division One status. This was guaranteed at Craven Cottage with a 1–1 draw on Easter Monday, and this despite his biggest mistake in a Forest shirt. The young defender slipped over, allowing Geoff Horsfield a free shot at goal, but Terry received a let-off when the big striker took an air shot and the ball trickled out of play.

After securing safety, Forest played some of their best football of the season to beat Port Vale 2–0 at home, and the last game of the campaign was a typical end-of-year affair as chances came thick and fast against Stockport County in an entertaining 3–2 win. Terry had played six games, starting five, as Forest won three and drew three, and the Chelsea starlet was certain they had turned the corner.

'There's a lot of talent at Forest and I can see them being up among the pacesetters next season,' Terry said in the *Sun*. 'I've tried to encourage the guys around me and made them believe in themselves. Forest have some great players but their confidence was a bit low when I came here. Hopefully they can continue where we've left off and get back into the Premiership.'

Platt was keen to sign Terry to help with this bid, but Chelsea rejected all the Forest advances and he returned to Stamford Bridge for the climax to the Chelsea season.

Back in the Premiership and in his favourite shade of blue, Terry made the bench for the last league game of the season and replaced Desailly after 55 minutes. It was an enjoyable run-out for the youngster as the Blues treated their home fans to some exhibition football. Derby were 2–0 down when Terry came on and the game finished 4–0 to give the Chelsea players a confidence boost ahead of the FA Cup Final.

Before the big game at Wembley, the Chelsea manager was philosophical about the season that was drawing to a close. 'Of course we want to win the Final,' Vialli said to assembled journalists. 'But I think this has already been a successful season in two competitions. By getting to the quarter-finals in Europe, we've been much further than a lot of important clubs in England, and we've reached the final of the FA Cup.'

The Italian continued: 'Obviously, we're conscious that we should have done better in the League, but it's difficult to play perfectly in all competitions. Look at the semi-finalists of the Champions League: not one of Barcelona, Valencia, Real Madrid or Bayern Munich are top of their domestic leagues. Like them, we concentrated too much on the Champions League, but then you're going to be more up for going out with Claudia Schiffer than with your next-door neighbour.

'At the start you weigh up the competitions you're in. I believed the Champions League and Premiership were on the same level. Then, as the season wore on, I saw we were more suited to Europe, so we gave that a higher priority. But if next season we're in the UEFA Cup and the Premiership, there'll be no hesitation: the League will be our target.

'The fact that the foreigners have now played in the Premier League and the English chaps have tasted the Champions League means everybody has experienced both styles. We can all improve next year, and we'll be looking to add some new players, hopefully younger ones, to the squad. But there won't be, as some suggest, a massive clear-out.'

Inevitably the press immediately attacked Chelsea's more recent acquisitions, the well-paid, well-known faces from far and wide, and the Blues' growing reputation as a European club which happened to be based in London. 'People need to get the facts straight,' said Vialli. 'We may have a lot of foreign players on our books, but we've also had nine home-grown guys in the team this year. Nobody should forget that. I can understand why English people would side with players from their country, but that is a fundamental mistake because we are not foreigners, we are simply Chelsea Football Club players.'

And on Saturday, 20 May 2000, the players of Chelsea Football Club won the last FA Cup Final at the old Wembley Stadium. The game against Aston Villa was billed as a battle between England and the Rest of the World, as John Gregory had built his squad with players mainly from the British Isles, in contrast to Vialli who had fielded an entirely foreign side on Boxing Day and regularly had only one or two Englishmen in his starting line-up.

Dennis Wise was the only Brit to start for the Blues at Wembley, but there was a more English feel to the bench where Terry completed a trio of home-grown players alongside Harley and Morris. Considering the build-up to the game, it was apt that the scrappy showcase event was decided by a mistake from one of Villa's England internationals and a piece of opportunism from one of Chelsea's more influential imports.

Having already made FA Cup history with the fastest-ever goal in a final after just 43 seconds in 1997, Roberto Di Matteo hit another landmark strike, the last Cup Final goal at Wembley before its renovation. When David James failed to hold Zola's free-kick in the 73rd minute, Di Matteo was on hand to lash the ball home from close range and become a Wembley hero for the second time in three years.

Leboeuf and Desailly held firm at the heart of the Chelsea defence and John Terry claimed his first medal. He may not have played in the Final but he certainly played his part in getting them there, being involved in the third, fourth, fifth and the sixth round, or quarter-final, where he claimed his first senior Chelsea goal.

The Cup Final brought an end to another long season of mixed fortunes for Terry. He had played only a couple more games for Chelsea than in the previous campaign, five from the start and four from the bench, but he had gained valuable experience in helping to save Nottingham Forest from relegation. And as an unused substitute he had won his first, and by no means last, medal with Chelsea. The Cup also secured European football for the Blues, providing them with entry into the UEFA Cup – the Cup Winners' Cup now being defunct – and saving them from the embarrassment of an early start to the season in the form of the InterToto cup.

Another pot for the trophy cabinet also improved Vialli's record as the most successful manager in Chelsea's history, sitting very happily alongside the League Cup, the European Cup Winners' Cup, and the European Super Cup won in 1998. But the proud Italian still wasn't happy.

'We have won the FA Cup but I still think we let everyone down in the League,' Vialli said to a press conference. 'I am proud of my record as a manager especially as I am young, inexperienced and still learning. But everyone has to learn.

'I want the best. I was a perfectionist as a player and that is what I want from this team. I want to win the Premiership. I will not be happy until that has been achieved. Next season we will have a better chance because we do not have the distraction of the Champions League.

'I have fantastic players and I want to add to the squad this summer. We had three home-grown players on the bench in Jody Morris, John Terry and Jon Harley. They give you enthusiasm, spirit and desire. But you must also have experience.'

The chairman Ken Bates clearly agreed with Vialli because, for all the youthful manager's enthusiasm, spirit and desire, he came up short in the experience department, and with the FA Cup freshly stored away in the Stamford Bridge trophy cabinet it came as a shock to everyone, including Terry, when the manager was sacked after only five league games of the new season.

CHAPTER FOUR
KING OF THE KING'S ROAD

'There did seem a lack of opportunities but I never contemplated leaving the club because I wasn't getting a chance,' Terry told the *Daily Mail*. 'When I signed professional forms, I set myself the target to play regularly for the first team by the time I was twenty-two. Then the new manager came in and told me I would get a chance. I believed him and kept working hard, and he kept his word. But I never expected my chance to come so soon – I'm buzzing at the moment.'

In December 2000, John Terry firmly established himself in the Chelsea first team, while making the transition from teenager to young man. He regularly played alongside Marcel Desailly, Frank Leboeuf, or both of the experienced Frenchmen, and he seldom, if ever, looked out of place. By the end of the season, the English defender had broken up the European Championship and

World Cup-winning defensive partnership and taken his place alongside Desailly in the Blues' back four, claimed the captaincy of the England Under-21 side and, for good measure, was named Chelsea's Player of the Year. All this and he was still just twenty years old.

A momentous season began in strange circumstances for Terry and his Chelsea team-mates, as Gianluca Vialli was sacked just five games into the new campaign. The Italian manager was given plenty of support over the summer and spent heavily on strengthening his FA Cup-winning squad before beating Manchester United 2–0 at Cardiff's Millennium Stadium to win the Charity Shield. This result saw Vialli's side installed as title favourites by many of the newspapers, but poor results after the traditional curtain-raiser tested the patience of his bosses and he was shown the door.

After beating United, the Blues put four goals past West Ham at the Bridge, but then travelled to Bradford and lost 2–0 to the Bantams, a startling reminder of the inconsistency which had plagued previous seasons. A week later, Vialli's side let a 2–0 lead slip against Arsenal at the Bridge for the second time in twelve months – this time to draw 2–2 – and the manager was as good as gone.

Once the Gunners got one goal back, a second seemed inevitable and watching that embarrassing collapse proved the final straw for chairman Ken Bates. Together with Colin Hutchinson, the club's managing director, Bates began the process of finding a replacement for Chelsea's youthful manager, and Vialli was sacked on Tuesday, 12 September.

It seemed a bizarre decision from the Stamford Bridge hierarchy; if they had so little faith in the manager as to show him the door after five matches of the season, then why had they not sacked him in the summer in order to let his replacement hire and fire in the close season, and use the pre-season to shape the team in his image? As it was, Claudio Ranieri took charge of a team seventeenth in the table with six points from six games and a squad filled with the previous manager's signings.

Over the summer Vialli had spent nearly £25m bringing in Jimmy Floyd Hasselbaink from Atletico Madrid, Mario Stanic from Parma, and Eidur Gudjohnsen from Bolton Wanderers. While Chris Sutton, George Weah, Dan Petrescu, Didier Deschamps and Neil Clement had left Stamford Bridge – a very busy close season for a man who was on the way out of his job.

Terry was recovering from an ankle injury as the results started to go against the Blues, but Howard Wilkinson had seen enough good work from the young defender in the previous season to warrant his inclusion in the England Under-21 squad for a friendly against Georgia. The Chelsea youngster missed the game at the Riverside Stadium through injury but his selection proved that his performances had been noted by people outside Stamford Bridge – and by people that mattered.

But in Vialli's final days at the Bridge, it was other

defenders that made the headlines. The manager had spent much of the summer courting Gareth Southgate, only to be rejected repeatedly by the England international's club – Aston Villa. Tired of the knock-backs, Chelsea swooped for Barcelona's Dutch defender Winston Bogarde on a free transfer. After strengthening the squad, the club accepted a bid for Emerson Thome, apparently against the wishes of the manager. The Brazilian centre-back had been signed from Sheffield Wednesday for £2.7m nine months previously and made more league appearances than Desailly or Leboeuf in that time. For all their fine distribution and composure in possession, the Italian manager felt that Thome's no-nonsense approach was far better suited to the English game, and he was reportedly very angry when Chelsea agreed to sell the defender to Sunderland for £4.5m.

As well as losing the confidence of his employers, the Italian manager was also having difficulty controlling the dressing-room. It is always tough to make the step up from player to manager at the same club, because one day you are on the same level as the rest of the squad and the next day you are the one calling the shots. Vialli was very popular as a player and friendly with all the other players, but as a manager he distanced himself from his team-mates and became increasingly withdrawn.

While in charge at Chelsea, Vialli had signed his former Juventus team-mate Didier Deschamps, and the Frenchman noticed a massive change in his old friend before he returned to his homeland. 'Towards the end, our relations were difficult, or even impossible,' Deschamps said. 'It was hard because I had a very different opinion of Luca as a player from the coach he became. At Juventus, he was Luca; we were mates. At Chelsea, he was intent on flexing his muscles.'

The Blues full-back Graeme Le Saux agreed that Vialli had changed but had a lot more sympathy for his departing manager and the difficult transition he had made. 'It is very hard to do,' Le Saux said. 'Especially if you try to do it at the same club. It brings its own burdens with it. You have to go from being in the players' dressing room to the manager's room and I can imagine that can be a very lonely place. Luca had a lot to deal with. What he wanted was the support and understanding of the players.'

Vialli was gradually losing the support and understanding of his players as well as his bosses, and with his contract not yet renewed rumours of his possible departure began circulating ahead of the Arsenal match. 'We have not started negotiating because there is still ten months to go before the end of my contract and in football things are very unpredictable,' Vialli said to assembled media, making light of the situation. 'We might beat Arsenal 5–1 and I might get a phone call from Ken Bates on Thursday morning. Or we might lose 5–1 and I might get a very different call from Ken Bates!'

His words may have been in jest but the spineless capitulation of the Blues brought exactly the same result as a 5–1 loss would have produced and, a week later, he was called to a meeting with Bates and Hutchinson during which he was dismissed.

'Gianluca was called in by chairman Ken Bates and managing director Colin Hutchinson and told it would be better if he went,' said Vialli's agent Athole Still. 'He accepted that he had lost the players' confidence and that it was Chelsea's prerogative to sack him because of the situation. Gianluca is a proud man, who is a winner. Under no circumstances is he a quitter and he would not fall on his sword willingly. He is not angry. He accepts the decision. He will be back, bigger and better than ever.'

The club statement read: 'Following discussions with Ken Bates and Colin Hutchinson, Gianluca Vialli has been released from his duties. He will continue to be paid under the terms of his contract. Chelsea have great admiration for his achievements in his two-and-a-half years in charge of team affairs and would like to place on record our appreciation for his services. However, the club feel that it is in our best interests to seek a change of direction. An announcement on the successor will be made in due course. For the immediate future the current staff will take charge of the team.'

So coach Graham Rix and assistant coach Ray Wilkins guided Chelsea to a 1–0 win over Swiss minnows St Gallen in the UEFA Cup first round. But they wouldn't be in charge for long and the tabloids began pulling names out of a hat in a bid to claim 'you read it here first'. Johan

Cruyff, Frank Rijkaard, Dino Zoff, Sven-Goran Eriksson, Glenn Hoddle, Terry Venables, George Graham, Walter Smith, Dick Advocaat, John Toshack, Aime Jacquet and Jose Antonio Camacho were all linked with the post before someone got it right by naming Claudio Ranieri.

Ranieri gave a big clue to the tabloid hacks when he was seen busily making notes in the directors' box at Stamford Bridge throughout the 90 minutes of the UEFA Cup-tie with St Gallen. The Roman coach was out of work, having left Atletico Madrid the previous season. Ranieri was almost the antithesis of Vialli, thus fitting the bill for Chelsea since the men at the top of the club wanted a complete change of direction. The son of a millionaire, who was brought up in a castle, was being replaced by a butcher's boy; a former World Player of the Year with 59 caps and winner of all three European trophies was being supplanted by a journeyman defender whose career highlight was a brief spell with Roma; but more importantly an inexperienced young manager in his first job was being superseded by a man with top-flight success in Italy and Spain.

Before Atletico Madrid fell apart with huge financial problems, Ranieri had transformed Serie C side Cagliari into a Serie A club, been in charge at Napoli and Roma, led Fiorentina from Serie B to the top flight and an Italian Cup win and in Spain he won the Copa del Rey while assembling the Valencia side which made it to successive Champions League finals. Considered a fine tactician with excellent man-management skills, Ranieri had the added benefit of having worked with Zola, Stanic and Hasselbaink at previous clubs, which would help him to win over the dressing-room which the outgoing manager had lost.

'I am very much looking forward to finding Zola again after almost eight seasons apart,' Ranieri said to a press conference, 'and I will obviously try to get Hasselbaink to score as many goals as last season. It is an honour to come to this great club and a dream come true to work in the homeland of football after my time in Italy and Spain.

'There is work to be done after watching the game on Thursday, but it could not be the best Chelsea performance against St Gallen because of the circumstances. I am looking forward to starting, although I also feel sorry for Gianluca Vialli because I know how much the first sacking hurts. I honestly hope to see him back in football soon.'

As the man who had given Zola his big break at Napoli all those years before, Ranieri also had a good eye for talent and wasn't afraid to give younger players a chance – surely music to the ears of Terry. 'I remember we had a reserve game against Coventry,' the defender recalled on Chelsea TV. 'We won 3–2 and there was a lot of talk about the new manager coming to watch the game and all of his staff. I just remember Ray Wilkins coming up to me before the game and telling me to just do the same as I had been doing all season in training – go out and impress him. That is what I did.'

Terry was very impressive in that game, and further good news came his way from the mouth of his new manager, although admittedly English wasn't his best language. Speaking through a translator, Ranieri said: 'I need to have a close look at what I have got before spending money. A new manager has to look at how the players react in tough times, and this is clearly a difficult time for Chelsea and all the staff here.

'I want to keep everyone who loves Chelsea. I have told them that big names and reputations mean nothing to me – only performance. I don't look at names, just how they play. I will be treating the youth team players just the same as the reserves and first-team stars. They will all be given a chance.'

As far as Terry was concerned, the new man was saying all the right things and it got better. 'The backbone has to be English,' Ranieri continued. 'If a team in Italy wins the championship, the backbone is Italian. The same happens in Spain. I must evaluate what players I have got and what English players to buy. I need to see if there are any good English players here.

'I was brought up on the image of English football with Bobby and Jack Charlton, and the temple of Wembley. I will definitely be considering the opportunities of the English-based players already here. It will take me a little time before I make up my mind about the side. It is impossible for me to say what is going to happen this season. My first job is to get the team to step up another gear. It is obvious morale has been affected by what happened.'

That morale was boosted by a 3–3 draw at Old Trafford but suffered yet another blow with a humiliating 2–0 defeat in Zurich to put the Blues out of the UEFA Cup. Terry was sidelined by a hamstring injury for these games and had to wait for his chance to show the new boss what he could do in the first team. In the meantime the Chelsea centre-back made his England Under-21 debut in a 2–2 draw with Finland. He almost helped his team to three points in their European Under-21 Championship qualifier, but volleyed a Michael Carrick corner just over the bar in the dying seconds.

The West Ham midfielder was a regular at Upton Park despite his tender years, and he felt sympathy for Terry at Chelsea, as he compared him to another of England's talented young centre-backs, Rio Ferdinand. 'Rio had a chance to prove himself at West Ham but other clubs just buy World Cup-winners which puts you down the pecking order a bit,' Carrick said at a press conference. 'What chance would Rio have had at Chelsea? I speak to John Terry and I can understand his frustration at being at Chelsea where young players don't get a chance. He's a top-quality player but he can't get a chance in the first team there. Rio got into the West Ham side at seventeen and played at the top level for five years. It makes me realise how lucky I am at West Ham.'

Terry had the chance to join the Hammers when he

was a schoolboy, but he saw Chelsea as a club on their way up. He would undoubtedly have played more often had he joined a smaller club, but Terry's future lay in west London not West Ham. His hopes of success at Stamford Bridge were boosted by the news that there would be no more signings, and the new manager would have to make do with what he had. As the Blues managing director Colin Hutchinson insisted: 'There is no money available for new players, unless there is another emergency like the Roberto Di Matteo situation [the Italian midfielder broke his leg shortly after Ranieri joined the Blues]. But Claudio is quite happy working with the squad he already has. At the start of the season, we knew we had to get the average age of the squad down. To a certain extent we have already started that but I am sure there are one or two who might benefit from moving on, especially with some young players like John Terry forcing their way into contention for a first-team spot.'

Terry had the opportunity to stake his claim for a place in the Chelsea first team soon after his international bow, when Ranieri chose the League Cup as an opportunity to see some of his less celebrated players in action for the first time. Playing Liverpool away in the third round, Terry showed his new boss sufficient promise to keep his place in the starting XI for the league game against Southampton at the Dell. And although Chelsea lost both games, 2–1 at Anfield and 3–2 against the Saints, Ranieri liked what he saw.

'Claudio's always taken time out to try to help me with my game,' Terry said in the *Daily Mail*. 'After a reserve game not long after he came, he got Ray Wilkins to translate for him and told me I'd get my chance in a couple of weeks against Liverpool in the Worthington Cup. I did. I played that game and the next but then I got injured. He told me: "Don't worry about it. When you're fit, I'm sure you'll be back involved again." That gave me confidence.'

The thigh strain kept Terry out of three games for the Blues and one for England Under-21s, but when he recovered the fine young stopper returned to the Chelsea defence and started ten consecutive matches, which established him as a first-team regular. Terry came into the back four alongside Leboeuf for the match against Manchester City, with Desailly pushed forward into a holding role in midfield, but after 20 minutes Ranieri showed his versatile approach to the game and played all three of them in defence, adopting a 5-3-2 formation.

Chelsea rode their luck, especially Terry who was lucky not to concede a penalty when he appeared to pull Shaun Goater's shirt in the area, and they came through the game at Stamford Bridge with three vital points after a demanding run of fixtures. It was a tough test for the young defender up against Goater and the unpredictable Paulo Wanchope in the first half, and the spiky Paul Dickov after the break. Terry received a booking for his handling of the diminutive Scot, but Ranieri kept faith with the nineteen year-old for the visit of Derby County, as Leboeuf served a one-game suspension.

The Blues were rampant against the Rams and won the game 4–1 with youth to the fore as Terry joined Sam Dalla Bona and Eidur Gudjohnsen as the pick of the players in an outstanding performance. The Estonian goalkeeper Mart Poom was Derby's best player as the shots rained in from all angles but Wise only had words for the Chelsea boys after the game.

'We've got a lot of young talent at the club and they've all done extremely well,' the skipper said after the match. 'The way John Terry played you'd have thought he had played a lot of first-team games but he hasn't. It's nice to have the youngsters playing. Some of us are getting on a bit and can't play as many games as we'd like to but we've got good youngsters capable of coming in and doing well.'

Wise wasn't alone in thinking that the future was bright for Chelsea and one of the Blues finest-ever defenders was equally impressed by Terry. Paul Elliott, who played for Chelsea, Celtic and Pisa, among others, before his career was cut short by a horrific knee injury, said in the *Daily Star*: 'It must give him great confidence to be picked ahead of Winston Bogarde who is a well-travelled international player. But you have to be careful with young kids. They have to be ready and you must not damage their confidence. You have to back the manager's judgement.'

It was Ranieri's decision to keep Terry in the team as Leboeuf was left on the bench following his one-match ban. Chelsea travelled to Middlesbrough seeking a first away win of the season, having only won once on Teesside since 1931. But another encouraging performance from Terry at the heart of the Blues defence couldn't stop Boro winning 1–0. The manager changed to five at the back for the second half in the North-east and kept all three of his classy defenders in the team for the next match against Bradford City.

Seeking revenge for the 2–0 reverse at Valley Parade earlier in the season, Terry and his team-mates enjoyed a much easier game at home, winning 3–0, but there was no time to enjoy revenge as the games came thick and fast over the festive period. Three days later, they were back on the road. The Blues were without an away win since April Fool's Day but, on Boxing Day, they appeared to have put their travel sickness behind them. Chelsea went 2–0 up after 17 minutes at Portman Road. But Ipswich were in fine form and refused to roll over – they pulled one goal back just before half-time and equalised 10 minutes from time. It almost got far worse, though, as Terry had to clear a Martijn Reuser header off the line to save a point in injury-time after De Goey flapped at a cross.

'I thought Ed had got a hand to it, but then I saw the ball coming to me. It was a good job I was there,' Terry said after the match. 'It was a game we could have lost. I don't know what the problem is; we just didn't kill them off.'

On their travels the Blues hadn't managed to kill anyone off for a long time and it was ruining their season.

Chelsea's away form was truly horrendous. On the road they had been knocked out of the UEFA and League Cups and had lost six and drawn four matches in the league – real relegation form. Their continued excellence at home, where they had won seven and drawn two of their ten league matches, meant that the Blues were tenth in the table but this wasn't acceptable for a team like Chelsea.

The press laid the blame squarely at the feet of the new manager. His English was improving but was still not good enough to communicate clearly with all of his players, and his excessive number of tactical changes looked farcical. Against Ipswich, Chelsea repeatedly changed formation; Terry played at centre-back throughout with either Desailly and/or Leboeuf, but other players moved around the park, seemingly changing positions at the drop of a hat. This made it very difficult for the Blues to maintain any momentum or retain possession as another two points slipped away.

'There is too much focus on me not speaking English,' Ranieri said. 'I find it strange. It only becomes an issue because we don't win away from home. I am learning more and more English and very few players can't understand me. But I can always make my point to them. Too much is made of it.

'Maybe some people in English football are too xenophobic. Just look at Terry Venables and Barcelona. He could not speak Spanish and yet was very successful. I believe in giving young English players a chance. We have very good young English players – John Terry, Jon Harley and Jody Morris. And Dennis Wise is a great captain. I believe that a championship-winning team must have a good core of English players. That is what I would like here.'

Terry was happy with the progress he was making under the new regime and he agreed with his boss on the home-grown issue. 'We have taken a bit of stick about not bringing youngsters through, but Ranieri has come in and given myself a chance, as well as Jon [Harley] and Jody [Morris],' Terry said.

'But sometimes we use squad rotation and certain players might be thought to be better against one team rather than another. So we all have to be patient,' he added, mentioning Chelsea's new flexible line-up. He was amazed that he hadn't been moved to full-back under his new coach. 'I would have thought it would be me changing positions not Marcel and Frank. I'm a bit surprised but I'm not complaining. The manager hasn't said anything to me about it.'

Ranieri clearly had faith in the young Englishman as he rotated Leboeuf out of the starting XI for the FA Cup third-round tie against Peterborough United. The Blues boss reverted to a more simple formation with four at the back for the visit of lower-league opposition and the change paid off as the Posh were humbled 5–0. Elsewhere in the Cup, Terry's brother Paul swapped shirts with his fiancee's brother Paul Konchesky as Charlton played

Dagenham & Redbridge in an entertaining tie. The Addicks won a replay 1–0 after a 1–1 draw at the Valley.

Terry's stock was continually rising and his valuable performances on the pitch had brought the first of many 'TERRY'S ALL GOLD' headlines, in homage to the plain chocolate confectionery assortment, as well as the more straightforward 'TERRY-FIC!' The press were definitely taking notice as the English youngster moved up the Chelsea pecking order at the expense of other more experienced defenders – Bogarde was increasingly marginalised and there was also talk of Leboeuf moving on.

Christian Panucci actually did leave the club. Having made only one league start since the end of September, the Italian defender, equally at home at full-back or centre-half, turned his back on Chelsea. He had joined the Blues on loan from Internazionale but agreed a new loan deal with Monaco, telling journalists: 'I made a big mistake in joining Chelsea. I was never really given a chance there. I was frustrated in Milan and just wanted to play football. But it did not happen. When Gianluca Vialli left, my career after that was never going to be at Chelsea. I cannot be angry at Ranieri, however, as he put a young player, Terry, in ahead of me.'

Other players were losing out to youth, and Terry's new status as Chelsea's second-choice centre-back, behind the still imperious Desailly, was further enhanced at Highbury a week later. After dominating the first-half, Arsenal were unlucky to take only a 1–0 lead into the break, but

Ranieri changed his side for the second 45 minutes and the Blues emerged with a deserved point in a 1–1 draw.

At the start of the match, Terry was in a back three, between Leboeuf and Desailly, but after the interval Chelsea changed to a back four and tellingly it was Leboeuf and not Terry who made way – another clear sign of the confidence that Ranieri had in the English defender – and Terry rewarded his manager with his first league goal to stop the Blues tumbling to another away-day defeat.

Wise whipped in a corner and David Seaman in the Arsenal goal got entangled with Martin Keown as Gudjohnsen got his head to the ball. It appeared to go over the line before Lee Dixon and Silvinho tried to clear, but Terry was on hand to nod the ball home. 'It was definitely my goal,' confirmed Terry after the game. 'I'm claiming it. It was a bit of a scramble, but I made sure. Yes, we were better in the second half when we changed our shape. But it was the manager's decision; we just get on with it.

'That's my eighth consecutive game and I feel more relaxed and part of the team now. The players are making me feel welcome. The new manager is giving the youngsters a chance. Of course it's difficult to come through with so many great players at the club but you do get to train with them and learn from them and, when you get your chance, you just have to try and take it.'

Terry was taking all the chances which came his way, and his team-mates were as impressed as the media. 'John did get a bit down when he was not in the side and I had to talk to him a lot,' Desailly said in the *Sun*. 'When he wasn't getting into the Chelsea team I was always talking to him in training, encouraging John and telling him: "You are the present and the future." Now his time has come, and this Arsenal team was a huge test for him. They have some magnificent forwards and it was his best game for us. He's played well before, but in games against lesser teams. This was a tough one because he hadn't come up against really quick players like Thierry Henry and Sylvain Wiltord, but he proved he could handle it. He didn't get too close in, because players like Henry can turn you and leave you for dead, and that shows what a quality player he is. He needs experience, but John can go all the way to the top. He's shown he can play at a high level now, but he's got to do it for a whole season, not just for three or four games.

'Once he plays for England, I'll be really happy for him. For now, it would be a good idea to get him into the England set-up, like we do with lots of our youngsters in France.'

Before Terry could make the step up to the full international side, he needed to negotiate a new contract to reflect his enhanced standing in the Chelsea squad. The contract signed in October 2000 gave Terry a basic wage of £5,000 a week, well below the team average, but it included a clause guaranteeing negotiations on a new contract after twenty first-team starts. The youngster said to the *Sun*: 'Once I do make those twenty starts, then it's up to me and the club to negotiate something that we're both happy with. Hopefully something will get sorted out as I'd love to stay here. Life just could not be better for me at the moment as I'm really enjoying myself on and off the pitch.

'Either Mr Ranieri or Angelo, his assistant, talks to me every day. Sometimes he gets someone to translate but mostly he talks to me in English. About football anyway,' Terry told the *Daily Mail*. 'His English outside of the game isn't as good but he knows most of the football terms. It's not really a problem for him now. In training sometimes or in the corridor, he'll hear an expression like, for instance, "Come on, lads." You'll hear him talking to himself, repeating it: "Come on, lads. Come on, lads."

'Claudio is always looking at the younger players. He is always at the reserve games. I think it is good that he should watch for the youngsters coming through, and now we are getting towards the right mix of youth and experience,' Terry said in the *People*. 'At the start of the season we were expected to be challenging Manchester United for the title. Yet we've been up and down all season, we've not been able to get a good run going – and we can't win away. But look at the table. We are not in an impossible position to push for a Champions League spot. We are not far behind. If we can maintain our impressive home form and sort ourselves out away, I'm sure we can go right up the table.'

Chelsea got a first away win of the season when they were drawn against Gillingham for the second successive year in the FA Cup. After going 3–0 up, everything got a bit tense as the Gills pulled it back to 3–2, but the Blues stood firm and claimed a late goal to win 4–2.

Having started ten consecutive matches, a heavy cold interrupted Terry's first-team run, but while on the sidelines he struck a new four-and-a-half-year deal with the club worth approximately £15,000 a week. 'I am delighted to pledge my future to Chelsea and hope to achieve a great deal of success with the club,' Terry said.

Chelsea were also very happy with the new deal as they attempted to move the club's image away from expensive imports to focus more on home-grown talents. 'John has earned this new contract. He has worked his way through the teams at the club and, since forcing his way into the Premiership side, he has done really well,' Hutchinson said to the press. 'His new deal is structured to reward him even further depending on appearances and how successful we are. With all young players, there are incentives in place for them to earn better deals as they progress and we hope John does just that.'

Terry returned, fit and raring to go, for the visit of Manchester United, his first match against the team he had supported as a boy and the team he had rejected as a fourteen year-old. 'I know I could have been playing with them, instead of against them,' Terry told the press, 'but I turned United down because I believed I stood a better chance at Chelsea. There has never been a time when I've thought about what I could have won.

'I've been content to wait and be successful here. It never bothered me when Chelsea brought in the foreign players,' he added. 'I knew my time would come. If I'm picked, then the United players won't faze me and they won't worry me. All I'll be anxious about is what I do myself. Too many teams worry too much about the opposition and, if you do that, you're going to lose.'

Terry had no reason to worry as he put in another outstanding performance at the centre of a three-man defence and the Blues took a point off Fergie's side. Under the scrutiny of the new England manager, Sven-Goran Eriksson, the Chelsea defender looked the most accomplished of the back three with his handling of Ole Gunnar Solskjaer and Andy Cole in the 1–1 draw. And by eclipsing the equally talented Brit, Wes Brown, at the other end, Terry further enhanced calls for inclusion in the Swede's first squad.

But Terry felt the press were getting a bit overexcited. 'Of course, I want to go all the way,' he said to the *Independent on Sunday.* 'But all that England talk's got a bit out of proportion. I'd be happy just to be selected for the Under-21s. I'm still looking over my shoulder – I don't feel that I've achieved anything yet. I don't think I will until I've played twenty or thirty games on the bounce.

'I got in when Frank was suspended, and played alongside Marcel and Mario. The manager obviously thought I'd done well and left me in, which meant that Frank was on the bench, which was pleasing for me. The manager always encourages us to play the ball out from the back and I've got Frank to thank for helping me with that. He's brilliant at it and so is Marcel. Defensively Marcel is very strong. He stays on his feet whereas Frank goes to ground a lot more when he tackles.'

He went on: 'I've always admired them both and they're always willing to spend time with you on improving your game. I've been able to learn from both of them.'

It wasn't only defenders who were caught up in the hype surrounding Terry at that time, and Chelsea's favourite Uruguayan also went on record with his thoughts about the young Englishman. 'Everyone is now looking at John Terry,' Gus Poyet said in the *Daily Mirror*. 'It's great for the club that John is getting regular games. It was difficult before as we had the two centre-halves from the World and European Champions. It's a credit to John that he's got into the side. That sends a message to the youth team players – try to reach the first team, because we need the English players to make it.

'When Gianluca Vialli was manager, he had so many foreign players it was easy to pick them,' the midfielder added. 'He didn't really need the English players, but at the end he was saying that he did need them to win the Premiership. That's what Ranieri has found as well.'

The Blues certainly weren't going to win the Premiership in Ranieri's first season, as they sat in ninth place in the table in mid-February, but they still had the FA Cup to defend. After two ties against lower-league opposition, Chelsea were drawn away against Arsenal in the fifth round. The Blues would really be up against it at Highbury, with the win over Gillingham in the previous round their only away win in the last ten months.

Facing Henry and Dennis Bergkamp in the home side's attack, Terry and Desailly had their hands full from the start but managed to hold the Gunners at bay for the first half. But they couldn't keep them out forever and Henry scored from the spot after Jesper Gronkjaer clattered into Lauren. It was the first goal Henry had claimed against Terry and the two would develop quite a rivalry over the coming seasons. 'Henry's world class,' Terry said. 'I realised how good he was from seeing him on television, but there were a few things that you can't really see on television – a few of his runs were unbelievable.'

Henry was often the star for Arsenal, but another brilliant game from Terry meant that the Frenchman's only real opportunity came from the penalty spot. Matt Dickinson, in *The Times*, described Terry as 'Chelsea's one outstanding performer' but even he couldn't stop Sylvain Wiltord's brace which made it 3–1, after Hasselbaink had scored a thunderous gem to level the scores.

A fine showing in the face of adversity, but it wasn't enough to keep the Blues in the Cup and it wasn't enough to get Terry into Sven's inaugural England squad. The centre-backs ahead of him in the Swede's thoughts were: Manchester United's Wes Brown; Rio Ferdinand, then at Leeds; Sol Campbell, then at Tottenham; Liverpool's Jamie

Carragher and Ugo Ehiogu of Middlesbrough. Still only twenty, the Barking-born defender was selected for the Under-21s with a number of other promising youngsters. Eriksson explained his decision by saying: 'It is better for them to play than sit on the bench with the senior team.'

But before Terry could join up with the other young Lions for their game against Spain he had his first experience of how his profile had risen in the nation's tabloids. After the FA Cup defeat at the hands of Arsenal, Ranieri had taken his squad for a five-day break in Tenerife and, when Terry and some of his team-mates had a night out in the Spanish resort, it made a splash in the *News of the World* the following Sunday.

'CHELSEA VILLAGE PEOPLE' read the headline after Terry and his pals took their tops off and led the dancing to 'YMCA'. Not much of a story really – there's nothing new in young men going out drinking, singing and dancing, but with fame comes responsibility and it certainly wouldn't be the last time Terry's name made it into the papers for non-footballing reasons.

Back on the pitch, Terry struggled in the first half of the England Under-21 friendly with Spain, and was replaced at the interval with the score at 2–0. The second goal came after 30 minutes when the defender was involved in a dreadful mix-up with Paul Robinson in the England goal, and the Chelsea centre-back didn't come out after the break at St Andrews.

Following such a calamitous display and after such a

long run in the team, Chelsea's Italian manager took the opportunity to give his youngster a break, and Terry started the next three matches on the bench. So the England Under-21 defender played only the last five minutes as the Blues finally broke their away duck in the league, beating West Ham 2–0 at Upton Park on 7 March – three weeks short of what would have been a most unwelcome anniversary.

Having waited so long for an away win, the Blues should have used it as a springboard from which to launch a late surge up the table to claim a Champions League spot, but instead they threw away a 1–0 and a 2–1 lead at home to Sunderland in their next match and lost 4–2 at the Bridge. Terry replaced Leboeuf 20 minutes from time with the game at 3–2, and the Frenchman's Chelsea career was effectively over as he picked up a groin injury during the ensuing international break.

Terry again joined up with his England Under-21 colleagues where Howard Wilkinson recognised the defender's natural leadership abilities and handed him the captain's armband. With the usual skipper, Blackburn's David Dunn, out due to injury, the Chelsea centre-back was given the honour of leading out his country against Finland at Oakwell. Terry was Man of the Match in the eyes of most observers and he capped a fine defensive display with the second goal in a 4–0 win.

He headed in Jonathan Greening's free-kick after 75 minutes at Barnsley's stadium and was thrilled with the result. 'A lot of people had a go at us after we lost 4–0 to Spain in the last game,' Terry said after the game, 'but we always said that was a learning process for us. We showed how much we learned from it and responded well. It was a real honour to be asked to skipper the side and getting the goal just rounded everything off. I am delighted.'

The coach was also pleased with the performance of his team, and his captain in particular. 'I made Terry skipper for the first time and he played a captain's game. I am delighted for him,' Wilkinson said. 'We looked like a team and, hopefully, we can carry that to Albania on Tuesday.'

Terry maintained his one hundred per cent record in charge of the troops as they beat Albania 1–0 with a Greening penalty in Tirana, and he returned to Stamford Bridge in far finer fettle than after his previous Under-21 break.

Following his good performances leading the young England side, Terry was even mooted as a future Chelsea captain by his club skipper Dennis Wise. But Terry was dismissive of his immediate chances. 'In the long term, I'd love to be captain,' he said in the *Mirror*. 'I've captained the reserves and England Under-21s. So, yes definitely, I'd love to captain Chelsea, even if Dennis has a few years left.

'Dennis is planning on staying and, if he does, then he will be captain. He's a great captain… He always talks to the youngsters and helps us on and off the pitch. If you're a bit asleep or something, he'll wake you up straight away.

That's what you need, someone to lift the players and encourage you. So he's perfect really.

'When you're a YTS, he's always there to talk to and, when you first break through, he's there if you ever want a chat. It's quite scary at first – even the big stars respect him so much. But even if you're a bit shy, he makes sure you know that he's always there.'

Wise was a fine servant to the club and a natural leader of men and, under his guidance, the Blues began climbing up the table at the business end of the season. With Terry restored to the side, Chelsea won four on the bounce and the previously slim chance of a UEFA Cup place started to look safe, but ever the optimist Terry aimed his sights higher. 'The Champions League is a real possibility now,' he said. 'For so long it didn't look like we'd be playing in Europe at all next season. But, while everyone has ignored us, we've sneaked up on the rails.'

Chelsea weren't quite sneaky enough to climb into third place, though, and defeat at Elland Road at the end of April effectively ended their hopes of Champions League football for the following season. But as April rolled to a close, there were plenty of positives for Terry with growing speculation surrounding Leboeuf's future.

Fully recovered from injury, the Frenchman was unable to claim a place in Ranieri's starting XI due to Terry's continued excellence, and Leboeuf was strongly linked with a return to his homeland. Terry certainly wouldn't be shedding any tears over the departure of his closest

KING OF THE KING'S ROAD

competition, as he revealed to the press: 'It's good news for me if Frank leaves because in football you always have to think about your own prospects. Maybe it's a good move for Frank too. I'm sure the lads will be upset to see him go because he's done well for Chelsea but I have to think about myself. I'm enjoying playing in the first team. The manager told me to be patient and I've taken my chance.'

Terry seemed to be improving with every game and praise was coming from all quarters. Chelsea's assistant manager Gwyn Williams, who played such a key role in the defender's decision to join the Blues, said: 'We believe that what we have in the club is another Tony Adams. They have the same approach to football, the same attitude. Ever since we converted him into a defender, he has shot up in height as if that was just what he was waiting for. But he can play; there are no doubts about that.'

One man who agreed with Williams was Adams himself. 'I love John Terry. He's a fabulous player,' the Arsenal captain said. 'I just hope he gets the guidance that he needs. He was my young player of the year. He could become one of the best centre-backs this country has ever produced.'

Terry lost out in the PFA Young Player of the Year voting to Liverpool's Steven Gerrard, but the praise from his idol was a phenomenal source of consolation. 'Tony Adams is one of the players I've always looked up to,' said the England Under-21 international. 'I've always admired the way he's played. He's just brilliant. It's wonderful he's said something like that about me. If I get the chance to watch him play, I always take it.

'I will still go down to Highbury to watch him when Chelsea don't have a game. I've seen plenty of him and I've tried to model my game on his. He's an Essex lad like me and, if I can become half the player Tony is, I will be well satisfied. Earlier this season, when we played at Highbury, I wanted to ask him for his shirt but I was too embarrassed. I'll have to make sure I do it next season now he's said it'll be his last.'

With the chance gone of playing in the Champions League in 2001/02, there was talk of an exodus from Stamford Bridge, with the big names said to be uninspired by the thought of another season without involvement at the top level of club football. But Zola committed himself to another year at Chelsea and many thought that the Italian virtuoso's actions would halt any mass departures.

'Gianfranco staying will encourage others to stay. Maybe they will realise it might be worth playing for Chelsea next year,' said Terry. 'There is good spirit in the team now and I'm sure we can go on to bigger things next season.'

Chelsea's campaign drew to a close with a battling 2–2 draw against Liverpool at Anfield, where Hasselbaink twice equalised goals from England's Michael Owen, and the result set Chelsea up to claim sixth spot in their final game of the season at Maine Road. 'From my point of view I found it very difficult trying to mark Michael Owen – but I'm not the first man to have discovered that,'

Terry said.

'It was a battling performance, the lads are delighted: we've come back twice and a draw was a good result. Now we need to get a win in our final game at Manchester City to make sure of the UEFA Cup place we all need.' That place was secured with a 2–1 win over the relegated Citizens and Terry's season was almost over.

Just two games for the England Under-21s stood between the young defender and his richly deserved summer holiday. The first was a friendly against Mexico and the second a European Championship qualifier against Greece. Wilkinson's previous skipper David Dunn had returned to the squad, but the coach kept faith with Terry as captain of the side. Wilkinson said: 'He's a natural leader and he gives us a presence. He has had a struggle at Chelsea but he has never allowed it to stop him fighting for a place.'

England beat the Central Americans 3–0 in a comfortable victory at Filbert Street, but Terry was one of six players replaced at half-time as Wilkinson made the mass substitutions now so common in international friendlies. The game in Athens twelve days later was an entirely different affair, however, as Terry and his team-mates came up against a talented Greece side. The young Lions were totally outplayed in the first half and were 2–0 down at the break, but after the interval things got even worse.

With an hour gone, Terry nodded a long ball back toward Stephen Bywater, only for the ball to squirm under the West Ham keeper's body. Terry was credited with the own goal but it was clear where the blame lay. The England players began to lose their cool at 3–0, and three of them were quickly booked for petulance and cynical fouls.

Carrick pulled one goal back after 85 minutes, with a fine drive from outside the area, but Luke Young was sent off minutes later for retaliating to a smack in the face, which was unseen by the referee. The Young incident sparked a twenty-man brawl and, once things had calmed down, Terry followed his team-mate off the pitch for an early bath. Fired up at the score-line and with his heart still racing after the melee, the Chelsea defender launched himself a little over-enthusiastically at Dimitris Salpigidis.

Terry claims he got the ball, but it was a dreadful two-footed lunge and the Greek player was fortunate to escape serious injury as he was scythed to the ground. The young defender's composure and self-control have always been evident in his game and, allied to his brilliant positional sense and timing, he has received far fewer bookings than any of the defenders he has played alongside. This dismissal, by Russian referee Joun Baskakov, was his first as a professional and, one of only two to date, his last. It must be put down to an uncharacteristic rush of blood to the head.

So the 2000/01 campaign ended in shameful circumstances for Terry, but it was a season which saw him make the transition from promising reserve to Premiership regular, from unknown youngster to a future

England player.

Who knows how things may have turned out if Vialli had stayed in charge at Chelsea? Terry might have played a few more seasons in the reserves and then been forced to move on, but that doesn't matter now, because Ranieri came in and put his faith in the Barking-born defender. 'Maybe I would still be a sub if Luca had stayed,' said Terry, 'but Claudio has given me my chance, and I'm not complaining.'

The manager had no complaints either as Terry had helped get the team moving in the right direction; his fine form in the second half of the season had helped the Blues move up from fourteenth to finish sixth in the table, and he was named Chelsea's Player of the Season. 'It's unbelievable to be voted player of the year when you consider the squad at this club,' the Essex lad said. 'It's a great honour.'

But even with all the accolades pouring in, John Terry would never forget the confidence placed in him by Claudio Ranieri, the man who gave him his first big chance.

CHAPTER FIVE
DARK DAYS

'I'm not going to sit on the bench for two or three years just watching people play in my position. That would be a step back for me. I want to play Premiership football week in, week out. I played twenty-three games last season in Chelsea's first team and I need to keep improving.'

John Terry, reported here in the *News of the World*, was understandably upset. After a fantastic breakthrough season in Ranieri's team, he was expecting to start the season as part of the first-choice defence. But the 2001/02 season was going to one of the hardest in the defender's career, if not on the pitch then certainly off it.

Following Frank Leboeuf's departure for Marseille, the English youngster wanted to form a new partnership with the Ghana-born colossus that is Marcel Desailly. But the Italian manager needed another centre-back following the departure of Leboeuf and Jes Hogh, so he signed William Gallas to bolster his squad.

Gallas, twenty-three, had caught the eye while playing for Marseille in the Champions League and Ranieri had moved quickly to sign the Frenchman for £6.2m. 'I have been reading about him in the papers,' said Terry. 'The fact that he is a central defender and he said he was looking forward to playing alongside Marcel Desailly has given me food for thought. I'm not sure what's going to happen next season. Will the manager play the new signing with Marcel or me? I just don't know. I'll now have to go back and prove to the manager again that I should be first choice.'

With quotes like these coming from the England Under-21 international, the sharks began to circle. Sensing possible unhappiness in a great young player, Steve McClaren tried to lure Terry away from Chelsea and up to Middlesbrough. Plenty of other clubs were also in the hunt. But Ranieri wasn't interested in selling his young protege; he was merely transforming the squad he had inherited less than a year before and strengthening it in places he deemed appropriate.

The other new arrivals were former Arsenal midfielder Emmanuel Petit and Dutch winger Boudewijn Zenden, both from Barcelona, but much more important for the future of Chelsea was the signing of Frank Lampard from West Ham United. The young England midfielder crossed London for £11m and was determined to make his mark for club and country. 'If you play against the top clubs in

Europe, it gives you that extra edge,' Lampard said to assembled media after completing his transfer. 'I want to be a regular for Chelsea and England and I know I can take the burden. I have always wanted to join a big club and Chelsea have huge ambitions, which have impressed me. I've proved I can do it at West Ham but I'm ready to move on and see this as a new challenge.'

The new challenge for Lampard, Petit and Zenden was to fill the boots of Dennis Wise, Gustavo Poyet and Jon Harley who had all moved on to pastures new. The whole squad was excited by the arrival of the new players and, having spoken to his manager about his position in the team, Terry couldn't wait for the new campaign to get under way. 'I am looking forward to the season,' he said. 'A club like Chelsea needs to be challenging for the title and the manager has signed some great players. We were a bit unlucky last year and suffered from our bad away form, but we will definitely be challenging this year.'

One man who tipped Chelsea, and more especially Terry, for the top was the Marseille-bound Leboeuf, who predicted his former team-mate would be one of the world's top defenders within two years. But Terry refused to get big-headed about all the praise that was coming his way. 'For someone like Frank who has won the World Cup to say that is a great feeling for me,' Terry said in the *Daily Star*. 'I am really excited about this season and I feel good about my own form. I don't know about the England team, but I wouldn't rule myself out just because I am still young. I will do my best and see what happens but it's nice to even be talked about in those terms.

'People might say I have seen Frank off but I don't see it like that. It's great for me if I am going to be in the team. But when Frank was around he gave me a lot of advice and tips that have brought my game on.'

With the signing of Lampard and the continuing development of Terry, Chelsea had two players who could form a world-class English spine to the team for years to come. In the defender's eyes, it was a clear signal of Ranieri's intent to re-establish the Blues as an English team. 'The manager has taken a lot of stick from people saying he doesn't use English players but I think you will see Englishmen become the backbone of the team,' Terry added. 'We have signed Frank Lampard and there are other young players here who will keep that English element strong.'

Despite the improving English presence, Desailly was appointed as the new Chelsea captain. Following the departure of Wise, the France captain seemed an obvious choice to take on the role and Terry started the season alongside his new skipper in the middle of the Blues defence. Chelsea got the campaign off to a bright start with home draws against tough opposition in Newcastle United and Arsenal. The Blues were quick to banish the previous season's dismal away record with a win against Southampton on the South Coast, but Terry now had other responsibilities after he was named captain of the England Under-21 side.

Following their atrocious display in Athens, Howard Wilkinson was sacked and his replacement was a man Terry knew well. The Chelsea defender had worked under David Platt in his brief loan spell at Nottingham Forest in April 2000, and the former England midfielder had seen enough of Terry to make him skipper of the Under-21s on a permanent basis. David Dunn, the former captain, was appointed vice-captain.

Terry and all of his young team-mates were delighted with the new coach. 'The lads respect him so much. His training is first class,' the Chelsea man said. Happy as he was playing for the Young Lions, Terry also had one eye on the future when he added, 'Playing for the senior England side is something I dream of. If I keep playing well for Chelsea, then maybe that chance will come one day.'

His performances on the field indicated that the wait wouldn't be too long, but his off-field misbehaviour would lead to a substantial delay in achieving his England dream. A first warning of things to come arrived in the aftermath of the terrorist attacks on America in September 2001.

'If you are having fun with your team-mates, you trust them more,' Terry said in the *Daily Telegraph*. 'A couple of times here, the lads have come in, trained and then gone their own ways. But sometimes we get the lads together and go for a meal. We went go-karting the other week and are trying to arrange paint-balling. It's good for team spirit; we came into training the day after go-karting and everyone was buzzing.

'There are different age groups in the squad and different people like to do their own thing. Manu Petit likes to spend time on his own before games. The young lads like Jimmy, myself, Eidur Gudjohnsen, Jody Morris and Frank Lampard tend to stick together, have a laugh and play little games of one touch.'

Unfortunately for Terry and his young pals, their 'having a laugh' occasionally got out of hand and this first came to light at the worst possible time.

On September 11, or 9/11 as is written in the American calendar, nineteen men affiliated with Osama bin Laden and Al-Qaeda simultaneously hijacked four United States domestic commercial airliners, two of which were crashed into the Twin Towers of the World Trade Centre in New York, causing the buildings to collapse. The third aircraft crashed into the Pentagon, home to the US Department of Defense, and the fourth plane, which was allegedly heading towards either Capitol Hill or the White House in Washington DC, crashed into a field in Pennsylvania, following passenger resistance.

The official records count 2,986 dead due to the largest suicide assault in the history of the world: 266 people died in the four planes – there were no survivors; there were 125 military and civilian personnel dead at the Pentagon; and the collapse of the World Trade Centre resulted in the death of 2,595 men, women and children.

The implications were almost incomprehensible: an overwhelming loss of life, the devastation of one of the greatest cities on earth and a truly distinct skyline that will never be the same again. The political, social, economic and military effects would be felt for many years to come.

One of the immediate effects of the atrocities was the grounding of aircraft across the globe, leaving holidaymakers stuck at airports around the world and, as far as the Chelsea players were concerned, the postponement of their UEFA Cup first round first leg tie against Levski Sofia at Stamford Bridge.

'UEFA today announced that all UEFA club competition matches scheduled to be played this week are to be postponed as a mark of respect for the victims of yesterday's terrorist attacks in the United States,' read a statement from European football's governing body.

Colin Hutchinson, the managing director of Chelsea, agreed saying: 'Football pales into insignificance at times like this.' So the training programme was changed for the players and the coach gave the Blues squad a heavy work-out on Wednesday and the afternoon off.

Once training was finished, a lot of the players went for lunch together and, with no match until Sunday, the beer inevitably began to flow freely. There's nothing wrong with a few young men enjoying some liquid refreshment with their lunch, but a couple of drinks turned into an alcohol-fuelled rampage and, as the young men were Premiership footballers, the story unsurprisingly made it into the papers. The Chelsea training ground, Harlington, is very close to Heathrow airport and the players' bar crawl took them into close proximity with many grieving Americans, stranded miles from home and unable to reach their loved ones.

As the papers were dominated by the tragic events on the other side of the Atlantic, the story took some time to break. But when journalists received information about the drinking spree, they tracked down eyewitnesses and took their reports to the Chelsea hierarchy.

The *News of the World* finally ran the article on 23 September with an opening paragraph which appalled many people:'Their football game had been cancelled as a mark of respect for the thousands massacred in America only 24 hours earlier – but four of Chelsea's top stars had no intention of mourning the dead. Instead the swaggering Premiership players went on an astonishing five-hour booze-fuelled rampage in the wake of the world's worst terrorist attack – stripping, laughing and vomiting in front of shocked and grieving Americans in a Heathrow hotel bar. The drunken stars – including England Under-21 players Frank Lampard, Jody Morris and John Terry – sneered and hurled abuse as numbed customers watched the disaster unfolding on TV.'

The report, which centred on Heathrow's Posthouse hotel and which also named Eidur Gudjohnsen and ex-Chelsea star Frank Sinclair as members of the party, detailed the footballers' offensive antics at a time when transatlantic flights were grounded and weeping Britons and Americans were desperately trying to phone New

York and Washington for information on loved ones who might have been caught up in the terrorist incident. The players were then reported to have gone on to the Air Bowl, a bowling alley next door to the Posthouse, where they annoyed still more people by sliding head-first down the bowling lanes.

The nation was outraged at such inconsiderate behaviour from supposed role models, and the people in charge at Stamford Bridge moved quickly to punish the young tearaways. Chelsea managing director Colin Hutchinson denounced the players' behaviour and imposed the maximum fine of a fortnight's wages on each.

'The players concerned have each been fined two weeks' wages and that money is being donated to the American appeal,' Hutchinson said to the press. 'Obviously we are condemning their behaviour by fining them. We have acted very quickly in this matter as we were only told about it last night. Claudio Ranieri and myself met the players first thing this morning. Normally we would not tackle disciplinary matters on the day before an important game against Middlesbrough.

'However, because of the seriousness of the matter, we have done it immediately. In the meeting with the players, we reminded them again of their responsibilities. They were categorical that in no way had they intended to insult any individuals and they said that they certainly didn't abuse anyone. They were loud between themselves but they, like everyone at the club, have been as hurt and moved by what has happened in the United States as anyone else. Their behaviour was totally out of order and irresponsible but there is no way that the players went out, in any shape or form, to insult or abuse anyone.

'The players have held their hands up,' Hutchinson added. 'They set a bad example for the youngsters who look up to them, and we have inflicted the maximum punishment we can under the rules.' The fine was the extent of the disciplinary action from the Blues. The manager certainly wasn't happy but he wasn't going to cut off his nose to spite his face; he still needed results and desperately wanted to maintain the unbeaten start to the season. The players had been fined as heavily as possible, and they were still available for selection. Terry, Lampard and Gudjohnsen all started against Middlesbrough at Stamford Bridge and Morris appeared as a substitute in the second half.

The Middlesbrough fans jeered the shamed players and the story was reproduced around the world. Letters poured in castigating the men involved and calling for them to be banned, further fined and even sacked. Other footballers criticised the players for the incident, but Chelsea stood by their men and those involved made their apologies and continued with their lives.

Terry released a statement: 'We wish it hadn't happened and we are sorry if we upset anyone. Our timing was awful, but we never wished to show any disrespect.' His fine amounted to approximately £30,000 but the serious damage had been done to his reputation rather than his wallet. It was a tough way to learn a lesson and only time would tell whether the lesson had truly been learned.

Back on the pitch, things were going from strength to strength for Terry and his team-mates. In the second leg of their UEFA Cup tie, the imposing centre-back registered his first European goal, forcing the ball over the line in Sofia after Desailly had nodded down a Petit corner. That goal killed off the tie after a 3–0 win in London the week before, and Chelsea eventually went through 5–0 aggregate winners. Things got a bit trickier for the Blues in the second round, though, as they were paired with Hapoel Tel-Aviv.

With the political climate as it was at the time, there were obvious security concerns about a trip to Israel. In the wake of the terrorist attacks on September 11 and America's resulting missile attacks on Afghanistan, a number of players were reluctant to travel for the away leg and, after consulting with the manager, William Gallas, Manu Petit, Graeme Le Saux, Albert Ferrer, Eidur Gudjohnsen and Marcel Desailly decided to stay at home.

The preparations weren't helped by the assassination of the Israeli Tourism minister Rahaban Zeevi just hours before Chelsea's players took off from Heathrow. That tragic event took place in Jerusalem, which is 35 miles away from Tel-Aviv, but fortunately for the Blues it was far further than that in terms of political unrest.

Ranieri wasn't at all concerned about travelling to such a supposedly dangerous place and compared it favourably to some of the other lively places he had stayed in throughout his life. 'I lived in Sicily for four years and in Spain,' he said. 'In Sicily they have the Mafia and they are very hard. In Spain everyone has heard of ETA. They target judges and other high-profile people. But I was OK there and I will be OK here.

'To me this place is just like any other city, like London or Rome. But it's OK for some players to stay at home because they will work even harder for the next match. We spoke to every player individually and it was a voluntary decision. I don't think it was the players' responsibility to have to make choices. It was UEFA's responsibility and choice as to where this match was to be played.'

European football's governing body gave the game the green light and Terry had no qualms about travelling. He held no grudges against his team-mates who had decided not to travel. 'I was always convinced it would be safe,' the centre-back said. 'It's the first time I've ever been anywhere like this, but I read stuff and watched the news and was always going to come.

'Once we're out there, warming up for the game, it will all go out of our minds,' Terry added. 'We'll focus the same way we do before every other match. The UEFA Cup is a big competition for us. We went out in the first round last year and we must focus on getting a good result to take back to London. We have a big enough squad to cope in every position and it's a great chance for some of the youngsters who have come out here with us.'

One of those youngsters was seventeen-year-old Uganda-born centre-back Joel Kitamarike. With so many Chelsea defenders choosing to stay at home, Kitamarike came into the starting line-up for the first time and there was also a debut for Mark Bosnich in goal. With such a youthful central defensive pairing – Terry was the elder statesman at just twenty – and a new keeper between the sticks, it was always likely to be a tough day at the office for the Blues. Mario Melchiot didn't help matters by getting himself sent off early in the second half for kicking out at an opponent, and the home side were firmly in control.

Fortunately for Chelsea, Bosnich was in inspired form on his first start and he made a number of spectacular saves to keep his team in the game and, after 89 minutes, it looked like the Blues would take a 0–0 draw back to England. But as the clock ticked down, the home side bagged two late goals to get a well-deserved win.

The first came when Terry handled a cross and Shimon Gershon scored the resultant penalty. While Chelsea were still reeling from this setback, Sergei Klaschenco headed home a Yossi Abuksis cross and the Blues returned to England on the back of an embarrassing 2–0 defeat.

Hapoel coach Dror Kashtan hailed the result as 'one of the greatest moments in Israeli football' and even with Chelsea's depleted side it was still a huge upset. The Blues were adamant that the first loss of the season wouldn't affect their league form and came out fighting in their next game at Elland Road.

Against a high-flying Leeds side, Terry and his team-mates battled to a 0–0 draw and the Essex youngster was impressed with the spirit and desire of the squad. 'The lads were so fired up before the game,' he said in the *Daily Mirror*. 'I have never seen anything like it. We need to be like that before every game to be at our best and achieve what we want to. That was our best performance of the season without a shadow of doubt and it goes to show what we can do when we are up for it. Everyone has talked about how well we played. Now we need to take things on and show that sort of commitment every week.'

The next match was against a struggling West Ham side, and it was time for Lampard to return to Upton Park for the first time since his £11m summer transfer. The subject of plenty of pre-match interviews, the former Hammer found time to comment on one of his new team-mates. 'I have been really impressed with John,' Lampard said. 'He will be in the England squad in the next year or so.'

Sadly for Terry, circumstances would conspire against the midfielder's prediction, and Chelsea also slumped to a first league defeat of the season, losing 2–1 after a lethargic display. It was their fifth game in fifteen days, and some people tried to blame the shoddy showing on the hectic schedule, but not Terry.

'We cannot use tiredness and the number of games as an excuse for our performance at West Ham,' said the centre-back. 'Sometimes we have to play two or three games in a week as professional footballers. There's no doubt we are fit enough and we have a big enough squad to cope, so we can't blame that.'

Chelsea were stuttering and, four days later, they drew with Derby County, their fourth away game in ten days, but the next game up was the home leg against Hapoel Tel-Aviv and Terry was desperate to turn the tie around. 'We owe it to the fans as we are such a big club,' he said. 'We need to stay in a big competition like this to prove we are among the top clubs in Europe. Hapoel were hard to break down in Tel-Aviv and they defended really well. There were only a few minutes to go when I gave the penalty away and they managed to get another one after that, so it's going to be difficult tonight.

'Nobody's holding anything against the lads who didn't travel,' Terry continued. 'There was no reason for them to say sorry. We respect everyone's decision. We all got a bit of stick after the game in Tel-Aviv and we had to prove a lot of people wrong, which I think we did with our response at Leeds. But everyone seems to be against us at the moment and that's given us the will to do even better... We know we've got to score three goals but we have to be careful not to let one in as that would make it even harder for us.'

Terry was extra-motivated to keep a clean sheet and try to beat the Israeli side because an extended UEFA Cup run would certainly benefit the England Under-21 international's chances of making it into the full squad. Other players had caught the eye of Sven-Goran Eriksson in matches against the continent's finest, and Terry was keen to push his claim.

'Mr Eriksson has spoken about young players getting experience in Europe,' Terry added. 'Ashley Cole got a nice run last year with Arsenal and the coach picked him and it's paid off. I feel as if I've been fairly consistent and need to keep it up. Maybe if Mr Eriksson sees me against the top-quality strikers in Europe this year, it will give me more of a chance.'

Unfortunately for Terry and Chelsea, Hapoel proved their first-leg heroics were no fluke and secured a 1–1 draw at the Bridge. The Blues enjoyed the majority of possession but failed to turn chances into goals and their European football was finished for another season.

Terry still had the chance to play on the continent, though, as England's Young Lions faced Holland in the UEFA Under-21 Championship play-off match. The first leg was in Utrecht and Platt's side showed great quality to fight back from 2–0 down to draw 2–2.

David Dunn scored a fantastic equaliser after 57 minutes and was revelling in his role as captain. Due to his suspension following the Greece game, Terry had missed some matches and, with vice-captain Dunn out injured, Aston Villa's Gareth Barry had taken over the armband for a while. But with Dunn and the Chelsea man both available, it was the Blackburn midfielder who was skipper now.

The second leg was played a week later in Derby, and

Early on in his career, John Terry had a short loan spell at the struggling Nationwide First Division side Nottingham Forest which proved useful in honing his burgeoning talent.

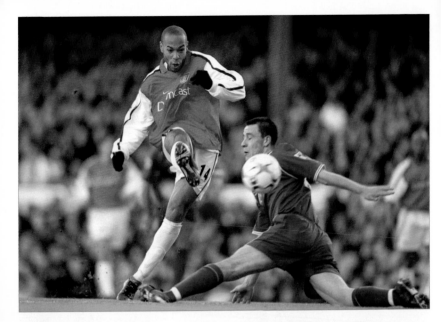

Above: Few strikers find success easy against John Terry, but he has always had a healthy respect for Arsenal frontman Thierry Henry, here firing a shot past his marker in January 2001.

Below: Defenders also score goals! Later in the same game, Terry celebrates scoring the equaliser.

England Under-21 captain John is sent off by the referee for a late tackle on Greece's Dimitris Salpigidis during the second half of their spirited European Championship match in Athens, June 2001.

John Terry, Harlington changing rooms, 2002.

John Terry takes some unusual exercise during pre-season training,
Harlington, 2002.

© *John Ingledew*

Looking pensive and stressed, John Terry arrives at Middlesex Guildhall Crown Court on 7 August 2002 for the third day of his trial, on charges including wounding with intent to cause GBH.

Fifteen days later and Terry, visibly relieved, leaves court after being cleared of all charges, and free to resume his footballing career in earnest.

John Terry secured his senior debut for England against Serbia Montenegro in June 2003, days after more tabloid speculation about his off-pitch antics.

the England Under-21 defence had to be on top form to guarantee the team's progress to the European Championship finals. Terry and King were at their best in front of Chris Kirkland and the young Coventry keeper was exceptional as the home side secured a 1–0 win that would take them to the Championship in Switzerland. 'I'm really looking forward to playing in the tournament,' Terry said. 'I'm sure it will be a fantastic experience.'

For any of the bright young England players that would miss out on the World Cup in Japan and Korea, there was now the compensation of the Under-21 European Championship. And although Terry would eventually miss out on both tournaments, he had played an integral part in the youngsters' qualification.

Since losing to Hapoel Tel-Aviv in the UEFA Cup, Chelsea had struggled to beat anybody. Following the defeat in Israel, Ranieri's side drew five and lost one of their next seven matches. And things got worse for the Blues as a 0–0 home draw with Blackburn Rovers ended with boos and jeers from the Stamford Bridge crowd – the fans were losing patience, and so were the players.

'If we are really going to challenge for the title, then we've got to stop drawing games,' Terry said, 'particularly against the likes of Blackburn. We are not creating enough but we have got to keep going and get the crowd back on our side. We owe it to them.'

The fans had always been good to Terry, voting him Young Player of the Year in 1998/99 and Player of the Year in 2000/01. As a Londoner, albeit from the wrong side of the capital, the men, women and children in the stands could relate to him, and he to them. He knew they were getting frustrated and he wanted to turn things around as much for them as for himself – and they loved him for it.

'Chelsea fans are no different to any other fans,' Terry said in the *Daily Star*. 'They want to see home-grown players on the pitch. There was Dennis before and now there's Jody Morris and myself who have come up through the ranks, but I'm sure there will be many more.

'It was a great honour to win Player of the Year when you think of all the other players at this club. The fans have always been good to me. When I first came into the side, I wasn't sure I'd done OK but they realised I was young and always encouraged me. When I came back into the team they were still OK with me and that gave me a huge lift.'

The team's poor form was in stark contrast to Terry's continued brilliance, and the bad results meant that the pressure on Ranieri was mounting. But a 2–0 win over Leeds United in the League Cup helped to alleviate some of the anxiety over the manager's position and the players were in no mood to see him leave. 'I would love to see him remain here and the other lads feel the same,' Terry said at a press conference. 'The coach has given me my chance and I owe him a lot. Claudio has been fine about everything and told us earlier this week that he was right behind the players.

'We have also been fine and when people talk of there being a crisis at the club, it is rubbish. We are all in it together and it is a good atmosphere. We wanted to put things right after the Blackburn game. The fans are entitled to their opinions but we're just as frustrated as they are.'

Before the match at Elland Road, the speculation about Ranieri's future had been increasing and there were allegations of offers of resignation and of training ground bust-ups but Terry was having none of it. The defender said: 'Things have been as normal this week at the training ground as they have been all this season.'

The Chelsea players would have to be united for their next match, away at Old Trafford. Alex Ferguson's side hadn't enjoyed the best autumn but were still expected to beat the Blues at home. The match against Manchester United brought Terry up against Ruud van Nistelrooy for the first time, and his team-mates warned him about the Dutch danger man.

'The day before a game, I look at the striker I am playing against,' Terry said to the *Daily Telegraph*. 'I try to learn whether they like to run at a defender or get close, hold the defender and then run. I have learned playing against Thierry Henry, Michael Owen, Emile Heskey and Ruud van Nistelrooy.

'Van Nistelrooy's all-round game is superb. Mario Melchiot and Jimmy Floyd Hasselbaink know Van Nistelrooy from Holland, and they were saying before we played United that his touch was unbelievable. I was thinking: "His touch can't be as good as Juan Sebastian Veron's or David Beckham's." But there were a couple of moments when I felt I could get the ball and he would take it away and I was thinking: "Yeah, Mario and Jimmy were right."

'You have to respect Van Nistelrooy and, if he is going to get a touch, keep him facing away from goal. He is the striker who has caused me the most problems this season. With Henry, it is not only his pace that is difficult to deal with; he is so clever with his runs. He and Patrick Vieira have a good link in midfield, with Vieira playing great balls through to him. Owen has pace and he uses it cleverly. His all-round game, touch and finishing are second to none among English players.'

Terry had a lot of respect for his opposition, but Chelsea put one over on the Red Devils in early December as they triumphed 3–0 in the North-west. It was the fifth league defeat inflicted on Ferguson's side and it wasn't even Christmas. The Champions had little chance of defending their title after such a poor first half of the season but a win at the 'Theatre of Dreams' gave the Blues' aspirations a boost. 'Talk of the championship at Chelsea isn't banned,' Terry said after the match. 'This was our best performance of the season and, if we can keep our form, we have a chance of winning the league.'

It wasn't just the Chelsea performance that had the critics purring. Terry continued to put in mature and commanding displays at the heart of the Blues' defence.

With Desailly out injured, the English defender took more responsibility alongside Gallas and, as the pair formed an excellent partnership, there was more talk of Terry moving up into the full England squad in time for the World Cup finals. 'It's far too early to talk about that,' Terry said. 'Mr Eriksson has said that everyone has a chance and that he will look seriously at some of the Under-21 team players. But first I have to keep playing well for Chelsea and then hope that other things follow.'

The young defender's fine form at the back for Chelsea and the injury to Desailly meant that other rewards soon came his way. Against Charlton Athletic at Stamford Bridge on 5 December 2001, John Terry led out Chelsea for the very first time.

'Claudio came to me the day before the game,' Terry told Chelsea TV, 'and it was a big surprise because at the time Le Saux was second in line, and there were obviously other players ahead of me, but Claudio came to me and said I had come on as a player and I was ready for that role.

'He said: "This is the game I am going to give it to you," and I remember Graeme coming up to me and wishing me good luck and saying how I was the future of the club and it was all about me. The manager and the players thought I was the right choice. Everyone was backing me, from Jimmy to Gianfranco, and when you have players like that supporting you then you can't go wrong.'

Unfortunately for Terry, things could still go wrong even with those brilliant players behind him, and Chelsea lost

1–0. It took a header from Kevin Lisbie 2 minutes from time to bring Chelsea's unbeaten home record to an end. There was no winning start for Terry as skipper, but the captaincy reminded the youngster just how far he had come, and how much faith Ranieri had in the England Under-21 international.

Now an established first-teamer and the only player to start every game that season, Terry pledged his future to Chelsea. He was as happy as he'd ever been and saw no reason why that might change. 'I would like to think I will always play for Chelsea,' he said to the *Sunday Express*. 'You don't get many one-club players nowadays but I definitely want to stay at Chelsea for the rest of my career if I can. Definitely.

'Obviously the World Cup is a dream… but I'm just taking one step at a time at the minute.'

As much as Terry tried to keep his feet on the ground and play down any suggestions of World Cup glory, the press were hell-bent on pushing the Chelsea youngster into the squad to face Argentina, Sweden and Nigeria in Group F of the summer's tournament in Japan and Korea. The media quizzed the men that matter and the replies were unrelentingly excellent. 'Physically tough, mentally strong, reads the game well and not fazed by either the cleverest or the quickest strikers,' said Platt, the England Under-21 coach.

Gwyn Williams was still singing the praises of the player he helped bring to Chelsea. 'It was when he filled out and shot up in height that we tried him out as a defender,' said Chelsea's assistant manager, to the *Mail on Sunday*. 'He's done extremely well. International football is different to the Premiership because strikers tend to sit off, so defenders have to be comfortable on the ball. He's excellent at that and when he has to get in a tackle he's tough and as brave as a lion. Certainly there's not another English centre-back we would prefer to have at Chelsea. Sven has watched him a lot. I think he knows all about him.'

Carlo Cudicini had established himself as Chelsea's number one goalkeeper with a string of clean sheets and he had great things to say about the man who helped keep the attackers at bay. The Italian said, in the *Daily Mirror*: 'If I was Sven-Goran Eriksson, I would definitely call him up for the World Cup. He is playing well and he certainly deserves it. John hasn't got a lot of experience like Marcel Desailly but he's playing with his heart. He's very strong and maybe he's older in his head than actual age.'

His maturity on the pitch belied his years, but Terry still had the youthful enthusiasm expected of a twenty-year-old, and, as the profile of the Premiership kept rising, he was just enjoying the chance to play against some of the world's finest footballers. 'It's matching yourself against players of such outstanding quality as Henry, Owen and Van Nistelrooy which adds to the education and experience,' the defender said in the Sunday *Mail*. 'The main frustration at the moment is our own irritating inconsistency. Last season we struggled to win away from home and this time we're struggling to win at Stamford Bridge. We don't seem to be able to put our finger on what's wrong.'

The manager was sure there was nothing wrong in the defensive area and he had an embarrassment of riches with Desailly on his way back from injury and Terry and Gallas conceding only one goal in eight games.

Ranieri said to the *Daily Mirror*: 'It will be difficult for Desailly to find his place. Last year I had Frank Leboeuf who was a fantastic player but for me John Terry was better and so I played John Terry. Now the defence is playing very well. I still want Desailly at his maximum but it's very difficult to put Marcel back in the team.'

The back four of Melchiot, Terry, Gallas and Babayaro in front of Cudicini had helped to make Chelsea hard to beat, and in the run-up to Christmas the attack started to fire as well. The Blues beat Liverpool 4–0 and Bolton 5–1 in two dominant displays at the Bridge and Ranieri's side were in top form for the trip to Highbury on Boxing Day.

Having not scored for Chelsea in the Premiership until the match against Bolton, Lampard made it two in two games with the opening goal after 31 minutes, but Sol Campbell's first Arsenal goal and one for Sylvain Wiltord took the Gunners back to the top of the table. Despite conceding two goals, the Chelsea defence continued to pick up praise, and the opposition manager was very impressed by the two young centre-halves.

Arsene Wenger said: 'Gallas is good at right-back, good at left-back and good at centre-back. He is very quick and a good all-round player. He will be one of the contenders to win a position in central defence when France rebuild after the World Cup.

'I think Terry is outstanding. They both did well against us on Boxing Day. We had to work very hard to create chances. Chelsea went to Leeds and did not concede a goal, did the same at Manchester United and the same against Liverpool. That's not coincidence. It shows the two boys have great qualities.'

Terry was worried at the start of the season that he might lose his place to the former France Under-21 international, but now it was Desailly who was finding it difficult to feature in the Blues defence. Despite starting every game for Chelsea in the first half of the season, Terry wasn't taking his place for granted. He said: 'It'll be interesting when Marcel is fit. I don't know what the manager is going to do and I wouldn't like to say any more.'

It had been a mixed few months for the young defender. Chelsea were sixth in the table and Terry had started all twenty-seven matches so far in the campaign, even leading the Blues out on occasion. He was also captain of the England Under-21s and was tipped by some pundits to make the step up to the senior side sooner rather than later. But away from the pitch Terry had embarrassed himself in the wake of September 11 and, as he entered the New Year, it became clear that as difficult as the fall-out from that episode had been for the Essex lad, it was nothing compared to what lay around the corner.

CHAPTER SIX
TRIAL AND TRIBULATION

'It was my life in the hands of the jury. Nothing can prepare you for going through it. I'm just so thankful that it's over and that they listened to me. It wasn't until the verdicts were read out that I finally felt free,' Terry revealed in the *Guardian*. 'I remember holding Jody's hand and giving it a really tight squeeze as our fate was decided. I looked back at my family, friends and girlfriend, and the tears were flowing again. The fact all twelve people on the jury voted in our favour on all charges speaks volumes for the injustice of the whole episode. But I've stopped looking in the past now – it's time to move on.'

John Terry left the courthouse in tears after being cleared of all charges. The Chelsea starlet had long been considered the new Tony Adams, and Terry had been on the verge of emulating his idol with a holiday taken at Her Majesty's convenience. Just twenty-one years old, he had faced the genuine threat of a custodial sentence if found guilty. But now, nearly eight months after the incident in question, the Chelsea defender could finally put the whole episode behind him.

It should all have been so different. On the evening of Thursday, 3 January 2002, Terry went out with two of his closest friends to celebrate the birth of a child. His team-mate Jody Morris was overjoyed at having become a father for the first time to a baby girl, Romy, and the two Blues headed for a meal in a nice bar-restaurant in Surrey with Wimbledon defender Des Byrne. Despite Chelsea having an FA Cup match against Norwich on the Saturday afternoon, the trio decided to head on for a couple more drinks after dinner. Few could have predicted where the night was going to end and the potential repercussions following what should have been such a happy occasion.

After the meal Terry drove the three of them from Epsom into London in his new car, so that they could continue the evening's entertainment. Appropriately for the Chelsea boys, they headed to Knightsbridge and, undeterred by the fact that their intended destination was closed, they headed to a private members club where Morris knew one of the directors.

The Wellington Club is the kind of place that is very popular with London's rich and famous, a place where three sportsmen could happily spend some of their vast disposable income surrounded by actors, fashion designers and assorted socialites. The vodka was slipping down quite easily as the lads listened to the latest trendy tunes and slowly made their presence felt in the club.

The young trio – Terry, Byrne, twenty, and Morris, twenty-three – moved on to shooters and cocktails and, after a while, the staff deemed that they had outstayed their welcome. The straw that broke the camel's back came when Morris allegedly spat out his drink at the bar, and soon the doormen were helping the troublesome triumvirate out of the club. As they left the premises, a fight broke out. The police arrived to find the entrance littered with blood and broken glass and arrested Terry and Byrne.

As the two defenders were still being questioned at Belgravia police station, the story broke in the national press the next day. The Chelsea centre-back had been in fine form throughout the season deputising for Marcel Desailly and even delaying the France captain's return from injury, but now he found himself in a police cell the day before a crucial FA Cup third round match – not exactly ideal preparation for a big game.

Of the three players, Terry had by far the most to lose after heading out 'for a couple' that fateful Thursday night. After all, he was the man keeping a World Cup-winner out of the Chelsea side: Blues midfielder Morris was out injured and Dublin-born Byrne was a player at Wimbledon, then in the second flight of English football. But Terry was the England Under-21 captain and he had been out drinking just 36 hours before an important cup-tie.

Chelsea had been knocked out of the UEFA Cup by Israeli side Hapoel Tel-Aviv and, with the club's debts spiralling, a successful cup run was vital to the Blues' progress. Funds were not available for any significant transfer signings but the revenue generated by some silverware could help Claudio Ranieri to keep hold of his key performers come the summer. For such a vital cog in the Chelsea defence to go out on the town so close to a game was downright irresponsible.

Following the trouble Terry had been in less than four months previously after the drunken binge at Heathrow, people at Chelsea and in the footballing world at large had genuine grounds for concern: just how much did the youngster want to play professional football?

In his programme notes the following week, Ken Bates wrote about Terry, 'He must ask himself if he wants to follow the path which is littered with drunks and wrecks of former players or emerge from this episode stronger and better for it.

'The problem is that most footballers come from working-class backgrounds and suddenly find themselves at a very early age earning money that their peers can only dream of. Unfortunately much of it is frittered away on fast cars, designer clothes and an attitude to pleasure reminiscent of the 18–30 holiday packages.'

Bates was right to be worried because it wasn't just his players that were getting themselves in trouble with booze and Bobbies. The idea of footballers acting as role models was becoming almost laughable now that instances of their misbehaviour were claiming almost as many front pages as back pages in the nation's newspapers.

The high-profile case of Lee Bowyer and Jonathan Woodgate ran for almost two years, from January 2000 until December 2001, and has continued to cast a long shadow over both players throughout their careers. In some quarters, this case was cited as the main reason behind the unedifying fall from grace of Leeds United from Champions League quarter-finalists to lower-league also-rans in a very short space of time.

There has also been an increase in the number of cases of alleged sexual misconduct among footballers, to go with the usual kiss-and-tell stories that the editors of the Sunday tabloids seem to enjoy so much, along with growing pressure on the England management to take action against players with off-field problems.

With this in mind, England manager Sven-Goran Eriksson announced, under pressure from his bosses at the FA, that no player facing legal action would be considered for selection until their case was resolved. Innocent until proven guilty in the eyes of the courts, Terry was being punished by his national coach for a crime he continued to deny.

Late in the evening of Friday, 4 January, Terry was released by the police but he would have to appear at Horseferry Road Magistrates' Court the following Wednesday to answer charges of assault causing actual bodily harm and affray – intentionally using or threatening unlawful violence such as would cause a reasonable person to fear for his safety. But Chelsea stuck by him, and Terry was named in the squad for the FA Cup match at Carrow Road, where he appeared as a second-half substitute in a 0–0 draw with Norwich. It was the first match of the season that Terry hadn't started and his manager certainly wasn't concerned about his protege. After watching him play the second 45 minutes, Ranieri said: 'John Terry played very well, just like usual. I have no worries about him. He's a good man.'

The press, however, disagreed with the amiable Chelsea boss and began to write off the defender's career. The news got worse for the Blues when Morris was arrested on Tuesday, 7 January and charged with the same offences as Terry and Byrne. This forced Chelsea's managing director, Colin Hutchinson, into action and he released a statement regarding his two players. 'John Terry and Jody Morris broke club rules by being in a nightclub at 1.30am, less than 48 hours before a match,' he said.

'They will both be fined the maximum possible, which is two weeks' wages. We are carrying out our own investigation. They are due to appear in court. For the moment, we will follow the guideline of innocent until proven guilty.'

Docked something in the region of £30,000, banished from the England set-up until further notice and with a court case hanging over his head – the full cost of the night out was increasingly apparent – John Terry may have been down in the dumps but he still had his football as Chelsea continued to stand by their man.

Hutchinson later commented: 'We took a barrage of adverse publicity that we shouldn't have played him against Norwich, but we knew that before we said to Claudio that he could still play him and that, whatever we did, we couldn't win.' It would be tough to get the press back on side and media relations were further strained when Terry and Morris both started in the League Cup Semi-final first-leg against Tottenham on the same day as their first court appearance.

Chelsea beat their London rivals 2–1 at Stamford Bridge after their two starlets entered pleas of not guilty in the morning. The three players – Byrne was also present – were granted bail, which meant they were available for their clubs under the conditions set out by district court judge Roger Davies: they had to stay at their then home addresses, they couldn't go within half a mile of the Wellington Club in Knightsbridge, central London, and they were not to have any contact with, or interfere with, prosecution witnesses.

Fortunately for Terry, Morris and their employers, Stamford Bridge is just over two miles away from the Wellington Club – so they could continue to play football, but in obeying their bail conditions to the letter of the law they would have to be very careful which route they took to and from home matches for a little while. The hearing lasted less than an hour and Terry could try and forget about the incident for the time being a the next court date was set for mid-February.

Chelsea were enjoying a very busy January; they had nine matches in the month due to their continued presence in both domestic cup competitions. With Desailly fit again, Ranieri took the opportunity to rest Terry for the FA Cup replay against Norwich, and he wasn't missed as the Blues won 4–0.

The English centre-back returned refreshed for the next game as Chelsea hammered West Ham 5–1 at Stamford Bridge, but there was a far less accomplished performance in the following match at White Hart Lane. The second leg of the League Cup Semi-final was a disaster for the Blues as they threw away a 2–1 lead from the first leg and were knocked out of the cup after a second-half capitulation.

Things started badly for Chelsea when a mistake by Terry in the second minute allowed Steffen Iversen to open the scoring. The defender dithered when Cudicini parried a shot to him, and the Norwegian striker nipped in to fire home from six yards. Tim Sherwood and Teddy Sheringham scored either side of half-time to make it 3–0, and Jimmy Floyd Hasselbaink was sent off in a case of mistaken identity: Mario Melchiot raised a hand to Sheringham and his compatriot saw red, before two more Tottenham goals made it 5–0. Mikael Forssell bagged a superb solo goal right at the death but it was little consolation after a dismal display.

Terry's uncharacteristic error had started the rout and it was the first sign that his off-field problems might be interfering with his performances on the park. All the new press from the arrest and the impending lawsuit meant that Terry was now much more famous than before, and receiving a lot more attention when out in public.

'It was quite difficult at the start,' Terry recalled to Chelsea TV. 'I would be out at places and I could feel people staring at me. Being quite new to it, it made me paranoid and uncomfortable, but I feel like I haven't changed – I'm still the same person. Sometimes I think people do look at me a bit differently. I feel if I do muck about in a restaurant, laughing loudly with my mates, they think bad things, but that's just me.'

Whatever the reason for Terry's mistake against the Lilywhites, it wasn't enough to dent the confidence of the manager and Ranieri continued to pick the youngster in the Chelsea back-line. Terry's form soon picked up and, after helping his side shut out Leeds on the way to a 2–0 win in west London, he was again making headlines for the right reasons.

Following his Man of the Match display against the Yorkshire side, the defender thanked his manager for standing by him. Terry said: 'The support Claudio's given me has helped a great deal and I owe him a lot. He could have dropped me but he didn't and the club have shown great faith in coming out and speaking publicly about the support they've given me. That's nice and I now owe it to him and the club. I've dipped in form a little bit in the past few weeks but I feel I've performed well in the last two games against West Ham and Leeds.'

He refused to blame his loss of form on the impending court case. 'I've not been affected by anything outside football. I don't want to go into that but it's not really affected me on the training ground or the pitch at all. It was just a dip in form; it's good to see that I've picked up again.

'Once I go out on the pitch I can focus on just one thing, and that's totally football. I'm not worrying about the other thing either; I'm just concentrating on my game. So hopefully that can keep on going well. We have suffered from inconsistency over the past two or three seasons, where we've performed well and then, against the so-called lesser teams, we haven't done as well. We can't put our finger on it but we need to go to Leicester and prove we don't just beat the big sides.'

Chelsea dug deep to beat the Foxes at Filbert Street and came back from 1–0 and 2–1 down to win 3–2 in the last minute, and they repeated the trick four days later to beat West Ham. In the FA Cup fourth-round replay at Upton Park, it was Terry's goal in the 93rd minute that stopped the tie going to extra-time and put the Blues through to the next round.

Claudio Ranieri was very happy for his troubled star and declared: 'John Terry is a strong character and a strong man. He was down after the Leicester game on Saturday, when he allowed James Scowcroft to score twice. So his winner was a very important goal both for his confidence and the club.

'The whole team showed a lot of character and we battled very hard,' the Roman added. 'I have won the Italian Cup and the Spanish Cup. Now I am dreaming of the FA Cup. They were all crazy goals, but sometimes there are games when it helps to score crazy goals. Every goal for Chelsea is fantastic, though. West Ham had conceded only seven league goals at home and only Fulham and Spurs had won here, so it was a big victory.'

West Ham's opening goal took a huge deflection off Terry on the way past Cudicini, and some watchers put it down as an own goal, so the imposing defender was even happier than usual to claim the deciding goal at the death.

'It was great to get the winner,' he said. 'I thought that corner in injury-time would be our last chance and we took it. As for the first goal, Jermain shot across the box, and the ball went in off my foot. I am happy to give it to Defoe – I didn't know anything about it.'

Having scored the winner, Terry was able to put the opening goal, whether an own goal or not, behind him and was happy with his hero's billing after all the bad publicity. 'It is nice to get the headlines for good reasons,' he said. 'On the pitch, I am able to forget about my problems off the pitch. Hopefully, they'll end fairly soon and I can just continue with my football. As soon as I am on the training pitch, it is totally out of my mind. Not that I worry about it during the afternoons, but I just want to concentrate on my football. I have received great encouragement from everybody. It was a huge relief for me to score.'

Terry added: 'I set myself a target of five goals this season and I've only got two, so I have a way to go yet. When I was young, I was at West Ham for three or four years. We had a fairly good team, but then we got a new Under-13 manager and no one enjoyed it. I left and joined Chelsea, so it was a big moment for me to come back and score and I'll be able to give my family a bit of stick for it now, as they're all mad West Ham fans.'

The wish to see the young defender maintaining his top form in the Blues defence wasn't held by Terry alone, as his team-mates were now fully appreciative of the youngster's talents. His good friend and fellow Eastender Lampard said: 'John is a very strong character. We knew he would always stay strong and, while people say there have been dips, his performances have been top class all season. Whatever goes on outside football, he will put it to the back of his mind on the pitch. We have tried to stick together and let him know we need him as he's that important to us.'

The importance of Terry in the Chelsea back four was becoming increasingly obvious, and the press were still of the opinion that the young centre-back would make a valuable addition to England's World Cup squad. The FA had not yet reached a verdict on whether to extend the suspension imposed on players facing criminal charges into the summer's tournaments and, if Eriksson was going to select Terry or either of the Leeds United pair, Bowyer and Woodgate, then he would want to see them play for England before the end of the season.

'It's a decision the FA and I have to take before the next game on Bowyer, Woodgate and Terry,' said Eriksson. 'We will have to get together. It's very difficult to say what's right and what's wrong. I think you should always listen to the critics. But you should try to have your own opinions. You must take a decision and then stand by it. We will be criticised whatever decision we take.'

Before any conclusion could be reached, the Chelsea stopper fractured a toe in his right foot against Aston Villa, which put him out of action for the foreseeable future. Terry sustained the injury in a tackle with Darius Vassell during the second half at Villa Park, and his absence from the team was a heavy blow to the Blues' fading Champions League hopes. It also brought to an end his run of thirty-five consecutive Premiership starts.

'John's got a crack in his toe and will be out for a month,' Gwyn Williams said. 'He went into a fifty-fifty block tackle with Vassell and he just didn't come out right. The X-ray didn't show a lot, so he had a scan and it's a hairline fracture. These things take time to overcome so you've just got to wait.'

It was the last thing Terry wanted. Football was the one release he had from the court case and, without training and matches to look forward to, the Essex lad only had time on the treatment table and appointments with his lawyer to fill his diary. The legal proceedings had got no further than preliminary hearings and Terry was now facing four charges over the incident in question.

Terry was already answering to charges of assault causing ABH and affray, and now the Crown Prosecution Service had added wounding with intent to cause grievous bodily harm and having a bottle as an offensive weapon. The wounding charge carried a life sentence as its maximum penalty, and things got worse for Terry when he again found himself in the news for all the wrong reasons.

'CHELSEA STAR TERRY IN NEW NIGHTCLUB SHAME' ran the *Sun* headline. 'Soccer star John Terry sickened nightclub revellers by relieving himself against a bar – after peeing into an empty beer glass. The Chelsea ace then pretended to drink the glass's contents as pals laughed and cheered. Defender Terry – an England Under-21 international – was thrown out by bouncers after a horrified woman employee spotted his vile antics. Last night a clubber said: "It was disgusting."'

Terry was escorted out of the Time and Envy club in Romford, Essex and left quietly by cab. Without football to keep him in check, he was back in trouble, but at least Chelsea were doing OK without him.

In the FA Cup fifth round, the Blues came from 1–0 down to beat Preston North End 3–1 at Stamford Bridge, and they followed that up by winning three out of four London derbies in the space of eleven days, the most impressive of which was the FA Cup quarter-final win at White Hart Lane.

Seeking revenge for the humiliating 5–1 defeat in the League Cup at the same ground six weeks earlier, Ranieri's side exacted brutal retribution, beating Tottenham 4–0. The two sides met again three days later in the league at Stamford Bridge with the same result, and the Blues made it three 4–0 wins in a row when Sunderland came to SW6 the following Saturday.

Terry returned to the Chelsea team over the Easter weekend and marked his comeback with a goal in the 2–1 win over Derby. He replaced the injured Gallas at half-time, and opened the scoring five minutes later, heading home Graeme Le Saux's left-wing cross from close range.

Having missed seven matches due to injury, a lot of frustration had built up in the young defender and grabbing a goal gave him good reason to vent some of that. It showed in his celebration. He was simply overjoyed to be back. It wasn't just Terry who went over the top after the goal; the reaction of the Stamford Bridge fans spoke volumes about their feelings for the increasingly popular defender.

'It's been frustrating with my injury but the response from the crowd was fantastic,' he said. 'It was great to be back and I'm delighted I was able to repay the supporters with a goal. You could see by my celebration that I went a bit mad. That was what it meant to me. It was a big release. These have been frustrating times, with the injury and everything off the field. It was nice to come back like that. I'd been injured for six or seven weeks and it had been frustrating getting fit again.'

Back in the side and at his influential best, Terry also helped to create the winner for Manu Petit five minutes from time. Andy Oakes palmed the defender's header on to the post and the Frenchman was on hand to guide the ball home for his first Chelsea goal. The win ensured three more valuable points to help the Blues' quest for fourth place in the league, which would also serve as a ticket into club football's top competition.

'We're confident we can make the Champions League,' Terry said. 'We have to wait for Newcastle to make mistakes or slip up, but all we can do is keep winning. I remember the big Champions League nights from a few years ago.

'I was involved. I wasn't even on the bench or anything, but I was involved and I'm looking forward to that again, if we make it. It would be brilliant for me to play in the Champions League. It is the biggest competition in Europe. Everyone wants to play in it and I'm no different. When the players are together, we talk about the Champions League – that's what we want. We're a massive club. That's what the fans want. That's what the players want. It will be a big disappointment if we don't get it.'

A win against Everton the following weekend helped towards that aim and temporarily lifted Chelsea into fourth place ahead of Newcastle, who faced Fulham two days later. Terry missed most of the match against the

Toffees, after coming off second best in a collision with one of the goalposts. The big defender left the pitch after 15 minutes and had to have twelve stitches to hold the wound together. But speaking after the game he was far more concerned with the three points.

'This is the first time this season we've been in fourth place and it's vital we hang on to it,' Terry said. 'Obviously we're relying on Fulham doing us a favour on Monday, but every time we win, it increases the pressure on Newcastle. I will be training normally – but I just can't head the ball! I think I'll miss Blackburn on Wednesday, but I should be OK for the semi-final next weekend.'

Terry made his first Crown Court appearance on the morning of the Rovers match, during which the judge set the next court appearance for June, but he still played at Ewood Park in a match which ended 0-0. The fact that the court case wouldn't start until the summer ended Terry's hopes of making the World Cup squad, and he wouldn't even have the reward of playing for the Under-21 side he had led to qualification at the European Championship finals.

'I am really gutted,' the Chelsea defender said in the *Sun*. 'Not just about not being in the senior squad but I have been a major part of the Under-21 side. I am so disappointed about not being allowed to go there. But that is something the FA have decided and I have got to live with it. I have been speaking to the Under-21 lads and I am hoping I can go out to Switzerland to support them.'

Terry quickly put his personal disappointment behind him, however, as he helped Chelsea go past Fulham and into the FA Cup Final.

Playing their west London rivals at Villa Park, Terry scored the only goal of the game after 40 minutes and helped keep the Cottagers at bay, ensuring it was the Blues that would be heading to Cardiff in May. Hasselbaink's right-wing corner struck Melchiot and broke to Terry on the near post – whose shot was touched over the line by Louis Saha attempting to clear. It was the defender's fourth goal of a very mixed season, and he summed up his feelings perfectly when he said: 'This will give me something to look forward to other than my court case.'

It was another superb effort by Terry, the overall performance by Ranieri's side was disappointing and they were outplayed in most areas of the park, but still the defence stood firm. The manager was delighted with his back line, and he said: 'Terry was fantastic, he played very well and scored the goal. But the whole defence played well. Desailly was magnificent – they all were.'

It wasn't just the manager who had noticed Terry's good form, however, and that point was highlighted at the PFA Player of the Year Awards Gala Dinner. The evening after the FA Cup semi-final, Terry attended the dinner as one of the six contenders for the Young Player of the Year Award. Nominated by his fellow players in the Professional Footballers' Association, he was up against Steven Gerrard, Ledley King, Michael Ricketts, then at

Bolton, Darius Vassell, and Newcastle's Craig Bellamy. The Welsh striker, Bellamy, walked away with the trophy but it was good to know that the other players still held Terry in such high regard.

By reaching the FA Cup Final, the Blues qualified for Europe because the other finalists, Arsenal, had already cemented a place in the top four and would thus be going into the Champions League, so the Cup-winners' UEFA Cup spot was guaranteed for Chelsea, unless they too could finish in the top four and have a run in Europe's premier club competition.

With three games left to play, the possibility of reaching fourth looked remote and it was all but out of sight after the Blues lost 3–0 to Manchester United at home.

Seeking retribution for their 3–0 reverse at Old Trafford in December, Ferguson's side dominated the match from start to finish and, if anything, the score-line flattered Chelsea. Terry certainly didn't enjoy himself against the reigning champions. 'I couldn't wait for the final whistle, to be honest,' he said. 'United were taking the mickey out of us and we got what we deserved. We should have been buzzing, but we weren't sharp at all.'

The result meant that Newcastle needed just one point from their final two games to secure fourth place in the league and, after such a dismal showing, the Chelsea players would be fighting for their places in the Cup Final team in the next match, away to Middlesbrough.

'It was going to be difficult before this game,' Ranieri

added, 'and now it will be very hard to reach fourth place and the final Champions League position. Now the next match is very important for us. It will be very important for the players.'

That game at the Riverside Stadium was much more straightforward for Terry and his team-mates as they wrapped up the points with a couple of goals just before half-time. After beating Boro 2–0 and having missed the starting line-up for only ten games in the season – nine while out injured and one due to his arrest – Terry was confident of starting the match at the Millennium Stadium where he would have to face Thierry Henry.

'Thierry Henry is definitely one of the best players in the world and the prospect of playing against him is quite frightening – although I'm looking forward to it as well,' Terry said. 'As a kid, everyone watches the FA Cup Final and dreams of being part of it. That's exactly what I did, so this will be a dream come true. Everyone realises how important the Cup is and it would be a great honour to win the trophy.'

Then he provided an insight into his very superstitious nature when he added: 'Every night before we play, I give the 2000 medal a kiss as a good luck superstition. I always look at it and think of that day; my best memory is definitely being part of that FA Cup-winning team.'

As an unused substitute at the 2000 FA Cup Final, Terry had already had a taste of the atmosphere and intensity of the big occasion but now he was looking forward to a playing role in the 2002 Final. Unluckily for the young defender, some more bad luck off the pitch conspired to prevent him from starting the match.

'I had a virus in the morning. It affected my ears and I lost my balance,' Terry said. 'I woke up dizzy, staggered into a chair and phoned the doctor. That was at 7am. But I was disappointed I didn't start the match. I had an injection to clear the virus, then had a fitness test and said I was 100 per cent but the manager decided not to go with me.

'It was five minutes before I was going down to the team meeting and I heard a knock on the door and I knew straight away it was the manager. I opened the door and he told me I wasn't in the starting line-up. After he'd gone, I felt like crying. It would have been a great achievement for me to start in an FA Cup Final but it wasn't to be. He just said to me that, with what had happened, he wasn't going to play me.'

Terry added: 'He said Celestine Babayaro, Marcel Desailly and Jimmy Floyd Hasselbaink were all struggling and, if he started with me, that would have been four players with fitness worries. It was a tough decision but he did what he felt was right. It seems like somebody up there doesn't like me.'

Starting a second Cup Final on the bench, Terry at least got onto the pitch in 2002, when he replaced Babayaro at half-time. The Nigerian full-back appeared to be struggling during the first 45 minutes and he didn't reappear after the interval as Terry went into the centre of defence with Gallas moving across to left-back. The reshuffled Blues found their feet quickly after the break and Arsenal were soon on the back foot, but when the first goal came in the 69th minute, it was the Gunners who took the lead against the run of play.

Ray Parlour picked up a neat reverse pass from Sylvain Wiltord and fired a stunning shot into the top corner from 25 yards as the defence backed off. The goal galvanised Arsene Wenger's team and, ten minutes later, they were 2–0 up after an even more impressive strike.

Edu played in Freddie Ljungberg and the Swedish midfielder decided to run at the Chelsea defence. 'I was the last man,' Terry said. 'Freddie cut inside myself and William Gallas, jinked right and left and then I slipped as we were jostling side by side, he got through and it was a good finish. Ljungberg is on fire, no doubt about that. I'd say Lamps is spot on when he says he is the best player in the country at the moment.'

The red-haired Arsenal midfielder scored seven goals in seven games as the Gunners marched towards a Premiership and FA Cup Double, and his cool, calm, curling shot past Cudicini was the pick of them. The game finished 2–0 and Terry had an FA Cup runners-up medal to go with his winners' medal from two years previously but the season wasn't yet finished as the FA had, in their infinite wisdom, moved the Cup Final forward a week to allow more preparation time for the World Cup.

The final league game of the season at home to Aston

Villa was a predictably lifeless game. Neither side had anything to play for. Chelsea had already secured their UEFA Cup spot and were unable to overhaul Newcastle to claim a Champions League berth, and Villa were merely fighting for eighth place in the league. Ranieri's players were understandably down after losing the Cup Final and failed to raise themselves for the visit of Villa, losing the game 3–1. With no international competition to look forward to, the season really was over for Terry and, while it had been a truly awful ten months away from football, he had still come on in leaps and bounds with his performances in that famous blue shirt.

'I have to look on the positive side,' Terry said to assembled press. 'It has been a good season for me on the pitch, not so good off it, but I have learned from my mistakes and will build from here. I still have three-and-a-half years on my contract and I would love to sign an even longer one if they offered it to me. I want to spend the rest of my career here and win things.

'I can definitely see the day when we are chasing the Double, just like Arsenal this season. Hopefully we can push for the title next season. The squad is good enough – we have just lacked consistency this season.'

Back in August many experts were tipping Terry to make a late run into the World Cup squad, but due to his off-pitch exploits the young defender would have to make do with watching the action on television. The Chelsea man certainly wouldn't have dislodged Rio Ferdinand or

Sol Campbell, but it is debatable whether both of the veterans, Gareth Southgate and Martin Keown, would have made the squad if Terry had been available. Wes Brown also made Eriksson's final twenty-three, his versatility giving him an edge over the other contenders and, while the Chelsea defender might not have been as good as his Manchester United rival at full-back, he was already head and shoulders above him as a centre-back.

Without Terry in the side David Platt's England Under-21s finished bottom of Group A in the Under-21 European Championship. They got off to a great start as they beat hosts Switzerland 2–1, but they then lost 2–1 to Italy and 3–1 to Portugal to crash out of the tournament. If the Chelsea centre-back had been there, the team would certainly have been more solid defensively but who knows how far they could have gone.

The senior side fared a little better at the World Cup as they moved on from the 'Group of Death' unbeaten, and dispatched Denmark 3–0 before succumbing to Ronaldinho's magic in the quarter-final, losing 2–1 to Brazil. The time for Terry to excel in the white shirt of England would come, but having enjoyed the football as a spectator like the rest of us during the summer of 2002, he now had little to look forward to other than his impending court case.

On 14 June 2002, all three defendants, John Terry, Des Byrne and Jody Morris, entered pleas of not guilty, the judge gave them bail and the trio were to stand trial starting on 5 August. Putting forward the case for the prosecution, Jeremy Donne told Middlesex Guildhall Crown Court that the three footballers had become aggressive after drinking cocktails and were asked to leave the club. He said: 'It started with the loutish behaviour of Jody Morris. It escalated into an attack upon a doorman by Byrne and Terry, supported by Morris, and it ended in a brawl involving all three.'

Morris was said to have told doorman Trevor Thirlwall: 'Do you know how much I earn? I earn more in a day than you earn in a week. Do you know who we are? We could get you sacked.'

The prosecution claimed that the three men were escorted to reception where they continued to misbehave, going so far as to mock another celebrity. Mr Donne said: 'After a few minutes, another customer came up the stairs [the actor Danny Dyer who starred in the film *Mean Machine* alongside Vinnie Jones]. Terry asked for his autograph and, once he had it and the man's back was turned, he threw the autograph on the floor and made a vulgar gesture, to the great amusement of his friends. To the doormen this confirmed what they had been told about the footballers' behaviour downstairs, and they again told the three to leave.'

It was alleged that Morris then became 'aggressive' and told the doormen to get the owner of the club, a supposed friend of his whom he called Jake. He is said to have told them: 'Just go and get f★cking Jake for me and we'll sort this problem out. I don't give a f★ck when the club closes, go and get Jake.'

After that the footballers tried to force their way back into the club but the ensuing fight spilled outside where Terry supposedly hit bouncer Thirlwall in the face with a bottle. Mr Donne said: 'Thirlwall was now grappling with Morris and, having pushed him away, he turned to see Terry lunge at him. Thirlwall put his hands up and told Terry to calm down at which point Terry swung a punch at him. What he had not seen, but others had, was that John Terry had a bottle in his hand.

'Thirlwall immediately felt what he described in a statement to police as an explosion of pain in his eye followed by the loss of vision in it. Miraculously the bottle did not break on impact – it is terrifying to think what could have happened if it had. As it was, Trevor Thirlwall's face was cut around the orbit of his left eye. As Shaun Brice [another bouncer] helped the injured and defenceless Mr Thirlwall into the club, at least one bottle was thrown at them smashing on the wall and the ground by the entrance.'

The jury was shown CCTV footage of the three men being asked to leave and much of the resulting melee, but the moment when Thirlwall was struck was not captured on film. The second day of the trial saw Thirlwall take the stand and he told the court how he and Brice had politely asked the accused to leave. They were eventually ushered out but they burst back in and a fight started in the reception area and soon spilled outside. He heard Mr Brice shout that Byrne had a bottle.

Mr Thirlwall said: 'It changes the whole ethos because you're now in extreme danger. I pleaded with him not to be so silly and to put the bottle down. I had been trading punches with Terry and had thrown Morris against railings. I then heard a voice behind me say: "You c★★t, you're going to get it."

'It all happened in a split second. As I turned to look at him I felt the sheer weight of a blunt object of some sort and it absolutely just shattered my eye and my cheekbone. That's what it felt like. The point of contact was over a wide space and my eye literally exploded with blood. The swelling came up in seconds.

'As he hit me, I knew it wasn't someone's fist because of the sheer weight of the object. It sunk me to my knees. I reached out because I certainly didn't want to be hit again. I pulled him towards me and buried my head in his chest. I remember holding him very closely. I didn't want him to strike me again and I remember shouting: "Can you get this f★cking twat off me?"

'Shaun pulled us apart and he was running me back to the club but when we got to the door we were absolutely showered with bottles. The glass was exploding and falling all around us.'

The doorman denied being provoked into an attack by Morris's mocking words because, as he put it: 'I have been threatened with the sack before and I have had lots of celebrities tell me how much they earn – it has no effect on me. Morris was acting like a spoilt little child and it was, "Go and get Jake, I'm telling you to go and get Jake." He began to wind himself up more and more and more. I had pleaded with them peaceably, justifying why I was asking them to leave and that was when their mood changed and they became violent.'

Thirlwall was shown shadow-boxing on CCTV and putting on leather gloves earlier in the evening but denied that fighting was in his blood, despite his brother being a professional middleweight boxer. He said: 'I don't use my fists. I know how to escort people from premises. I'm not a good fighter. On that night I defended myself. I put in retaliation. It is one thing shadow-boxing and another thing to actually strike a person.'

Desmond de Silva QC, defending Terry, claimed Thirlwall had goaded his client into a fight and was merely looking for a quick buck by suing the Chelsea player. Mr de Silva said: 'The story you have given this court that John Terry bottled you in the left side of the face is a complete fabrication. You are lying. I'm suggesting that's been done by you to get him convicted and make a claim against him.'

Mr de Silva went on to insinuate that the doorman was a criminal with connections to numerous shady characters, and Thirlwall didn't respond kindly to this line of questioning. In an outburst that may have damaged his credibility in the eyes of the jury, he shook with anger and glared at the QC as he said: 'Not only is that slanderous but it is a defamation of character. I have been accused of being a thug without any reference or credible evidence. We're losing the point. I am the victim – I am the victim of a very violent crime. I have not come here for financial gain. I didn't ask to be put in this position.'

'I am the witness and a victim of a very violent crime perpetrated by the gentlemen behind you,' Thirlwall said, pointing at the accused trio in the dock. Referring to the parts of the fracas captured on the CCTV cameras, he went on: 'Byrne attacked me in the door as it is plain to see on the CCTV. Stop it, pause it, play it, do anything – he attacked me. John Terry did indeed stab me in the face with a bottle.

'I am here because I am the victim. Because of that I have been branded a thug, a violent man, a racist and now a criminal. I want the police to come forward and put my police record to the jury and the court. I am not a criminal.'

Highlighting the fact that he had no criminal record, Thirlwall added: 'I have, in the past, helped the police with their inquiries. I object strongly to you taking these facts and twisting them to slander my reputation in the media and in the public eye to get these defendants off the violent crimes that they committed against me. When helping police with their inquiries as a matter of formality [when] they arrest people – I was helping the police with their inquiries. There is a difference, which you wish to exploit. I have no criminal convictions of any kind and I'm not awaiting prosecution for any offence. I have not made an agreement with any newspaper or any other media organisation for the sale of my story.'

On the sixth day of the hearing, Mr Brice gave his evidence, which agreed with Thirlwall's account that Terry had attacked the doorman with a bottle. Other witnesses were called to describe the footballers as being drunk, cocky and generally unpleasant on the night in question. On the eighth day the transcripts of the police interviews were read out in court. When questioned after his arrest Terry said: 'Two or three people came from inside the club and ganged up on Des. I stepped in to break it up.

'Punches were thrown. I can't remember who I hit or who hit me. I just threw one punch. I remember getting hit two or three times on the head. It was over seconds after that. My intention was to stop things more than anything. I think I saw a couple of people on Des and it was unfair and I tried to put a stop to that.'

He was then shown photographs of injuries to Mr Thirlwall's face and asked if it was possible that he had caused them. Terry replied: 'Of course it's possible. I don't know if that's definite, I'm saying it's possible. I threw a punch, I'm not going to stand there and let someone hit me, am I?' But he strenuously denied hitting anyone with a bottle or throwing any bottles as the two bouncers retreated into the club.

The ninth day saw Des Byrne take the stand. The Dublin-born defender said that Thirlwall had shouted abuse at him, at which point he got very angry, but was then hit several times in the head in an unprovoked attack.

He said: 'Brice said we should just go home and I said I was outside the club and he couldn't tell me where to go. The other one said: "Just go home, you f*cking Irish prick." When he said that I wanted to confront him.

'I got a little bit angry. It just came from nowhere. I wanted to confront him face to face and see what the problem was with me. I took a couple of steps and Brice had two hands on me and pinned me to the door. Thirlwall came over and gave me a dig in the head. I fell backwards out of the doorway – I wasn't expecting a punch.

'I remember my top being pulled over my head. I remember getting a couple of digs, it happened like a blur. I just tried to get myself out of the doorway. I remember getting a dig then behind my left ear, I remember being on the floor, then flat on the floor. I was trying to get away and I saw three of them attacking John. John had Mr Thirlwall on him now, he was scrapping with John, I remember John swinging his hand and he caught Mr Thirlwall in the face with a dig. I thought, to be honest, great dig.'

Byrne insisted Terry did not have a bottle in his hand at the time, but as the Irishman got up, he found a bottle at his feet, which he threw towards the entrance. 'I remember picking it up and smashing it on the floor in the direction of where they were going,' he went on. 'I don't know why. I was upset and angry. It was more in frustration than anything. There were loads of things going through my mind. I was in the middle of Knightsbridge; I had taken a few digs to the head. I don't know why I did it but I did it and that was that.'

On the tenth day of the trial, on the eve of the new Premiership season, Terry came to the stand. It was an extremely emotional experience for the Chelsea defender – he was the one defendant facing a significant jail term – and after two-and-a-half hours in the witness box he buried his head in his hands and began wiping away the tears that were rolling down his cheeks.

His voice choking with emotion, Terry said: 'They are all lying. I never picked up a bottle. Not at any time did I use a bottle. There is no truth in that because I didn't pick up and use a bottle that night.

'I saw Des being punched and kicked on the floor. I thought it was two on one and that's unfair. I had seen the young reception guy kick Des and I thought he was going to kick him again, so I ran over and got Matthew Thirlwall [Trevor's brother] off him. That's when the three of them ganged up on me and started to attack me. I threw a punch. It was a normal punch, but it was fairly hard. As far as I remember it, I hit him in his head, his face. The sole purpose was to get people off. I was being attacked by two, if not three, of them.'

Terry stood by his claim that he was acting as peacemaker,

trying to calm things down rather than start any trouble and the effect of giving evidence was clear for all to see as his voice often dropped to a whisper. The judge went so far as to ask if he wanted a break – and Terry stood down ten minutes before the scheduled end of proceedings.

In regard to the very serious charges of wounding with intent to cause grievous bodily harm and having a bottle as a dangerous weapon, Terry's defence was helped by the evidence of Chelsea's medical officer, Neil Fraser, who examined the player's hand the day after the fight. He told the court that an X-ray revealed Terry had suffered a fracture to his hand that would come as a result of punching someone or something very hard, ruling out the use of a bottle.

Dr Fraser said: 'The injury suggested he had broken that bone having put some degree of force through it. He had an X-ray and saw a specialist and it was confirmed he had a fracture. In the medical textbooks, it's referred to as a boxer's fracture.'

Terry was also helped by an excellent character reference from his team-mate Graeme Le Saux, an experienced international with thirty-six England caps who is well respected throughout the game. His statement read: 'I have seen John in a social context and he behaves politely and I consider him to be of a gentle disposition. My view is, if the allegations were true, it would be genuinely out of character. I have never seen him behave violently or aggressively to anyone.'

Le Saux went on to say that he felt Terry would have been picked for England's World Cup squad if not for the proceedings, and in summation de Silva highlighted the talent of his client. Speaking to the jury, the QC said: 'His ability to serve his club and his country and to win for himself the great prizes of sporting life are just around the corner. But that future, and that life, is in your hands.

'The whole case against John Terry stinks, it is rotten, rotten. Beware. Some of those prosecution witnesses, I suggest, have crawled out from under the stones of London nightlife and now parade themselves as virtuous victims. They are in fact fraudulent thugs.'

Terry's legal representative pointed out that not one witness told police at the time of the arrest that the star had used a bottle. 'Why? Because it didn't happen and they hadn't yet worked out their story,' de Silva said. 'It was all a subsequent invention to try to demonstrate the bouncers were the real victims.'

Of the nine prosecution witnesses, eight were on the Wellington Club payroll and the ninth was a friend of Thirlwall and Wellington director Christian Panayatou. de Silva claimed that these people had combined to tailor their stories in a bid to cover the fact that they were serving drinks out of hours, and that Thirlwall wasn't a licensed doorman at the time of the incident.

'There was a conspiracy to cheat and deceive the police by the whole group – the staff and the management,' said the barrister. 'There can be no doubt about that. They took positive steps to pervert the course of justice by hiding the truth from the police. They were faking, deceiving and cheating. If the truth had come out, the club could have lost its drinks licence and lucrative celebrity trade.'

The case against Terry was created to cash in on the fame of the player, De Silva alleged, as he said: 'Let's not beat about the bush. Newspapers pay large sums of money for stories that concern sporting celebrities.'

But the judge, Fabyan Evans, told the jury of eight women and four men that no special treatment should be given to the accused just because of their fame and, on their second day of deliberation, the twelve good men and women true returned with their verdicts.

On Thursday, 22 August 2002, the fourteenth day of the trial, seven-and-a-half months after the incident in question, John Terry was found not guilty on all four charges. Morris was also cleared. Byrne was found guilty only of possessing an offensive weapon, fined £2,000 and ordered to pay costs of £1,000.

Terry was delighted and a statement was read out on his behalf, by his solicitor, Steven Barker: 'Anyone who saw him give evidence in that witness box will have no doubt of the enormous stress and strain he has been under for the last eight months because of some monstrous allegations that he took a bottle to a bouncer. He is extremely relieved and pleased at this verdict. His words were that justice has been done. He wants to thank his legal team, Chelsea Football Club and, last but not least, his family and friends. He has been under enormous strain – that is clearly visible on this young man's face. Now he wants to get on with what I believe is a glorious career in the game.'

The Chelsea hierarchy were also overjoyed at their players being cleared. 'We are delighted at the outcome of the trial,' said Ken Bates. 'Chelsea Football Club always believed in the innocence of the two players. It is unfortunate that the Crown Prosecution Service took eight months to bring a relatively straightforward matter to court. Irrespective of the fact that both have been found not guilty, Jody Morris and John Terry have suffered eight months of agony. Terry's international career has also been damaged.

'It is a sad commentary on our criminal justice system. The matter is now over. They will return to training tomorrow and rejoin our squad and be available for selection as and when the manager wants.'

But before he returned to the football pitch, Terry wanted to let the public know how the trial had affected him and to assure them that the jury's decision had been right and true. He did so by selling his story to the *Sunday Mirror* for a fee believed to be in the region of £50,000 – more than one-and-a-half times his fine for being out drinking on that fateful January evening.

Speaking about the day of the verdict he said: 'I had my

bag packed all ready for prison. I had my toothbrush, my wash stuff, a book and a radio. I knew I was innocent – but I had to be ready in case the jury went against me.

'Being in that cell was horrendous. I remember being woken by three or four fights in the corridor and crying most of the time. I was shivering, it was freezing cold and I felt totally alone. I didn't have a clue what was happening… I was in there for 22 hours. I kept thinking during the trial: If a day in there was that bad, what would a year or two years or whatever in prison be like? I tried to stay strong for my family and my friends but deep down I was a bag of nerves.'

Terry also spoke of how he had been almost addicted to watching the grainy CCTV footage from the night in question, willing the three young men on the screen to walk away and take his seven months of anguish with them. 'I couldn't help myself. I kept putting it on and freezing it at different bits. Every time I saw it, I would say to myself: "Go home, lads, go home now before it gets nasty, get a taxi and go." If we'd gone then, none of this would have happened.

'Sometimes it takes an experience like this to make you sit up and take notice of things,' he went on. 'I had a good think about what I was doing and I've changed my lifestyle around now. I haven't drunk alcohol for six months now and that's the way I think it will stay. I haven't been to any nightclubs either… I've decided I owe it to myself to change things round.

'The players at the club have been fantastic. They have kept me going when I was really low. Throughout the case they have texted me on my phone, supported me and told me to keep my head up because things were going to be all right. They never had any doubt I would be found not guilty; they always talked about me being back and playing and that helped.

'I can't really put into words how scared I was. It was the worst experience of my life.'

The relief was palpable but the trauma of the trial had affected Terry greatly. It was obvious to him that he couldn't continue misbehaving in any way if he wanted to realise his dreams of winning trophies with Chelsea and playing for England. Like all men of any stature, Terry had learned from his mistakes and he would never let drinking affect his career again.

To be a professional footballer at the highest level you must have aptitude and attitude. Terry had always had the ability and now he adopted the mentality to take him to the very top.

Des Byrne had been released by Stockport County in 1999 after an incident in a nightclub; he then returned to St Patrick's Athletic in his native Ireland until Wimbledon stepped in, but two months after the 'Wellington Club' trial finished he was given a free transfer to Carlisle United. Byrne was in the North-east for less than five months before his contract was terminated for breaking the club curfew and, at time of writing, he can be found playing centre-half for Dublin's Bohemian club in Ireland's Eircom Premier League.

Jody Morris left Chelsea in July 2003 to join Leeds United, but the accusations and allegations of off-field misbehaviour continued to haunt the player and, one year later, he joined Millwall on a rolling contract after a brief loan spell with Rotherham United.

In May 2005, John Terry lifted the Premiership trophy.

CHAPTER SEVEN
ENGLAND AT LAST

'I waited a long time to get my England debut but when it finally came I was the proudest man ever – it was a fantastic achievement. When you talk as a kid about playing for your country, that's a dream come true. But if you speak to every kid, they'll also tell you that to be able to play in a World Cup tournament would be the biggest thing ever, and that definitely goes for me.'

In June 2003, John Terry made his long-awaited first appearance in Sven-Goran Eriksson's England team, and he was soon looking to the next challenge. Never one to rest on his laurels, the Chelsea defender had endured a difficult season with injuries, but still managed to achieve a great deal with his club and, at last, his country.

The campaign got off to a very tough start for Terry: not only did he have his court case to contend with, but he also had a troublesome knee injury which required an operation. It was another heavy blow to the defender's spirits, but the way the problem flared up in the first place was quite amusing.

'Me and the lads were watching the tennis down at the training ground when Tim Henman was playing Lleyton Hewitt in the semi-final,' Terry recalled in the *Sun*. 'I think he was two sets down when someone called suddenly to me from behind. As I turned around I felt something go in my knee. It was painful but I didn't think too much of it.

'I managed to train but the problem got worse and worse throughout the day. By the time our afternoon session came around, I couldn't train on it. I went to see a specialist and ended up in hospital. I can't blame poor Tim though – he's taken enough stick this summer.

'I've had a bit of a clean-up inside my knee,' the centre-back added. 'The doctors told me that I would be out for three weeks and that was seven days ago. I've had to take it easy for the past week but am back at the training ground tomorrow. I can start running in a few days and doing weights so there's no long-term problem.'

The operation, in a private north London clinic, put Terry out of a pre-season training camp in Italy, as his team-mates jetted off without him. There were very few new faces in the Chelsea ranks for the forthcoming season, due to the Blues' new status as Premiership paupers, but paradoxically Terry thought the lack of big-name signings would strengthen Claudio Ranieri's side.

'We have pretty much the same team as last year,' he said

in a press conference. 'I feel this team is strong and we stay together as a unit. We will carry on from where we left off last season and the fact we all now know each other's game will help us. All the players want to bring some silverware back to Stamford Bridge for the fans, the club and ourselves. We all want to win things. We are hoping we can do that this year. I was gutted when I saw Arsenal lift the FA Cup and I must admit to being jealous of their success because that is what I want.'

If Chelsea were to achieve any of that success in the short term, it was imperative that the players stuck together and improved upon the understanding they had already built up. As the debts continued to grow, the massive wages of players like Marcel Desailly and Jimmy Floyd Hasselbaink were crippling the club. To compete financially with the biggest clubs in the league, it was vital that Chelsea qualified for the Champions League. But at the start of the 2003/04 season, with massive payments still outstanding on all the big transfers from the previous summer, Ranieri had to make do with the signings of Enrique de Lucas, on a free transfer from Espanyol, and Filipe Oliveira from FC Porto for £500,000.

Club chairman, Ken Bates, tried to calm the fears of the fans over the lack of transfer activity, as the *Express* reported: 'You can't keep on spending. You only buy if you have something to buy that will fill a weakness. Now we have got a period of consolidation. The stadium, by and large, is finished. There is money owed but the assets are earning money so who cares? We have a bigger European scouting network so that we will look to buy players before they become stars, rather than buying established stars that are perhaps overpaid and we pay too much for.'

Bates went on: 'The transfer market is usually led by Spanish and Italian clubs but they haven't got any money. So they haven't spent any money in England buying players and that means there isn't any money filtering around in the system. Everybody has to sell as well as buy. We have thirty-one players in our first-team squad – there is no point in buying any more players just to sit them on the bench.'

The only bench that Terry saw in the early part of the season was in court, but as August drew to a close he could finally put the whole sordid chapter behind him and get on with his life and his football career, whose progress had been halted at an international level by the false accusations levelled against him.

'It's a challenge for me to get back in the Chelsea team and I'm just relieved and happy that I have that opportunity,' said Terry to the *Sunday Mirror* after his not guilty verdict. 'And you can't imagine how relieved I am that that opportunity is there for me because my career could have been in ruins if that verdict had gone against me.

'This, in a strange way, is a new beginning for me and I don't want any opportunities in football that come my way to pass me by,' Terry finished. 'I'm determined to push on as a player, to show people I have the ability to play at the highest level. I didn't want to miss out on the European Championships. But I hope I can start playing well for Chelsea and get back to playing with the Under-21s, as I am eligible for another two years. Last season was the sort of progress I was looking for, but the challenge is to keep improving, and hopefully get into the full squad. At the first opportunity I will be banging on the England door and, if the chance comes, I will grab it with both hands.'

But first he would once again need to force his way past two Frenchmen to get into the Chelsea team, since Marcel Desailly and William Gallas had developed their own excellent partnership in the Blues defence. Ranieri's side began the season in impressive form and were unbeaten after six games, including draws against Arsenal and Manchester United. But Terry's recovery from knee surgery took longer than he had hoped and, with further complications such as the dizzy spell he suffered before the FA Cup Final, he didn't feature in the first team until October.

'I have been told by a specialist it is nothing to worry about any more,' said Terry to the *Sunday Express*. 'But back in the summer I had to stop my training a couple of times because I was still having the same problems that I had on the eve of the Cup Final. Sometimes when I lay down at night, my head started spinning. It came and went in just a few seconds and then I was OK. But it was a great relief when the specialist said it will just clear up in time.'

After his lengthy absence, Terry took to the field for his first match of the season away against Viking Stavanger in the UEFA Cup. Chelsea travelled to Norway with a 2–1 lead from the first leg but the last-minute goal they conceded at the Bridge would come back to haunt them as they lost 4–2 on the night and 5–4 on aggregate to crash out in the early stages of European competition for the third year in a row. Terry was clearly short of match practice and had been rushed back to cover for the injured Desailly.

In the absence of the colossal Frenchman, the Blues' back line had an unfamiliar look to it as Gallas played at right-back and Robert Huth, a German from the Chelsea youth team, partnered Terry at the back. The new look defence struggled to subdue the Norwegian side and they went in 2–1 down at half-time, level on aggregate thanks to Frank Lampard's goal just before the whistle. Viking went back in front after an hour, but Terry scored two minutes later, heading home a Graeme Le Saux corner to give Chelsea the advantage on away goals.

That should have made things safe for the Blues but they failed to take their chances throughout the match and, with three minutes left on the clock, Erik Nevland made them pay for their profligacy with another late goal. The defence was criticised for conceding four against such inferior opposition but the good form of Gallas had seen him called up for the French national team. Terry was thrilled for his young team-mate.

'I just can't believe it has taken so long for William to be called up for France,' Terry said to the *Sunday Express*. 'When they had their last friendly I hadn't seen the game, but I asked William how he had got on. He told me he wasn't involved and I just could not understand it because he was brilliant last year. I'm delighted he has got his chance.'

He added: 'We believe in each other and I know the partnership works. At times last season we felt invincible. I just felt no-one could get past me, but if someone did, William was there and vice-versa.'

Unfortunately, Terry found he was unable to renew that partnership with Gallas since he was about to be relegated to the reserves in search of some much-needed match sharpness.

With Terry out of the side, the tabloids did what they do best and began linking him with a move to another of the Premiership's big fish. He was named as a transfer target for Arsenal, Liverpool and Newcastle but he only had eyes for the Blues. 'As far as John is concerned,' said his agent Aaron Lincoln, 'he is committed to Chelsea and focused on winning his place back in the side.'

Gallas and Desailly performed admirably in Terry's place, and the English centre-back had to make do with substitute appearances as the two Frenchmen kept clean sheets in five consecutive league matches. Barring the odd 10 or 15 minutes in the Premiership, Terry's only chance to impress came in the League Cup.

In the third-round tie against Gillingham, Terry showed

he had fully recovered from his injury problems as he and Gallas stifled the Gills attack again and again. Marlon King scored a last-minute consolation goal for the visitors but a well-taken brace from Carlton Cole ensured it was Chelsea's name that went into the hat for the next round.

Terry again deputised for Desailly when Everton came to the Bridge in the fourth round, and the Blues dominated from start to finish to win the game 4–1. It wasn't just the Frenchman's place in defence that the youngster took for the visit of the Toffees; he also took over as skipper, much to his delight. 'It was a huge boost for me to be given the armband,' Terry said to the *Daily Mirror*. 'The bad times are behind me and now I'm looking forward to good times. The chairman, manager and everyone at the club stood by me and I take my hat off to them. I want to have a long future here at Chelsea. Marcel and William are both playing well but hopefully I'll get my place back soon.'

The captaincy was a fine early present for Terry, coming three days before his twenty-second birthday and, although the manager still had plenty of faith in him as shown by the fact he'd picked him to lead the side, Ranieri was loath to change his winning formula, so Terry was back on the bench for the trip to Goodison Park on his actual birthday.

Chelsea beat Everton 3–1, the three points lifting them to second in the table, and although supporters don't often enjoy a team turning up and taking away all the spoils, one of the home fans in particular warmed to Terry a lot more than most. The five-year-old lad, Mark Turner, was shivering in the stands until the Chelsea defender offered him his coat and gloves to keep him warm during the game. 'His granddad looked at me as if to say, "My grandson's not wearing this,"' Terry said. 'But it was so cold, he let him put them on.' The young Evertonian was suitably grateful, and said: 'Wayne Rooney used to be my favourite, but now John Terry is the best.'

Terry had plenty of time to make friends in the stands as he only played the last quarter of an hour and he was getting increasingly upset with his new position at number three in the pecking order. 'It's frustrating, having been a regular in the side for two years,' he said. 'But the pair of them are playing brilliantly, as are the whole team. The club hasn't been able to spend money this season and I think that's helped. We haven't had new players needing time to settle, and we're all familiar with the system the manager wants to play. It's strange, but a lack of cash has worked in our favour.'

But it would take more than a few weeks on the sidelines to damage the Barking-born defender's feelings for Chelsea. 'I've still got two years left on my contract and I'm staying,' Terry went on. 'We will be discussing a new deal next year and I want to stay because I still have a big ambition of captaining Chelsea on a regular basis and then making the step up with England.

'I know it's within my capabilities but that will only

happen once I'm back in the Chelsea team. It's frightening to think that all my plans could have been taken away from me this year. But now everything is back in my hands, I'm even more determined to make the most of every opportunity that comes my way.'

Having been cleared of all charges, Terry was sure that supporters of some of Chelsea's rivals would still try and wind him up over the incident that had threatened to bring a premature end to his promising career. 'I know there's going to be some fall-out from what's happened. I'm going to get stick from some fans,' he said. 'I've also decided to cut out the drinking. My birthday last Saturday was the first time I'd had a drop since the incident. If I'm going to make the most of my career, I've got to focus on my football and not let outside influences get in the way. That's the way it'll be from now on.'

One person, who had been a very good influence on Terry, was Gianfranco Zola. The Italian veteran was defying the ageing process with another fine season at the age of thirty-six. 'Gianfranco is the perfect role model, whatever age you are,' Terry said. 'He sets a great example for everybody. He has affected the culture of the club. We can all see that his body shows all the benefits of years of doing the right thing. Even players in the reserves and youth teams are taking notice.

'Nobody could be a better example. One of the biggest things to have happened, due almost entirely to his influence, is that there is hardly a member of the team

164

these days who touches a drop of alcohol. We all feel so much better for it. I'm teetotal, clean as a whistle. We've all made mistakes in the past. I'm quite prepared to hold up my hands on that score, because there would be no point in denying it. But I have to say, in all sincerity, Gianfranco has been the main man in putting the likes of me on the straight and narrow.'

The defender went on: 'This is a person who has looked after his body properly for years and years, which is why he continues to perform at the highest level with his thirty-seventh birthday in sight… He is fantastic, and it wouldn't surprise me if he was still playing in ten years.'

Sir Stanley Matthews played on for Stoke City until after his fiftieth birthday but football is a lot quicker now than in the days of the 'Wizard of Dribble' and, in the end, Zola wouldn't last quite that long.

Terry's long wait for a Premiership start was soon over, however, as Desailly missed the game against Middlesbrough for personal reasons. In the Frenchman's absence, Terry was once again made captain. Ranieri was happy to give his stand-in skipper a chance. The manager said: 'John has been suffering a lot this season but he has always been fantastic in training.'

A win against Boro would take Chelsea to the top of the table for the first time in three years and undoubtedly help keep their title bid on track, but the Italian refused to look any further than the game at the Riverside Stadium. 'My focus is only on Middlesbrough and, of course, my own team – only the next match,' he said. 'My players want this pressure, the pressure of being at the top. But I don't want to say Chelsea can win as the FA don't give me 10 more points just for saying it. I would like to win the title, to do better than I did with Valencia or Fiorentina, but it is too easy to speak now. Wait until April – if we are top then we can talk about it.'

But the Blues didn't claim top spot as the points were shared in a 1–1 draw. Geremi opened the scoring for the home side with a fabulous free-kick, but Terry equalised just before the break, sweeping home from Hasselbaink's corner. 'It is great to be back in the team and to be captain of a great side like this, and scoring the goal rounded it off,' Terry said. 'For the manager to give me the captain's armband was a great boost. The lads are delighted with the way we played, especially in the first half. Now all I can do is keep working hard in training and when I get a chance to come back into the side I've got to do well. Middlesbrough is always a hard place to come and we are pleased with a point.'

Terry was taking nothing for granted, however. 'Marcel will be back in a couple of weeks. When I came back in the side, it was great that the manager gave me the captain's armband. It makes me very proud.'

With Desailly still missing, Terry would lead the side out against Manchester United in the League Cup quarter-final, and he was confident of the team's chances of getting a result.

'We can't wait to go up there,' he said. 'It should be a great tie because both sides are in the middle of really good runs. We won at Old Trafford last year and we can do it again so it holds no fears for us, and I'll be ready if needed at United.'

Terry was indeed required, but neither he nor Gallas could stop Diego Forlan from hitting the only goal of the game, 10 minutes from time, to put Chelsea out of the Cup.

Chelsea were out of two knock-out competitions before Christmas but the result failed to upset the Blues' good league form and they won the next match, 2–0 against Aston Villa, to extend their unbeaten run in the Premiership to ten games. In Desailly's absence, the manager continued with Terry as captain, but Ranieri's ever-improving English let him down slightly, when he said: 'I spoke with Zola and Le Saux and asked if I could give the captaincy to John Terry because, for me, he is our captain for the future. They said they were happy and I gave him the handbag.'

Desailly returned for the next match to reclaim the handbag, or armband as it's better known, from Terry but the English defender retained his place in the team for the visit of Southampton. Chelsea drew 0–0 but Terry was relegated to the bench for the next two matches as the Blues' unbeaten streak came to a spectacular end. Ranieri's side lost the final match of 2002, 2–0 away to Leeds, and the New Year didn't start much better when they were beaten 3–2 by Arsenal at Highbury.

Terry returned to the side for the FA Cup third-round tie against Middlesbrough, as Gallas moved across to left-back to cover for the injured Le Saux. The English centre-back was lucky not to get a red card after a quarter of an hour when he brought down Jonathan Greening with a tough challenge, but Chelsea went down to ten men after 64 minutes as Cudicini was sent off for allegedly retaliating to a shove from Dean Windass. The Blues were already ahead through a first-half goal from Mario Stanic and they held on to win 1–0 despite their numerical inferiority.

A season of injuries continued for Terry in the next match against Charlton, when he fell awkwardly on a very sandy surface at the Bridge and had to be replaced after 16 minutes. With no defenders on the bench, Jody Morris came on in midfield and Emmanuel Petit moved into the back four. 'I was worried when John Terry asked to come off midway through the first half,' Ranieri said, 'but Manu was fantastic and Jody came on and did really well. We don't know what the matter is with John but he will be checked tomorrow – he seems to have a problem with his back. It could have had something to do with the pitch – it was very difficult for the players to keep their balance on the surface.'

The surface looked more like a beach than a football pitch, and Alan Curbishley considered lodging a complaint, but both teams had to play in the same area inside the white lines and the Blues won 4–1. The sandy conditions were certainly not part of any Chelsea master plan and Terry was as surprised as anyone at how bad it was. 'We only saw the pitch on the day of the game,' he said after the game. 'I spoke to my mate Paul Konchesky the night before and he asked if the pitch was going to be a problem. I said: "Not as far as I know." He said it would suit them anyway.'

The pitch certainly didn't suit Terry and his new injury meant he missed the trip to Old Trafford and the defeat that saw Chelsea fall to fourth in the table. Fortunately it was the only game he missed. Terry was fit to replace the suspended Desailly against Shrewsbury Town in the FA Cup fourth round and he led his side to a comfortable 4–0 win. That game proved a turning point for the English defender as he put his injury troubles behind him and went on to start the next fifteen matches.

It was a timely return for the Blues since the games were coming thick and fast. In fact they had just 48 hours after their cup-tie before entertaining Leeds in the league. Many of the players complained about having so little time to recover between games, but Terry was pragmatic. 'If the match is there we want to win it,' he said. 'We can't complain about it because that's the way things are in England. We are all professional and we are fit athletes. We'll be going into training, having a massage and a little jog and we will be ready for Leeds. We owe them big time. We were on a good run when we went up to Elland Road and it set us back a few weeks.'

The Blues had to fight hard not to be beaten again, and

twice came from behind to win 3–2. Terry's return to first-team action once again had him linked with the England squad, but he was more concerned with sorting out his future at Stamford Bridge. 'I had a meeting with the chairman in the summer and he told me: "You're not leaving this club. And if you do, I'm going to break your f*cking legs,"' Terry said in the *People*. 'But he didn't smile afterwards, so I don't know if he was joking or not!

'That's the chairman all over. I've got two years left on my contract here and at the moment we're trying to sort things out. We were fairly close but it's just broken down again, so I don't know when we're going to talk. I'm just concentrating on my football but I'd like to see out my career here. I love Chelsea. I've been here since I was fourteen and I've seen a lot of changes. To captain this side in the next five to ten years would be brilliant. Obviously I want to stay but things have to be right for me.'

The club had stood by Terry during his hard times and he was keen to repay them on the pitch for all their kindness over a very difficult twelve months. 'I've grown up an awful lot in the last year,' he added. 'I've learned from my mistakes and benefited from them. During the trial I found out who my true friends were. I give thanks to them and a lot of people at the club were very helpful to me as well. If I make the England team, I'll dedicate it to the players, the manager, the chairman and Trevor Birch [Chelsea's chief executive] and all my family.

'All the bad times are behind me now and I'm looking

to the future. I've dreamed of playing for England since I was a boy. When I couldn't play in last year's European Under-21 Championships, I was devastated but I knew all along I was innocent. If I were selected now, it would make me the proudest man in England. It would be the greatest day of my life and my family's too, I'm sure.'

Terry missed out on the squad for the friendly against Australia in February, but given the 3–1 loss and the subsequent bad press, he was probably better off out of it. With his Chelsea team-mates, Terry followed up the win over Leeds with a draw against Tottenham and an away victory over Birmingham to get the Blues' league campaign back on track after three losses in four games over New Year.

The Blues were up against it in the first half at St Andrews and were grateful to goalkeeper Cudicini that they were still in the game before a limping Zola scored two minutes before the break. 'There was never the slightest doubt Gianfranco would put that chance away, even though he was hurt,' said Terry. 'When we scored again within three minutes of the second half, Birmingham's hearts were broken. This was the kind of show to underline the fact we're making progress. We are moving up the table, a little closer to the leaders, in a nice, quiet fashion.'

Arsenal, Manchester United, and Newcastle led the way in the Premiership, but Chelsea were hot on their heels. 'All three of them were in the high-profile games on Sunday,' Terry added, 'while we played 24 hours earlier and just got on with the job of winning. We'll keep doing that, staying out of the limelight, and looking for a slip by the big three that will allow us into the race. But it remains important Gianfranco is fit, and it is even more important he is persuaded to sign a fresh contract for next season.'

It says a lot about Terry and the good spirit at the club, that not only was he keen to see the Italian maestro continue at the Bridge, but he also wanted to see the player who had been keeping him out of the side stay on. 'William's probably the best signing made by anyone over the last two or three years,' he said of Gallas, to the *Sun*. 'He's a brilliant player with so much pace. I'm always watching him and Marcel in training and matches and learning from them. I just have to take my chance when it comes.'

Terry enjoyed his fifth successive start as Chelsea secured a place in the FA Cup quarter-finals with a 2–0 win over Stoke City at the Britannia Stadium. But just as everything was looking rosy again, the Blues crashed to a 2–1 home defeat at the hands of Blackburn. Chelsea were almost unrecognisable in the opening 45 minutes against Rovers, and Terry revealed after the game how upset Ranieri was. 'We were shocking in the first half to be honest and when we came in at half-time the manager couldn't even talk to us. After the game he didn't even come in and say a word to us either – so that shows how badly we played.'

And despite some excellent saves from Brad Friedel in goal for the visitors, the manager wasn't any happier when the dust had settled. 'It was, I think, our worst match of the season,' Ranieri said. 'I am angry. Everybody is angry. Now it's important to forget everything and look forward. That's my philosophy.'

Looking ahead to the next game, Chelsea had the opportunity to close to within one point of Newcastle as they travelled to St James' Park, but instead they saw the gap extend to a massive seven points when they lost 2–1. Terry led the side again in the absence of Desailly and he soon proved he was growing increasingly accomplished in the art of post-match analysis. 'We really should have come away with something today,' the skipper said. 'The result has put a major dent in our hopes of taking one of the top-four places. But it's not a dip in form. If we keep playing like that, we will win more games this season.

'We know we're one of the best four teams in the League and we have shown it on numerous occasions. We have to be more consistent. The only way we're going to end up in the top four is by coming back from this. We will, I assure you. We have a lot of heart and steel. We've had the upper hand over Newcastle in recent seasons, so I suppose it was only a matter of time before they beat us.'

Ever the optimist, Terry focused on what the Blues needed from their final nine league games to claim that vital fourth place. 'It's in our own hands,' he said. 'We need six wins and hopefully to get a run going. It's important for the club from a financial point of view and all the players are desperate to play in the Champions League.'

His desire to play at the top level was unwavering and, with a new contract yet to be finalised, the talented young defender was again linked with a move away from the Bridge. But Terry had no thoughts of leaving. Reported the *Daily Mirror*: 'I've agreed everything with Chelsea and I'm just waiting for them to get back to me,' he said. 'The ball is in Chelsea's court but we've spoken about it and I'm ready to sign for a few more years.

'I can't see me ever leaving so it's not a problem. On New Year's Eve, before we played Arsenal, I went to see the manager and he told me that I was his captain for the future. That was reassuring to hear and it would be a dream come true. It's a privilege to captain Chelsea.'

He continued: 'The club have been good to me and I never thought about leaving. They stood by me through some difficult times and you want to repay people's faith in you. You expect tough competition at top clubs so I know I'm not guaranteed a place. Pre-season, I had a bit of an injury on my knee and had an op. When I came back, Marcel and William were playing brilliantly so I had no complaints. I think I've come through everything a lot stronger for the experience and will learn from it in future. I love it here and I think we are going places this season. We believe we can get into the Champions League and there's the FA Cup tie with Arsenal.'

Playing the Gunners in the Cup for the third successive season, Chelsea travelled to Highbury determined to get revenge for the defeat at the Millennium Stadium ten months before. Ranieri's side got off to the perfect start when Terry headed home a Gronkjaer cross after three minutes. Arsenal hit back through Francis Jeffers and a Thierry Henry pirouette, but Lampard equalised seven minutes from time to force a replay.

Before their second bite at Cup retribution, Chelsea swept aside West Bromwich Albion, 2–0 away, and Manchester City 5–0 at home, with Terry claiming his fourth goal of the season just before half-time at Stamford Bridge. The young defender's good form since returning to the first team had not gone unnoticed and, despite being overlooked by Eriksson for the friendly the previous month, Terry received his first England call-up for the Euro 2004 qualification double-header against Liechtenstein and Turkey. The Swede was without Sol Campbell and Wes Brown for the vital games, and he liked what he saw in the Chelsea man.

'John is playing better and better,' Eriksson said. 'Earlier this season, he played very little. Since then he has had his chance and done well. I am happy because he is getting stronger and now he is the captain. He is a good defender and is improving his passing as well. Someone told me he wants to be captain of Chelsea and England. They are good ambitions.'

There was no denying Terry's desire to lead his club and country. 'I'd love to be England captain, it's always been a dream of mine,' said the England new boy, in the *Daily Star*. 'Any player will tell you they want to play for their country and being captain is the ultimate achievement.'

The defender still harboured resentment over his period of international suspension but insisted the whole ordeal had helped to make him a better player. Terry said in the *Daily Express*: 'I've come back stronger. I resent the way I was treated by England a little bit. I knew I was innocent and it was really upsetting that I couldn't play. I made a mistake being out that night, but I didn't deserve to be treated like that.'

The court case had proved a significant hindrance to his international ambitions but Terry was delighted finally to get the call, and his team-mates were equally happy to see him make the step up. His defensive mentor, Desailly, said: 'I feel so good for John. I have said for three years he should play for his country, and I have tried to set the right example for him to follow.'

And the younger defender was as complimentary as ever about his illustrious team-mate. 'Marcel is a pleasure to play with,' Terry said. 'He has proved he can still do it and he is still the best for me. Being next to him has taught me so much. Without that, I wouldn't be where I am today.'

But before Terry could join up with his new England colleagues, there was the considerable obstacle of Henry's Arsenal and an FA Cup quarter-final replay. However, the Chelsea manager had no doubts about the ability of his young defender to handle arguably the world's finest attacker. 'When I was in Italy I said I had seen the Muhammad Ali of football, because Henry could float like a butterfly and sting like a bee,' Ranieri said in the *Daily Express*. 'But Terry is like a man from Mars. I have never seen a centre-forward dominate him, not even Henry.

'John can mark them all, the big strong guys and the quick ones. He can become England's regular central defender for years to come. When I first came to the club three years ago, I saw John in the reserves and knew he would become a fantastic player. Not only can he defend, but he can score goals from set-pieces too. And against a team as fantastic as Arsenal we will need him to be at his best.'

'Arsenal will play their hearts out, but then so will we,' Ranieri went on. 'And if they fight as Arsene Wenger says his team will, until the last drop of blood, then so will we. I want a fight, and so do my team.'

Terry was ready for the fight and celebrated his England selection by continuing his rich vein of form in front of goal, and was on the score-sheet twice against Wenger's team. Sadly for Terry and his team-mates, the first one was an own goal.

Midway through the first half, Arsenal broke quickly from defence and, running back towards his own area under pressure from Francis Jeffers and Sylvain Wiltord, Terry turned Patrick Vieira's cross past Cudicini. Things got worse for the Blues as they went two down before the break, but in the 66th minute Pascal Cygan was sent off for hauling Hasselbaink to the ground and Terry made amends for his own goal with a fine header past Stuart

Taylor with 11 minutes left. But all hopes of a Chelsea revival were dashed soon afterwards as Lauren scored a rare goal to make it 3–1.

With only the league left to concentrate on, the Chelsea players channelled their disappointment into claiming that last Champions League spot which had proved so elusive in recent years. Terry wasn't involved in either of the two England matches when he joined up with the full squad, as Rio Ferdinand, Gareth Southgate, Campbell, and Jonathan Woodgate were all ahead of him in the eyes of Eriksson. But the Chelsea defender gained valuable experience training with such quality players and put that all into practice in the league.

The Blues beat Sunderland and Bolton to narrow the gap with Newcastle to just one point, and keep their European destiny firmly in their own hands. 'It would be unbelievable,' Terry said in the *Daily Mirror*. 'It's been too long since we were in the Champions League. We had a disappointing season last year, to be honest, and this time everyone has been saying that the Champions League is the most important thing. It's vital financially for the club, so hopefully we can do it for the club and all the fans. All the players desperately want to play in the Champions League. Newcastle have lost two on the bounce and we've won two, so it's interesting with us being a point behind them.'

But Chelsea faltered on their way to the finishing line, drawing at home to Fulham and losing away games against West Ham and Aston Villa, despite Terry scoring his sixth goal of the season at Villa Park. But the Blues still had Champions League qualification within reach as they faced Liverpool, now their closest rivals, on the final day of the season.

The two sides were level on 64 points after 37 games and knew that whoever won the game would take fourth place in the league along with the final Champions League spot. The loser would be heading for the UEFA Cup. Chelsea had a superior goal difference so they only needed a point and, playing in front of a sell-out Stamford Bridge crowd, they would be roared on by vociferous home support. But nothing could be taken for granted in what was effectively a Champions League play-off, worth more than £10m in revenue to the winning team.

Although the extra money would be incredibly beneficial for the club in negotiating contracts, signing new players and relieving debts, Terry was only interested in the challenge of playing against the world's finest footballers in Europe's top competition. 'To help in my continued development,' he said, 'it is imperative that Chelsea qualify for the Champions League. I can't help but think what it would be like to pit my wits against the likes of Ronaldo, Raul and Figo.'

The manager certainly wasn't underestimating the importance of the big match either. 'The game against Liverpool is a Cup Final and I like this but I would have preferred to have done it already,' Ranieri said. 'The Champions League is important for everyone. We have some experienced players here but we also have some youngsters who have never played at that level and it will be good for them if we qualify.'

The Blues were in desperate need of the money that the Champions League would generate since there was talk of Ranieri having to sell off some of his best assets – Gallas, Hasselbaink and even Terry – so it was a great relief when they did qualify with a 2–1 win over the Reds. First-half goals from Desailly and Gronkjaer gave Chelsea the points after Sami Hyypia's opener. It meant Gerard Houllier's team would have to make do with the UEFA Cup.

Terry missed the big clash due to a thigh injury but he was fit to join the England squad for their end-of-season matches. The Chelsea defender was left out of the game against South Africa in Durban but he was on the bench for the next friendly a week-and-a-half later and he came on at the interval to make his full England debut.

At Leicester's Walkers Stadium on Tuesday, 3 June 2003, John Terry replaced Gareth Southgate at half-time to come on for the second 45 minutes of England's friendly with Serbia & Montenegro. The score was 1–1 when the Chelsea defender entered the fray, but playing alongside Matthew Upson in the middle of a back four, Terry helped to keep the Serbs at bay, and West Ham's Joe Cole hit a brilliant free-kick eight minutes from time to win the match.

In the build-up to the game, Terry was again linked by tabloid reports with off-field misbehaviour: he had allegedly been involved in an altercation at the hotel where the England squad were staying while at a training camp in La Manga, but his agent was keen to play down the incident. 'John hasn't apologised to anyone – he hasn't got anything to apologise for,' Aaron Lincoln said. 'John told me that a guy went up to Rio and tried to grab a cue off him – it was nothing. John walked away, then went back to the room. He wasn't involved.'

Following his earlier problems, Terry was very keen not to be involved in any more headline-grabbing exploits and, fortunately for the future Chelsea captain, whatever happened in La Manga was sorted out quickly and quietly.

'I knew I had to sort myself out,' Terry said, speaking about the effect his court case had had on his lifestyle. 'I've obviously made mistakes, and I hold my hand up to that. But I've really knuckled down this year. I'm doing a lot of extra work in the gym, and looking after myself in what I eat and drink… I've been playing a lot of golf with Gianfranco, and we've had little chats on the course. He has told me I have a big future with Chelsea and I have to work a little bit harder.'

His new healthy lifestyle had helped him to achieve an even higher level of consistency on the pitch and, despite his injury problems in the 2002/03 season, had won him many admirers. As well as making the breakthrough on the international stage, Terry had been linked with a move to all the big clubs in England.

'It's nice to be linked with big clubs like Arsenal,' Terry said to the *Daily Mirror*. 'Am I going to leave Chelsea? I hope not, I really do. I've told Chelsea I want to stay and hopefully they'll get back to me in the summer, but I'm not too sure. I don't know what's going on and I need to know. I've always said I wanted to stay a Chelsea player but it's not always in your own hands.

'I want to stay but you wait around and nothing happens. You have to look after your own interests. The manager says he sees me as a future captain but it's time to get things sorted. I've been at the club since I was fourteen. I've got two years left on my contract and they tell me they want me to sign a new one – but nothing's happened.

'It's a little bit frustrating when Chelsea's future is looking good and things aren't being sorted out. You see players at other clubs being rewarded for doing well. I don't feel as if I've been rewarded for what I've done over the last few seasons. I've had the same deal for two years and, if things can't be resolved, I'm going to have to start thinking about my own future. I don't want to be up there with the likes of Jimmy and Marcel. I just want to be on a nice level.'

Terry had certainly proved his worth to the Blues in a season blighted by injury; he only started twenty-five games but still managed to score six goals. All the people in charge at Chelsea appreciated what a gifted young player they had on their hands and Terry would still be at the Bridge for the 2003/04 season, but a new investor in SW6 meant that money would no longer be an issue. Chelsea were about to become the richest club in the world.

CHAPTER EIGHT
THE RUSSIAN REVOLUTION

'People are waiting for the first person to be unhappy, but the manager had a meeting with all the players at the start of the season. He told us that he couldn't keep everybody happy, that he was going to rotate and I think everybody's got to accept that. It's down to the players to prove to the manager they should be in the starting XI and, if they do that, then they've not got a problem. The manager doesn't want to see players sulking. The best way to prove yourself to the manager is to keep your mouth shut, get on with it, work hard in training and prove it to him that way.'

After playing two seasons with basically the same squad, John Terry now found himself surrounded by new faces. By early September, Claudio Ranieri had made twelve signings as the Blues were transformed from the paupers of recent seasons into Europe's biggest spenders. With all the newcomers plus the seven first-teamers who had been shown the door, it really was a new squad for a new Chelsea.

The Blues finished the 2002/03 season by securing a place in the Champions League qualifying round. The club had massive debts and the extra revenue from playing on European club football's biggest stage would enable them to keep hold of their players, although there would be few, if any, funds available for new signings. What wasn't apparent at the time was that by finishing in the top four of the Premiership they had also caught the attention of a certain Roman Arkadievich Abramovich and new players would soon be arriving almost daily.

The Russian was more than three months younger than Gianfranco Zola and worth several billion pounds. He had obtained his vast fortune by acquiring shares cheaply in freshly privatised companies following the fall of Soviet communism and, in early July 2003, Abramovich became the majority shareholder of Chelsea Village holding company, making him the owner of the Blues and simultaneously rendering the club debt of approximately £80m inconsequential.

A spokesman for Abramovich said that he had run the rule over several clubs before opting for Chelsea. 'This is not a snap decision,' Jonathan Clare said. 'His people have been looking at a number of football clubs. They were looking for a club that was already good but also had the capability for further development to the highest levels of the game.'

It was the Champions League involvement that had swayed the decision Chelsea's way. And with the financial backing of one of the world's richest men, the Blues would again be able to compete with Europe's richest clubs in the transfer market and would emerge as genuine title contenders for the first time in years. But the first thing to do was to secure the existing assets, which meant tying down Chelsea's best players to new contracts: Terry was at the head of the queue.

After eight months of on-and-off, back-and-forth negotiations, Terry signed a new four-year deal worth £50,000 a week. It was a staggering pay rise and showed how valuable the young defender was in the eyes of his employers. Terry was delighted.

'It's such a relief it's all over now,' he said. 'I always wanted to sign and now it's great – I can just focus on playing for Chelsea and on the Champions League next season. I love this club and I never wanted to leave. I always said that I wanted to re-sign at Chelsea as long as it was right for me. It looks great for the future and I'm looking forward to it.'

Terry added: 'The club are going to give a new contract to Eidur Gudjohnsen and hopefully William Gallas will re-sign as well. If you look at the last couple of seasons, we have improved each year and last year we found some consistency, which was vital. We're getting the younger players signed on and, if we can bring new players in, then I'm sure we can push for the title next year.'

The new players were definitely on their way; in fact

they were arriving thick and fast. Over the summer, they turned up in their droves from near and far, but Ranieri was still determined to keep a British feel to the club. The majority of managers shy away from buying domestic players due to what they perceive as inflated prices, but that was of no concern to 'Chelski'.

The first two men to join Abramovich's Chelsea were the goalkeepers Jurgen Macho and Marco Ambrosio, whose deals had been negotiated under the 'old' Chelsea regime. They would soon be forgotten under the avalanche of money that brought in so many fresh faces. Glen Johnson was signed from West Ham on a £6m deal that was meant to be £3m up front with a further £3m depending on appearances, but the day after the transfer the whole £6m arrived in the Hammers' coffers.

Wayne Bridge was next, a second young English full-back, this time from Southampton for £7m. Having strengthened the defence, Ranieri turned his attentions to midfield and signed Geremi for £7m from Real Madrid [although he had spent the previous season at Middlesbrough adapting to English football] as well as Blackburn's exciting Irish winger Damien Duff for a massive £17m.

With all the new players coming in and the impressive contracts handed out to existing top performers, things were almost perfect for the Blues, but not quite. Stamford Bridge's favourite Italian, Gianfranco Zola, had been out of contract at the end of the previous season and, with the then cash-strapped club unable to offer him a realistic new deal, the little genius had negotiated a return to his native Sardinia to play for Cagliari. A man of pride and honour, Zola had given his word to the Italian club and, even though he had signed no contract, he stuck by his promise and returned home despite a fantastic last-minute bid from Chelsea who were now funded by Abramovich. 'I think I have made the right decision,' Zola said. 'My reputation with the Sardinian people was at stake.'

Before the season began, the future of another Italian was also thrown into doubt as the pressure mounted on Ranieri. The world's best coaches were being linked increasingly with the Blues as new players flooded in, but Ranieri took a realistic approach. 'To be honest, I don't know anything about the proposals made by the club for other coaches,' the manager said. 'I know the rules of the game and I know that, when a club changes owner, anything can happen.'

It didn't make much sense to let one manager sign so many players if he was only going to be replaced before the season kicked off, which meant Ranieri just got on with his job and that included guiding his team to a first trophy. In the Premier League Asia Cup, Chelsea beat the Malaysian national team 4–1 and then defeated Newcastle United 4–3 on penalties when the game finished 0–0 after 90 minutes. The spot-kicks went to sudden death and it was Terry who held his nerve to win the final, making him the captain who lifted the first Chelsea trophy of the new era.

Back in London at the start of August, with six new players at the Harlington training ground and with more being linked on the back pages every day, Terry was asked how the players felt about all the rumours. 'Are we worried or excited? I can honestly say the players are fine about it,' he said. 'We are happy and the team spirit is still good. These are among the most exciting times Chelsea has seen in terms of what could happen in the future. No-one knows how far it will go. What is certain is that we're assembling a great squad. Everyone knows how many games there are, what with Europe and the Premiership. The manager will pick his players and he has good options in every position.'

Ranieri's options increased further as Juan Sebastian Veron and Joe Cole joined to give the Blues that something extra in the final third, and Romanian striker Adrian Mutu signed from Parma to provide competition for Hasselbaink and Gudjohnsen up front. The squad was still far from complete, though, and Ranieri splashed some more cash bringing in Argentinian striker Hernan Crespo from Inter Milan, Real Madrid's French midfielder Claude Makelele and Alexei Smertin from Bordeaux, although the Russian went straight out on a season-long loan to Portsmouth.

The players were all good enough to play Champions League football which they secured by beating MSK Zilina 5–0 on aggregate in a qualifying round. Chelsea were then drawn in Group G where they would face Sparta Prague,

Besiktas and Lazio. The league campaign also started well, and Chelsea won six of their first seven Premiership matches, drawing the other 2–2 with Blackburn.

Having spent more than £100m on players for the new season, Chelsea were viewed by many as a team trying to buy success at any cost and, as such, were losing as many friends as they were making. 'Everyone is waiting for us to get turned over,' Terry said. 'We are the talk of the town at the moment and it is a good pressure to have, but if we can keep performing well we can do good things and stop the talking. The manager has made some great signings and we have a great chance for the title.'

Throughout the spending spree, several centre-backs were linked with the club, but despite all the millions at his disposal, Ranieri kept faith with Terry, Desailly, Gallas and the young and improving Robert Huth. Terry was back at the top of that list and was starting almost every game, but other players weren't so lucky and there were concerns that such a large squad would cause some players to become disheartened with Chelsea's Russian revolution. Not according to Terry, though.

'The spirit has been really good,' he said. 'When the lads first signed I was really impressed by the way everyone gelled together… There's no bitchiness or anything like that, which is good to see. For the first eight games, we were quite lucky; we didn't have any injuries and the manager has had more or less a full squad every game. Now, as the games have been coming thick and fast, we've picked up a few knocks, but with the players and strength of squad we've got it's great for the club.'

And with regard to the speculation surrounding Ranieri's future, Terry was unequivocal in his support for the man who had put so much trust in him. 'We want to do well for Claudio and show he should stay as manager,' the defender said in The *Times*. 'He gave me my chance at Chelsea and I feel he deserves to stay. There has been a lot of speculation about Sven-Goran Eriksson but Claudio has done superbly to get us where we are with no money. Now he's got lots of money, so hopefully he can take us that step further.'

Terry's season had started brilliantly at Chelsea, and he was once again involved with Eriksson at international level as England attempted to secure their passage to Euro 2004. The young centre-back was involved in every game for the Three Lions throughout autumn as he proved his worth to his country. The friendly against Croatia at Portman Road on 20 August was Terry's first start for England and he took his club form forward with a display as confident and composed as anyone could have wished for. He was the only man to play the whole match and was even handed the captain's armband for the final ten minutes. England won the game 3–1, making it six wins on the trot, perfect form heading into vital European Championship qualification matches.

Against Macedonia in Skopje, Terry continued his international development with his first competitive start for England. Playing alongside Sol Campbell in the middle of defence, the Chelsea stalwart proved valuable in the opposition box as well, winning the penalty from which David Beckham hit the winner after 63 minutes. Four days later, Terry helped England to make it eight wins in a row as they beat Liechtenstein 2–0, also securing a first clean sheet for his country alongside Birmingham's Matthew Upson.

The win over the European minnows meant that a draw in Istanbul would leave England on top of the group and guarantee their place at Euro 2004, as well as force Turkey to take their chances in the play-offs. Terry was a very promising defender but, at the time of this crunch tie, Eriksson's first-choice centre-backs were Campbell and Rio Ferdinand who had both performed so brilliantly at the World Cup in 2002 and who were still very dominant. Unfortunately for Ferdinand, his club and his country, the Manchester United defender had missed a drugs test and, before he was formally banned, the FA deemed his call-up 'inappropriate'. He was thus unavailable for the crucial clash.

'Rio is someone I look up to,' Terry said of his international team-mate. 'Whenever Manchester United are on the TV, he is someone I look out for.'

The Group Seven decider was Terry's biggest chance yet to show what he could do and, despite his continually assured performances for Chelsea and now England, many people thought that Terry was too young, too unfit and too slow to really make it as an international defender. Some critics were mourning the loss of Gareth Southgate and Martin Keown to injury, both considerably more experienced centre-backs who would be far better prepared to face a daunting trip to the Bosphorus. But John Terry was about to prove all the doubters wrong, when playing against Turkey in the Sukru Saracoglu Stadium on Saturday, 11 October 2003 he came of age for his country.

Turkey had finished third at the World Cup in Korea and Japan, and Terry was winning his fifth cap, making just his fourth start for England. But his partnership with Campbell was impressive from the first minute to the last and few onlookers would have imagined it was only the second time the two had ever played together. Sure they had both been through Senrab FC, but with more than six years separating them, Campbell was a Tottenham Hotspur trainee before Terry even thought of joining the east London boys club.

For a game of such massive importance, chances kept coming far too easily at both ends, but during the first half all of the Turks' efforts came from distance, with Terry and Campbell defending the edge of the box as if their lives depended on it. England had the perfect opportunity to relieve some of the pressure at the other end when Tugay brought down Steven Gerrard in the area, but as David Beckham ran up to hit the penalty, he slipped and sent the ball sailing over the bar.

A goal would have made things a lot easier on the nerves of spectators, but you can't lose a game if you don't concede – Terry and Campbell stood firm and the match finished 0–0, sending England to the European Championship finals. The press were unanimous in their praise of Terry after the game: 'KING JOHN,' read a headline in the *Sun*; 'RIO WHO?' asked the *Daily Mirror*.

The blood-spattered face of Terry Butcher is ingrained in the mind of any England football fan and the former international centre-back led praise for the new kid on the block. 'I thought he was immense,' Butcher said of Terry. 'Especially the way he handled Hakan Sukur. He was the one defender to hold the line and push the team forward in the second half. England were being pushed back towards their own goal because Turkey had the ball so much and pushed men forward. After that sort of performance, he has staked his claim to be a starter. Rio Ferdinand wasn't missed at all.'

The England goalkeeper was equally complimentary about the performance of the men in front of him. 'I thought the defence was very solid throughout,' David James said. 'It was the best defensive display I have played behind for club or country. It meant that I could enjoy it. I was never over-extended which is fantastic when you consider they had to win. JT and Sol were superb… I've said many times how highly I rate JT as a defender and he has shown the strength of the squad when he can come in and play like that.'

And the praise didn't stop there. In fact it came from the very top. Sven-Goran Eriksson said: 'John was absolutely fantastic. All four at the back did a wonderful job but Terry was excellent. He and Sol dealt with absolutely everything Turkey threw at them.'

With all the acclaim directed at Terry, it would have been easy for him to let it go to his head, but not many footballers are as well grounded as the Chelsea youngster. 'It was the game of my life and one of the toughest I have ever played in,' he said. 'They pushed a lot of players through with three up front but we did the job.

'It was great. There was a little bit of added pressure on me because of all the hype around Rio. I knew that, if I did make a mistake, people would have said: "Rio wouldn't have done that," or whatever. That was one of my biggest tests so far in football and I came through it. I've been playing well for Chelsea, and my confidence is high. I knew I could do well.

'Before the game Rio sent a message to wish all the lads good luck, and we all wanted to do it for him. Everybody is aware of the commitment we showed to Rio and it was good to see. That result was for him. I am a great admirer of his and I will keep watching and learning from him. I know that he and Sol are Sven's first choice, I just have to keep working hard and do well when I'm called upon.'

Back to the hard graft of the Premiership and Chelsea had the chance to go top with a trip to Birmingham City. Going into their game in hand over league-leaders

Arsenal, they were just one point behind their London rivals with a superior goal difference. The opposition were managed by one of the finest defenders in recent years never to have received his country's call, Steve Bruce. And the former Manchester United centre-back had been impressed by Terry's heroics just three days previously.

'He's a top player who turned in an exceptional performance, despite a lot of disrespect being shown to him,' Bruce said. 'I thought the way he conducted himself was marvellous. If anyone doubted him – and I'm not saying many did – he's answered them. He was massive against the Turks. And to think that he's the skipper of Chelsea at just twenty-two. All I can say is, thank God he's English!'

The Birmingham manager added: 'I think Sven-Goran Eriksson has gained something from all this. He's been given a nice kind of headache by Terry's performance. Rio is the costliest player in the country and obviously he's been in the first-choice pairing for quite a while. But Terry has given everyone something to think about. Rio must have a fight on now to get back in the team.'

Birmingham had started the season well and, with both sides looking a little tired after the international week, the game ended 0–0. But a point was all Chelsea needed to take top spot, much to the satisfaction of the players. 'I hope we can stay where we are,' Terry said. 'We are aiming to keep going and keep progressing. That's our target. It would be silly after all the hard work we've put in to throw away our good start. We've closed the gap on the sides above us from last season – United and Arsenal are the target for everyone. But I think we are now the team that everyone wants to beat. We won't be allowed to relax for a second.'

The next hurdle Terry and his team-mates had to overcome was Arsenal, as the table's top two came head to head at Highbury. Chelsea had never beaten Arsene Wenger's side during Ranieri's reign, the last league victory over the Gunners coming back in September 1995.

To rub salt in the wound, the Blues had been knocked out of the FA Cup by their London rivals in each of the previous three seasons. Chelsea's only recent successes against Arsenal were in the League Cup, 4–3 on aggregate in the semi-final in 1997/98, and 5–0 in the fourth round at Highbury in 1998/99, so history was against them.

The Blues also had to contend with some serious bad luck on the day, as Terry suffered a hamstring injury during the warm-up and Mario Melchiot took his place alongside Huth in the centre of defence. The makeshift back four was soon a goal down as Edu's free-kick deflected home after four minutes. A brilliant strike into the top corner from outside the area, courtesy of Crespo, had Chelsea level three minutes later, but an error from Carlo Cudicini in the 75th minute gifted Thierry Henry a winner when the ball rolled through the goalkeeper's legs.

The result took Arsenal back to the top of the table, but

Terry refused to blame his keeper. 'There is no other goalkeeper in the Premiership that I would rather have,' the England centre-back said. 'As a defender you know that, if a striker gets past you, it will still be extremely difficult for him to score if Carlo is in goal.'

It was Chelsea's first league defeat of the season, and, coming two weeks after an unfortunate 2–0 defeat in the Champions League at the hands of Besiktas, some people suggested the bubble had burst and it would be back to the inconsistent Chelsea of previous seasons... and of course others suggested that Ranieri wasn't up to the job.

The players responded to the criticism in the best way possible with a defiant performance against Lazio at Stamford Bridge. The Blues showed their spirit as they fought back from being a goal down at the break to win 2–1 with goals from Lampard and Mutu. 'The manager wants us to be able to fight when the going gets tough,' Terry said. 'I think we showed we can do that against Lazio.'

The spirit that the players showed against Lazio helped the Blues to embark on a run of seven successive victories in all competitions, including an excellent 4–0 win in the return match against the Roman side in the Stadio Olimpico as Claudio Ranieri enjoyed an auspicious homecoming. And it was a good evening, too, for one of Chelsea's favourite former players, as Gianfranco Zola watched from the stands. After the game, he met up with his old team-mates in the dressing room, much to their delight.

Since the little Italian playmaker had moved on, a lot of new players had come into the Chelsea line-up. And Claude Makelele, for one, was making a big impression on his new team-mates. 'Maka's form has been a big part of our great start to the season,' Terry said. 'He's great for defenders. He sees midfielders running through and picks them up. He's always there. He always wants the ball. It's the same in training. Maka is relaxed, laid-back. He's quite a funny guy. He's settled in really well.'

The team was very settled and, although the run of victories came to an end in the Champions League against Sparta Prague, a 0–0 draw extended the sequence of clean sheets to five. In the press conference, Terry was confident about their next match against the Red Devils. 'We look forward to Manchester United next,' he said. 'We'll go into it with a will to win. It's a chance for us to prove ourselves. We're confident that we're as good as them. We lost at Highbury, so it's important to prove we can beat one of the big two.

'They don't come any bigger than this. When the champions come, everybody is up for it and, as soon as the Sparta game was over on Wednesday, the manager was telling us about the need to focus. That's what we've had to do. There's respect between the sides and it should be a great game. People will be looking to see if we can match United. They did that before we went to play at Arsenal. We lost that game and there were some people who wrote us off and said: "That's it; they're out of it." This is a chance to prove ourselves. We can compete with the best, as we've shown in the Champions League.'

Terry continued: 'We have to be utterly switched on all game. Playing United is like an international game. If you make one mistake, they will punish you. That's why they've been the best in the league, because they do that. They've got great players throughout the side and one mistake can be costly. Maybe Ruud van Nistelrooy's all-round game makes him the hardest opponent I have to face in the Premiership, although Thierry Henry and Michael Owen are the other two that stand out and are big tests too... But I'm not going to talk about what I feel I've learned from the tapes – until after Sunday!'

Van Nistelrooy was equally generous with his praise. 'John Terry has been outstanding,' the Dutch striker said ahead of the game. 'He has always performed brilliantly for Chelsea and I think he's given them that solid base from which to work. He has been the vital link with the old Chelsea. I didn't think Chelsea would do as well as they have. But the important thing is that they've been solid. With all those new players coming in, you knew they could score, but they also keep it tight at the back.'

The Blues only got one against Ferguson's side, but that was all they needed as Terry and the other defenders kept Van Nistelrooy and company quiet. Lampard hit the winner from the penalty spot in the first half and, with Fulham holding Arsenal to a draw at Highbury, a good day got even better. Chelsea's three points took them back to the top of the table at the end of November.

'We've made a big statement here,' Terry said after the victory and a sixth consecutive shut-out. 'There's a long way to go, but psychologically this was brilliant for us. It's another clean sheet and the defensive lads are well happy. But we put eleven together a few years back, so there's still a way to go for our record. There was a lot of hype that this was our biggest test so far, and we got a fantastic result from it. United put us under a lot of pressure towards the end but we soaked it up, and we came out on top.'

Nine days later when they beat Besiktas 2–0 'away' in a neutral venue in Gelsenkirchen, Chelsea also came out on top of Group G of the Champions League. Safely through to the knock-out stages of the competition, Terry was enjoying his first season in Europe's Blue Riband competition. 'This is all about proving myself in big competitions like the Champions League and international games,' the England centre-back said. 'Mr Eriksson has been saying for a long time he likes his defenders to be involved in the Champions League. I've played quite a lot at this level now and that can only benefit me. Straight after the game the lads were all happy at what we'd done, but the boss came in and told us we had to forget about Besiktas. He said Bolton were a good side and told us to start thinking about them. The boss said there was no point in going back to the Bridge after having won 2–0 at Besiktas and then throwing it all away by not beating Bolton.'

Unfortunately it was worse than that as Chelsea lost 2–1 to Sam Allardyce's battling side. Bolton fought back valiantly from being a goal down, and their winner came in the last minute as Henrik Pedersen's shot deflected off Terry and went past Cudicini, a truly cruel way to surrender their unbeaten home record in the Premiership. Chelsea were unlucky against Bolton, but in their next match away to Aston Villa in the quarter-final of the League Cup the players just didn't perform and again they lost 2–1.

The Blues showed remarkable 'bouncebackability' three days later to beat Fulham 1–0 at Craven Cottage, but they made it three defeats in four matches on Boxing Day when they crashed to a 4–2 loss at The Valley. Terry equalised after nine minutes with a fine header from Mutu's free-kick, but it was at the other end that the damage was done as the Addicks ran the Blues defence ragged. This festive blip undermined the great progress the team had made in the first half of the season, but Ranieri's men were third in the table, and still very much alive in the Champions League, with the FA Cup to come.

On the international stage, things continued to go well for Terry and, in Ferdinand's continued absence, the Chelsea youngster had made himself very much at home in the England defence. In mid-December, Ferdinand received an eight-month ban after his failure to submit to drug testing and, although he still had an appeal, the chances of him featuring at Euro 2004 looked increasingly slim.

'I have a lot of sympathy for Rio and his situation,' said Terry. 'He is the main defender in the country I look up to. He is so comfortable on the ball; he is very solid; he is good in the air and he is quick. Any time that he is on TV he is the player I watch, and I try to learn things from his game and put them into mine. Sol Campbell is a great player, but Rio is the one I look up to and admire. Those two are the best in the country, and it is down to me to prove myself to Mr Eriksson.'

Everyone was impressed with the young defender's performance in qualifying for the European Championship, and his manager had no doubts about his ability to deliver on the big stage. 'Terry proved against Turkey what we always knew about him,' Ranieri said. 'And he came back a bigger and stronger player. Now he is getting experience of Champions League football he can only get better... Every time he has moved up a level, he has grown in confidence. That is good for him, for Chelsea, for England and for everyone.'

Even Terry's England and Chelsea team-mate Lampard, who grew up alongside Ferdinand, backed his current club colleague to fill the boots of his old mate. 'John is more than ready,' Lampard said. 'He has shown he can do it for England in the past and he will do it again. I grew up with Rio and know just how much he loves his football and how ambitious he is. What has happened to him is a big loss for England. At the same time, John would have been pushing hard for his place − especially after his performance against Turkey. Since then there has been a natural improvement in his game. He is now a stronger player who has a real presence about him. He had to fight to nail down a place in the Chelsea side in the face of stiff competition from Marcel and William Gallas and that made him an even better player.'

It had been a very busy year for Terry. As 2003 drew to a close, the twenty-three year-old told the *Sun* about his taxing twelve months. 'When I stop to think about everything that has happened it is exhausting,' he said. 'There have been so many landmarks, so many milestones, that 2003 has flown by. My England debut, Roman Abramovich taking over at Chelsea, the Champions League, qualifying for Euro 2004 and my brother Paul getting his big break at last with Yeovil made last year momentous.

'I just hope 2004 is as exciting… There's the possibility of winning the Premiership, the FA Cup and hopefully going with England to Euro 2004 and winning that too. But if you can't have it all, and I could only have one, it would be the Premiership title without doubt.'

But Terry was also enjoying his first campaign in the Champions League, and was getting impatient ahead of the knock-out stage. 'I can't wait to face Stuttgart in the next round,' he added. 'Beating Lazio 4–0 in Italy was like one of those landmark moments too. To go there, lead out the team and watch the way we performed sent a message throughout Europe that we mean business in every single match we play.'

Terry had been going about his business brilliantly and had started twenty-six of Chelsea's thirty games in the first half of the season. The manager decided to give him a rest in the FA Cup third round – not only that but Ranieri told him that he wouldn't even expect him to turn up for the game. Terry hated to miss a match at the best of times, but took his manager's orders with good grace and asked if he would be allowed to come to the match just the same. The dedication of Chelsea's No. 26 to the club cause had never been questioned, but attitudes like this highlight the obsessional loyalty of Terry.

The Blues defence wasn't the same without their home-grown centre-back and they conceded two goals in a draw with Watford at Vicarage Road. Terry returned to the team for the next match, but still the poor form continued and Liverpool stole three points from the Bridge with a 1–0 win.

The sudden rush of bad results added fuel to the flames burning under Ranieri, but the wins came back to the Blues almost as quickly as they had vanished. Chelsea put together a run of six victories and a draw in the next seven, to go through to the FA Cup fifth round and to within a point of Manchester United, who were second in the Premiership. After beating Portsmouth 2–0 at Fratton Park, Chelsea's next two games were against the Gunners, the first in the FA Cup followed by a league match the following Saturday.

'It was absolutely vital for us to win after Arsenal had beaten Southampton the previous night,' Terry said. 'This result keeps us in touch at the top of the table and sets us up nicely for a massive cup-tie on Sunday. Arsenal are a great team but the way we are playing at the moment, there's no reason to believe that we can't beat them.'

Chelsea were back on track on the pitch and, with the transfer window open, they were back on track in the player market as well. Abramovich got his cheque book out again in January to strengthen the squad with the signing of Scott Parker from Charlton. The young English midfielder had impressed in the Blues' defeat at The Valley, and Ranieri thought he would be a valuable addition for the club.

But even with their enhanced squad, Chelsea were unable to overcome Arsenal. The Blues lost to their London rivals in the FA Cup for the fourth consecutive season, and lost again in the league six days later when the Gunners came to Stamford Bridge. In both matches Chelsea had taken the lead and, in both matches, Wenger's side had come back to win 2–1.

In the space of a week, Ranieri's men had been knocked out of the FA Cup and had their title hopes shot down, so the persistent whispers about the manager's future were getting ever louder. But the cheery coach refused to be dismayed by the constant speculation. 'My future is not important, I am concerned only about the future of Chelsea,' Ranieri said. 'I am confident with Chelsea, with Roman Abramovich, with Peter Kenyon, with everybody. People continue to write something different, but what more can I say? I don't think about a trophy. I repeat that I want to build.

The players certainly still had faith in their boss and Terry led the shouts for the Chelsea hierarchy to persevere with the Italian coach. 'I'd just ask the board to be patient,' the defender said in the *Daily Mirror*. 'We have the quality to win the title, but we need time. When we come back for pre-season I want him there as manager, 100 per cent.'

'For me personally, he's been great. He's the man who gave me my chance. He's played a massive part in my career. I owe my life to Claudio. I won't forget the man. Everything about him is great. He's always got time for the players.'

The England defender added: 'I think that's the same for all the lads. You ask anyone in that dressing room. People talk about the pressure on Claudio, but at the end of the day it's up to the players to get the results. Claudio can pick the team but it's then down to us on the pitch. Claudio has done a great job. He's also made some great signings. But it takes time.'

Arsenal were running away with the title, but Chelsea were still in the fight for second place in the league, which would allow them to build on their return to Champions League football. And their next match was in that competition as the Blues endeavoured to put their domestic disappointments behind them with a trip to Germany.

Playing VfB Stuttgart away, Chelsea received some incredible good luck, the type which had abandoned them the previous week, and won the game 1–0 through an own goal. Fernando Meira smashed the ball past his keeper from a dangerous Johnson cross and, after the goal, Terry and the rest of the team held firm, showing their desire to progress in the one competition which they still had a chance to win.

Ever the optimist, Terry saw no reason why Chelsea couldn't claim the big trophy in May. 'We've got a lot of European experience here,' he said. 'We've gone from strength to strength. A lot of people didn't expect us to go to Lazio and win. We didn't just win, we kept the ball, we were patient, won our tackles and were better all round. When you beat teams like Lazio and Besiktas away, you can only take confidence from that.

'We really want to put Chelsea on the map as one of Europe's top clubs. We have a great squad and that strength in depth is going to help us… The Champions League is a new experience for the home-grown lads but you can really see the eyes light up in the foreign lads like Crespo and Adrian Mutu. Deep down, every player believes we can win it. But all the talk surrounding the coach's future hasn't helped. He is the right man for the job and has the support of the players. I just hope that he is given more time.'

Victory was just the thing Ranieri's men needed to pick them up, and they showed their character in putting together another fine run of results, like the one that saw them sitting pretty at the top of the table before Christmas. Manchester City were brushed aside in the league, 1–0, before the Blues secured their place in the Champions League quarter-finals with a resolute display against Stuttgart at Stamford Bridge, ending in a 0–0 draw. Chelsea were in the last eight along with two Spanish teams, two French teams, one from Portugal, one from Italy and one other English side, Arsenal.

Most Englishmen wanted the two teams to stay apart for as long as possible to maximise the country's involvement in the competition, and most Chelsea fans wanted to avoid the team that had done so much damage to their hopes of domestic glory in recent years. But one of the first men to speak out about keeping the two London clubs apart in the draw was the Arsenal manager.

'It's a huge compliment by Wenger to say he hopes to avoid Chelsea in the draw,' Terry said in the *Sun*. 'It would be frustrating if we met them in the next round but to have come this far we know we have to beat the best sooner or later. We could give them a great game. I'm not scared of Arsenal. I think we've really pushed them this season – even though we didn't get the right results against them in the Premiership or FA Cup.'

Although there was only a one-in-seven chance of Chelsea being drawn out of the hat to play Arsenal, nobody was surprised when England's top two were paired together. When it came to cup draws, the clubs had an almost magnetic attraction. And given what was to happen, it seemed fate had given Ranieri one last chance to beat Wenger's team.

Regardless of the opposition standing in their way, Terry was adamant the Blues could bring the Champions League trophy back to Stamford Bridge and, for him, it would mean almost certain salvation for the man to whom he owed so much. 'Every player in that dressing room is going to try their hardest to win the competition, and that would make it almost impossible for them to replace Claudio,' the defender said. 'The club should come out and say something. Claudio has been great to Chelsea and it wouldn't hurt for Chelsea to come out and support him… Every day there's a link with Chelsea and Eriksson, or whoever. It's frustrating for Claudio because he works so hard.'

Chelsea got the best possible preparation for the quarter-final first leg with back-to-back Premiership wins, and Terry was at his imperious best putting in gargantuan performances against Bolton and Fulham. He even hit the opening goal at the Reebok Stadium, volleying home a Duff cross at the far post, a perfect way to atone for his last-minute own goal when Allardyce's men had stolen three points from the Bridge in December. The game in the North-west finished 2–0 and, when the Cottagers came to SW6, they were beaten 2–1. But the next visitors were Arsenal.

The Gunners were in incredible form and were still on course for the Treble as March came to an end. They sat at the top of the Premiership unbeaten, they were in the semi-final of the FA Cup, and they faced Terry and his team-mates in the Champions League having already beaten them three times that season. But it was time for Ranieri's revenge and in the biggest of all their clashes.

Arsenal were slightly ahead after the first leg, their away goal giving them the advantage following the 1–1 draw, and with Desailly suspended for the return match after his late red card. But there was nothing to separate the two sides on the pitch in west London, and that gave Chelsea confidence for the second leg a fortnight later.

The Blues kept the pressure on Arsenal in the league as well, with wins over Wolves, 5–2 and Tottenham, 1–0. That made it 15 points from five games since the two teams had met in the league. Ranieri was named Barclaycard Manager of the Month for March, and Eriksson had signed an extension to his England contract – ending the 'SVEN TO CHELSEA' headlines the papers had been running since the start of the season – everything was going well, and it was only going to get better.

Terry had never played in a team that had beaten Arsenal, and Chelsea hadn't beaten the Gunners in the last seventeen attempts but all that was about to change on a memorable night at Highbury. Jose Antonio Reyes put the visitors ahead in first-half injury-time, but after the break it was all Chelsea. Frank Lampard equalised when Lehmann failed to clear Makelele's long-range effort. Arsenal were on the ropes, and Chelsea drove forward searching for the knock-out blow.

Ashley Cole made a miraculous goal-line clearance from an effort by Gudjohnsen after 85 minutes, but two minutes later Bridge charged up the left wing to score the most important goal of his career. The former Southampton full-back played a one-two with Gudjohnsen on the edge of the area, and the beautiful return pass from the Icelandic international received the finish it deserved: the ball nestled in the Arsenal net. With only three minutes left, the home side needed to score twice to rescue the tie, but it wasn't to be. Chelsea were through to the Champions League semi-finals.

Just as Terry had insisted previously, the boys were doing all they could to keep Ranieri in his job. 'We've said all along we are right behind the boss,' the centre-back told reporters. 'He has done a great job already and we'll wait and see what happens. He has got the lads together and that is vital. We'll keep fighting until the death. Arsenal are a great side with great players and I'm sure they'll bounce back. But if we keep putting pressure on them, then who knows what will happen? They cracked last year.'

It could have been the ecstasy and relief of finally beating Arsenal, or the thought of facing Monaco in the last four of the Champions League, or perhaps even the fact that the Gunners bounced back the following Friday to beat Liverpool and shatter any remaining hopes the Blues may have had of catching them in the league; any one of these reasons could have accounted for Ranieri's men losing focus. Whatever the explanation, Chelsea went off the boil in the league and picked up only two points from their next three games.

This wasn't ideal form ahead of the biggest game in Chelsea's history, but in a last four featuring AS Monaco, FC Porto and Deportivo La Coruna, the Blues had to fancy their chances of coming away with the trophy. But Monaco had beaten Real Madrid in their quarter-final, overcoming a 4–2 first-leg deficit, so Terry and his team-mates wouldn't be taking anything for granted. 'Their win over Real showed they are no mugs and it will be tough for us,' said the Shed hero. 'We have to prepare right but we do look solid throughout the team and the lads want to win and die for each other.'

That fighting spirit was indeed needed in the Stade Louis II as Monaco went ahead after 15 minutes. The goal spurred Chelsea forward and they were level six minutes later through Crespo's close-range finish. The equaliser put the Blues in the ascendancy and they dominated the rest of the half, with Lampard magnificent. But no further goals came and, with the score 1–1 at the break, Ranieri tried to mix things up by replacing Gronkjaer with Veron. The substitution handed the initiative back to the home side and they started the second half brightly, but the French side were reduced to ten men when Andreas Zikos was sent off for clashing with Makelele after 52 minutes.

In the run-up to the game, Ranieri found out that Chelsea had a secret meeting with Jose Mourinho, the talented young Porto manager, and the Italian was desperate to win the match and prove his worth to his employers in spite of their recruiting efforts. Sensing a weakness, the former Valencia coach went for the jugular with the opposition a man down. Unfortunately for the Blues, his two additional changes, Hasselbaink for Melchiot and Huth for Parker, only served to disrupt the shape and structure of the side. Monaco played most of the second half with ten men, scored two more goals and, against the odds, won the match 3–1.

'We are down but not out, not by a long way,' Terry said after the game. 'We are all positive – disappointed but positive… When we get them back to Stamford Bridge, with the support of our fans behind us, anything is possible. It's going to be tough because they showed they are a good side and disciplined but we are going to be positive.'

'The Tinkerman' had made all manner of changes to his formation, personnel and tactics during his time in charge of Chelsea but never previously had he come as spectacularly unstuck as he did in that first leg. He was distraught, but he manfully accepted responsibility for the defeat. In his book *Proud Man Walking*, Ranieri revealed his reaction: 'OK, chaps, my fault!' he told his players. 'This time I got it wrong. I misread the game, and made the wrong changes at the wrong times, but now we've got to forget Monte Carlo. We've got to stay calm and do enough in the return leg to get us to the final and, if there's a team that can do it, that team is us.'

But Terry couldn't stop thinking about the first leg. 'I haven't slept for thinking about the game,' he said. 'The first night I stayed awake all night chatting with some of the lads about what happened. It is so frustrating as I felt we had control of the game. We were saying at half-time: "We can go on and win this game" – and what a great result that would have been with the home leg in front of our fans to come.

'It just wasn't to be. But we are optimistic we can still win… For ourselves, the manager, the fans and everyone at the club.'

The loss in the French principality added to the speculation surrounding the manager, and Mourinho's name was increasingly mentioned in links with Chelsea. However, Terry had come out in support of Ranieri throughout the campaign and he wasn't going to stop now. 'The situation involving the manager hasn't changed,' said the England defender. 'It has been the same all season, and we have dealt with it from the word go. He has had a lot of stick all year… But if we could beat Monaco and go through to the final, it would be a very special night for Claudio.'

Terry went on: 'There will be no excuses. We were disappointing over there but now we have the chance to prove just how good we are. It was a dream for me just to play in the Champions League this season. But the belief is there that we can go through to the final… The Monaco players are also under pressure. They know they have to come here and put in a good performance. So the pressure will be on them.'

A goal after 22 minutes added to the pressure on the visitors, as Gronkjaer's fine left-footed cross looped over the Monaco keeper and into the top corner. Chelsea continued to push forward, maintaining the high tempo associated with English football and searching for the goal that would put them in the final.

As half-time approached, Lampard added the perfect finish to a crisp move involving Melchiot, Gudjohnsen and Bridge and, for the first time in the tie, the Blues were ahead, courtesy of the away-goals rule. But their joy was short-lived as Hugo Ibarra pulled a goal back deep into first-half injury-time.

Seconds away from the chance to regroup and focus on the 45 minutes that stood between them and the Champions League final, Ibarra's finish knocked the stuffing out of Chelsea. They had one chance to score early in the second half, but Monaco scored again with 30 minutes remaining and it was game over.

The visitors' first goal had done all the damage. 'It killed us,' Terry said of the strike in added time. 'If we could have gone in at half-time with a clean sheet, it would have given us a great boost. I thought we played brilliantly in the first half, one of the best games we've played. It's just disappointing that we switched off for a couple of minutes and they went and scored.'

As the season drew to a close, Terry had no time to mope around since he had to try and lift himself and his team-mates for a trip to Old Trafford. Arsenal had finally confirmed their status as champions a fortnight earlier, and Chelsea needed one point from Manchester United to secure second place in the league. 'It's going to take a couple of days to get the Monaco result out of our systems,' Terry said. 'But we need to forget it as soon as possible. We'll be going for the win at Old Trafford anyway, but one point will be good enough to give us second place and, if we can do that, maybe it would give us a little lift. For many years in the league, it's been all about United and Arsenal in the top two. It would be good to put an end to that.'

That they did with another resilient display. Cudicini saved a penalty and the Blues had to play the final 17 minutes of the match with ten men, but they still held on for a 1–1 draw, thanks to Gronkjaer's first-half opener. Chelsea were the second-best team in the country in the 2003/04 season. Arsenal had been in incredible form and went through the thirty-eight Premiership matches unbeaten to claim the title. It was an historic year for Wenger's team, but Terry could be proud of the achievement of his side since they were better than everyone else bar the north Londoners. Sure there are no trophies for second-best, but the Blues had made great progress and Arsenal's unbeaten season was the kind of freakish thing that only happens occasionally in sport. If Chelsea continued on their current track, they would get the rewards they deserved.

'You look around and the squad is full of great players and great people,' Terry said. 'It might take another season but slowly and surely we're improving. If it wasn't for

Arsenal having a perfect season, maybe it would have been us winning the title.'

Terry had once again shown great improvement: his seamless transition to full England international and his maturing performances as Chelsea captain, with Desailly missing more than half of the games, proved the fact. He had only scored three goals, but had started fifty-one of Chelsea's fifty-nine games, and his continued excellence was once again recognised by his peers when he was nominated for PFA Young Player of the Year.

He lost out in the final reckoning to his recently acquired team-mate Parker; possibly because he was an England defender, a lot of Terry's fellow players may have thought his mature performances ruled him out of the voting for the Young Player award. But he was clearly well thought of: Terry was the only one of the six nominees for the trophy to feature in the PFA Team of the Year.

It had been another fine twelve months on the pitch for Terry and his Chelsea pals, but the defeat by Monaco still rankled with the youngster and he couldn't bring himself to watch the Champions League final. 'I knew it should have been us out there,' he said. 'But I think it has been a good season – it has gone well for me. I've made the step up with England, which has been a dream come true. We are disappointed we didn't win anything but have made a big move from last year, coming fourth and then second.'

But second place wasn't good enough for Abramovich, and it wasn't unexpected when Ranieri was sacked. A new man would be coming in to spend some of the Russian's roubles, and the man who had put so much trust in Terry was leaving. The two had developed a fine working relationship in the Italian's four years at Stamford Bridge. The young defender would never forget what the coach had done for him, and he had shown his appreciation to his mentor earlier in the season with an incredible gesture after the England match in Istanbul.

In his book, Ranieri told a story about the time he had seen his young protege with a package at Harlington. It turned out to contain Terry's England shirt from the match against Croatia, his first start for his country. This was mounted in a glittering frame with England emblems at each corner. The Italian said: 'Well done, JT! Look after it always, it's a lovely souvenir. And framed like that, it looks really good.'

A couple of days later Terry returned to the training ground with a gift for Ranieri. The manager wrote: 'Mounted in a frame, just like the one I had admired, was his England shirt from the qualifier against Turkey in Istanbul, with a dedication: *To Claudio. I will never forget the man who gave me my first chance. John Terry.*'

But without any serious trophies to show for his time at Chelsea, it was time for Ranieri to move on. It was a season of almosts, ifs, buts and maybes, – everything was heading in the right direction but not quickly enough for Abramovich. The Russian wasn't the only one who wanted to see some silverware at Stamford Bridge. 'It's not good enough for me,' Terry said of the second-place finish. 'Even before Roman took over, everyone wanted to win things, and I'm no different. I want to win trophies and, at the end of my career, that's the only thing that I want to have – one being the league title, the second being the Champions League. As a player you dream of winning things and, when you don't, it's so frustrating.'

Soon it would be time to stop dreaming and start achieving.

CHAPTER NINE
EURO HEARTBREAK

'We have to believe we can go all the way. I was a supporter for the last World Cup, sitting there watching it on a big screen in Dubai, and it was a massive target to be here for this tournament. Thankfully, I am. It's a tough group but we go there full of confidence and we aim to enjoy it.'

John Terry travelled to Portugal for the European Championship finals as one of Sven-Goran Eriksson's twenty-three man squad. The Chelsea No. 26 was given '5' as his shirt number, reinforcing his position as one of the first-choice centre-backs for the upcoming tournament. Twelve months previously he didn't have a single cap to his name but now the centre-back's assured international performances would have been considered impressive coming from a seasoned veteran. Still only twenty-three years old, the Chelsea vice-captain was mature beyond his years, on the pitch and off it.

He had truly arrived as an international footballer with his performance in Istanbul, the match that secured England's place in Euro 2004. And after a string of friendlies building up to the summer's main event, the Blues defender had made the position in the middle of the back four his own, something Rio Ferdinand's enforced absence allowed him to do. In November, Terry played 90 minutes against Denmark. Eriksson experimented with his team and formation and watched his adopted country lose 3–2 at Old Trafford.

Terry missed the game against Portugal in February due to injury, but was back in the side to face Sweden at the end of March. The Chelsea defender only played the goalless first half, but Zlatan Ibrahimovic scored the only goal of the game after 53 minutes and Eriksson's mother country inflicted a first defeat on Steven Gerrard at international level.

As the domestic season came to an end, the squad was announced for Euro 2004. Terry was named as one of four centre-backs alongside Arsenal's Sol Campbell, Ledley King of Tottenham and Liverpool's Jamie Carragher. The build-up to the tournament had begun in earnest but Terry was still thinking about the dismissal of his club manager. 'I am here today in the England team because of one man, and that man is Claudio Ranieri,' the Chelsea defender said. 'The new manager might not favour me, but

I will just work hard and hope to be in the starting XI at the start of the season.'

Terry had forced his way into the England side during Ferdinand's suspension, and the Chelsea man was expected to partner Campbell on the Iberian Peninsula when the tournament finally got under way with a big cross-channel clash. England had been drawn in Group B with Croatia, Switzerland and France, and the anticipation ahead of the opening match between England and France in Lisbon had been growing almost exponentially since the fixtures had been announced.

With such a large number of French stars plying their trade in England, the match would have a strong Premiership flavour. Club mates were pitted against one another: Terry was set to line up alongside Frank Lampard, with Claude Makelele, William Gallas and Marcel Desailly in the opposition line-up. 'I have a special partnership with William on and off the pitch,' said Terry of his French colleague. 'Off the pitch we talk a lot and phone each other. We have a laugh. He's a funny guy.'

But Desailly was coming in for a lot of stick from the French press and, as the tournament approached, he was booed by French fans in some of the warm-up games. Terry continued to hold his senior team-mate in high esteem. 'Marcel is still right up there,' the England centre-back said. 'He's getting on, as he would be the first to admit, but he's such a true pro. He's still got great desire. There's nobody else who's done what Marcel's done. And he has always had the time for me. When I was seventeen or eighteen, he was there to help when I was nobody. And hopefully I will be able to pass my experience on to others in the future.'

But it wasn't just Chelsea players in the French squad's Premiership contingent: Robert Pires, Patrick Vieira, Mikael Silvestre, Fabien Barthez, Louis Saha and Thierry Henry also featured in Jacques Santini's twenty-three man squad.

Henry was at the height of his incredible powers in 2004 and played a huge part in Arsenal's unbeaten season, but Eriksson was confident his Chelsea defender would be able to handle the mercurial forward. 'Terry is a young Tony Adams, that is exactly right,' the England manager said. 'He has the spirit, he is strong, and he is not the quickest in the world but he is very difficult to beat.

'Against Thierry Henry you have to be a little bit careful but the good thing is that the players know Henry. They play against him at least twice a year and see him on TV every week. Sol plays against him every day and John played against him four times this season. Terry's improved as a player very much over the last year. He's much more mature and quicker than he was eighteen months ago. He is a big, big talent and still very young. Hopefully, he's going to be in there for a long time now.'

Terry was in the team for a friendly against Japan at the City of Manchester Stadium for one of the final preparation matches before Euro 2004. The Chelsea centre-back lined up alongside Campbell and came close to scoring his first goal for England after five minutes when he met a David Beckham corner with a firm header. The ball appeared to be over the line before it was saved by goalkeeper Seigo Narazaki, but the referee didn't think so and the game remained scoreless until Michael Owen hit the back of the net after 25 minutes.

Gerrard unleashed a low shot from outside the area and the eternal predator Owen was on hand to tuck it home from six yards. England couldn't hold on to their lead however and Shinji Ono hit an equaliser early in the second half. The result left Eriksson's side without a victory in five matches since beating Liechtenstein in September, not ideal form for a team supposedly capable of winning the European Championship.

But England had one more dress rehearsal before their heavyweight bout with France and, unluckily for Iceland, the Three Lions chose the perfect time to roar. Again at the City of Manchester Stadium, England beat the visitors 6–1 to win the FA Summer Tournament. Terry missed the game with a hamstring strain, but like many other observers he was in awe of the young star of the show.

Wayne Rooney scored two goals and constituted a real threat throughout the first half; if he hadn't been replaced at the interval, it would have been a question of how many he scored, and he was still just eighteen years old. 'Wayne is an unbelievable talent,' Terry said. 'His second goal today was special but, to be honest, we see that from him in training every day. The fact he is eighteen doesn't matter. France will know all about him and be wary of him – and so they should be.

'He's lightning-quick, brave and he doesn't let defenders bully him, no matter how big and experienced they are. He's a nightmare to mark in training and I'm just relieved he'll be playing for us and not against us in Portugal this summer.'

All the pundits were tipping the young Evertonian as one to watch in Portugal, but the biggest concern for England in the seven days before the tournament started was Terry's fitness. In big tournaments, the games come thick and fast so it is always imperative to have your players one hundred per cent fit. With the opening game against France looming large on Sunday and the match against Switzerland just four days later, it was important not to risk forcing the Chelsea defender back too soon since a set-back could end his tournament.

'He will probably not be fit for Sunday but we are sure he will be fit for Thursday,' Eriksson said. 'He trained a little bit with us and did some fitness work and he'll train again with us tomorrow, but it's too short a time and we think it's dangerous to risk him. But that's life and we hope he'll be okay for the second game; we're almost sure he'll be ready for it.'

As time was running out on Terry in his race for fitness, one person who thought he would be back in time was French striker Henry. 'I am playing against one of the best central defensive pairings in the world in John Terry and Sol Campbell,' the Arsenal hit man said. 'That's how highly I rate them. It doesn't mean you won't play well against them or you will play well. People have said that Terry has played well against me when I play against Chelsea but I am marked by William Gallas because he is on the side where I play – and Mario Melchiot too – but my scoring record against Chelsea is still good. I know more than anyone that England are capable of winning Euro 2004. So many people think the English league is easy, but I know there are many quality English players.'

Terry didn't recover in time to play against Henry and his team-mates, so Ledley King replaced him in the England defence. Eriksson's men exceeded expectations in their big game and led for most of the match after Frank Lampard headed home a David Beckham free-kick in the first half. But it was not to be their day and France won, thanks to two late strikes from Zinedine Zidane.

Beckham even had a second-half penalty saved with the score at 1–0, but it was his Real Madrid team-mate Zidane who had the last laugh with a fantastic free-kick in the 90th minute and a cool, calm and collected penalty deep into injury-time. The spot-kick came after a Gerrard back pass sold David James very short and the Manchester City keeper brought Henry down in the area.

It was a cruel end to an otherwise excellent England display, and Terry was very impressed by his deputy. 'It was a great performance by the lads against France,' said the rapidly recovering defender. 'Overall we were the better side and were very unlucky not to win the game. I thought Ledley was brilliant. He was very comfortable defensively. He won some great headers and tackles and looked good with the ball at his feet. I couldn't see any way France were going to break the back line and score – Ledley and Sol were magnificent.

'To pick up a little injury before probably my biggest game was very disappointing. I went more or less the whole season without getting any injuries and I was fully fit and looking forward to being a part of the team. We were very cautious over the injury but I'm thankful for that – if I'd played, I might have pulled it and I would have been out for four or five weeks. My tournament would have been over. Just to be here is a great achievement for myself and my family, and they're all over here watching.'

The Terry clan were soon able to watch their most famous son in action as England concentrated on qualifying for the quarter-finals by trying to beat Switzerland and Croatia. The Chelsea defender returned to the line-up for the second group game, but it was Wayne Rooney who dominated the match against the Swiss. The teenager announced his arrival as an international force, on the biggest stage, with two goals in a 3–0 win. The first, after 23 minutes, made him the youngest player to score in a European Championship finals match and the second made the game safe with a quarter of an hour left to play. Gerrard added a late third but all the talk after the game was of Rooney.

'Wayne was unbelievable out there in Coimbra,' Terry said. 'I look at him and wait for the signs of nerves and he is just not affected by all this. All he wants to do is get to the next game, so there is someone else to beat, another occasion to rise to. I felt when I was injured and sat watching the France game that he had been fantastic.'

Terry had enjoyed his first match at a major tournament and, although he looked a little rusty, he combined well with Campbell to keep the opposition quiet. Switzerland didn't have anyone of Rooney's ability, which was good news since the Chelsea defender had had enough problems with the teenager in practice. 'Wayne is a nightmare to mark and I should know because I've had to do it in training!' the defender said. 'All of Europe is now aware of him and I'd love to get him to Chelsea next season. I've not got the money to buy him but I think there are others connected with Chelsea who may be able to raise the cash!'

Rooney wasn't the only England player to be linked with a move to the Bridge: Liverpool's midfield dynamo Steven Gerrard was also rumoured to be on the move from Merseyside to west London. 'I think Steven is one of the world's best midfielders,' Terry said. 'He drives the team forward, he is great on the ball and his range of passing is brilliant – probably up there with David Beckham. As a defender and as a midfielder, you need to be close to people off the pitch as well, like I am to Sol, Gary Neville, Ashley Cole and David James. And Gerrard and Lamps' relationship is strong.'

He continued: 'As a pair they complement each other. They can both drive forward and get goals but, if one of them goes, they are both intelligent enough that the other holds. They've both got great stamina and even in the 89th minute they're capable of making a run in behind the defence to get that crucial goal.'

There was no transfer talk concerning Terry. He was happy as could be at Chelsea and he was fully focused on England's job in hand, beating Croatia – the team that Terry played against when he started his first England match in August 2003. They had Monaco's Dado Prso up front and the striker was trash-talking the England defender in the build-up to the game. 'If you'd told me when I made that first start ten months ago I'd be playing them again in the European Championships with everything on the line, I wouldn't have believed it,' admitted the Chelsea defender. 'The thought that it might be up to me and the rest of the defenders in the last few minutes is exciting. As a player, you want to rise to the occasion.

'I learned from playing against Prso in the Champions League,' Terry continued. 'Coming off the pitch when I've kept a striker quiet is a buzz for me and the only two who I feel have really got the better of me were Thierry Henry and then Fernando Morientes in that game against Monaco.'

None of Croatia's players got the better of Terry in

Lisbon and, although England went behind after six minutes, Rooney again guided his team to victory. Paul Scholes equalised after 40 minutes and the young Evertonian scored his third goal of the tournament on the stroke of half-time. In the second half, Rooney made it 3–1, and Lampard added a fourth after Igor Tudor had halved England's lead. The 4–2 win gave Eriksson's team second place in Group B, and they were through to the quarter-finals where they would play Portugal.

Terry picked up a knock in the victory, but was sure he would recover in time to face the tournament hosts. 'My knee locked up when I went for a header and I landed on one foot,' he said. 'But it is all OK – definitely. I don't think it's going to be a problem. I'm sure I will be fine.'

The Chelsea defender was indeed fit to play in Lisbon, and Eriksson picked the same side for the third successive game. England got off to the perfect start when Michael Owen latched on to a defensive error to open the scoring after three minutes. But the team was seriously compromised with less than half an hour on the clock, when the inspirational Rooney was forced off injured. The talismanic forward had broken a metatarsal in a collision with Jorge Andrade and his tournament was over.

Sadly for England, the team looked clueless without the teenager and they would soon be following their best player out of the Championship. Without Rooney as the focal point of every move, the team had no shape and no structure and seemed unable to retain the ball. The players didn't look interested in adding to their lead and simply invited the opposition on to them. Predictably, this led to Terry and the rest of the defence being put under constant pressure.

Along with Neville, Campbell and Cole, the Chelsea defender dealt admirably with everything that was being thrown at them, but eventually Portugal found a way through and it was no less than they deserved. After 83 minutes, Helder Postiga headed Simao's cross past James and the crowd went wild.

There was still time for England to push forward, though. With the attack still looking toothless, it took a set-piece for them to come close to a winner. Owen headed Beckham's 90th-minute free-kick against the bar, and Campbell bundled the ball over the line. In a spooky coincidence, similar to the game against Argentina at France 1998, the last-minute goal was disallowed for a foul on the keeper. Sadly for England, the referee Urs Meier saw an alleged push by Terry on Ricardo and the game went into Silver Goal extra-time.

The first half of the added 30 minutes was nervy as neither side was willing to commit too many men to attack, but after 110 minutes Rui Costa hit an unstoppable drive from outside the box into the top corner of James' net. With only ten minutes left, England had to attack and, five minutes from time, they hit an equaliser thanks to the Chelsea connection.

Terry nodded down a Beckham corner and Lampard

was on hand to swivel on the edge of the six-yard box and smash the ball home. Having helped the team level, the boys from the Bridge stood up to be counted when the tie went to penalties five minutes later. Both men scored from the spot but England were let down by Beckham and Darius Vassell and they lost the shoot-out 6–5.

The Chelsea defender took the seventh penalty, England's fourth, and sent it high into the back of the net, unlike his illustrious skipper who sent his effort high over the bar when his standing foot dislodged the ball as he ran up. Vassell's penalty was well struck and well placed, but Ricardo pulled off a brilliant save and then got up to score the deciding kick. England were knocked out of a fourth major tournament on penalties and it hurt. Portugal went through to the semi-finals and eventually lost the final to Greece just to emphasise how winnable the competition might have been for England. 'I'm devastated,' Terry said. 'It's a terrible way to go out of the competition, especially when we thought we'd done enough to go through. I thought it was our night but, in the end, we didn't get it.'

He went on: 'I thought I would be fifth, sixth or even seventh to be sent up for the penalties. But, in the end, the boss came up to me and told me I would be fourth. It was no problem; we had practised them in training the day before the game. I've never taken a penalty for Chelsea before because there are a few others ahead of me in the pecking order. But I was happy to take one on this occasion. Every time someone took a penalty the next one up had to pad down the turf. The area around the spot was too soft and you could tell that by the penalties that were missed.'

Terry was insistent that he wasn't allocating blame. 'It takes a lot of bottle for someone to take a penalty in a situation like that. David was the first to put his hand up and say he'd take the first one. That shows great character and confidence. And even after he missed his penalty, he was still there encouraging us all on, which says a lot about his character.'

Terry was adamant he hadn't pushed the keeper in the 90th minute. He said: 'I certainly didn't commit a foul and I've no idea why it was disallowed. I didn't touch the goalkeeper and neither did Sol.'

Following his injury troubles, the Blues defender had never really hit top form in the tournament but he was delighted with the form of his club mate, Lampard. 'Frank had a fantastic season for Chelsea,' Terry said. 'Then he came here and kicked on again. He played four games and scored three goals: one with his head, one with his left foot and one with his right. A few people doubted his ability – but no-one in the dressing room did. I just hope things are sorted out with Chelsea and his new contract as soon as possible. It takes some players eight or ten games to find their feet at international level but Frank has taken his chance and been absolutely brilliant.'

The form of the two Blues throughout the previous season and the extra experience picked up in Portugal were sure to be of great benefit to Chelsea in the campaign to come. Terry wanted to make sure this season would end with silverware. 'As you come to terms with what happened in Portugal you have a stark choice – you can either let it get you down or get on with life and try to take some benefit from it,' the England defender said. 'No experience is ever wasted and I've come through Euro 2004 battered but unbowed. I know my team-mate Frank Lampard feels the same. I've suffered a lot of hurt on the pitch in the last year. Going out of the Champions League to Monaco when we were just one step away from the final was painful.'

Terry explained: 'Surely my luck has got to change sometime. I've got youth on my side and ambition and, with it being a young squad, we all feel the same. Immediately after the game, the England lads met in the dressing room and we decided there and then not to dwell on the result or what had just happened. We said: "Let's take this and use what we have learned to build a better, more experienced squad to take to the World Cup." We're capable of doing that, and it won't be long before the qualifiers are under way and we can forget about Euro 2004.'

England had many talented players, but without an obvious left-sided midfielder, playing with three very similar attack-minded men in the middle of the park and overly reliant on Rooney, they had been knocked out of a tournament that they had the quality to win. But as

Terry said, it was all valuable experience and, with a new coach on the way in to SW6, he was only looking forward. 'When I went back to Chelsea for pre-season last year, the club was the talk of football because Mr Abramovich had arrived. We moved up a step with his arrival,' he recalled. 'Now we have to see what will happen with Mr Mourinho. It's a fresh challenge and, hopefully, I'll be too preoccupied with everything going on there to think back too often about Portugal.'

With everything that was about to happen at Stamford Bridge the following season, Terry's Euro 2004 disappointment would disappear before his suntan.

CHAPTER TEN
CAPTAIN MARVEL

'When we were flying out on the way to America, he pulled me to the back of the plane. I didn't know what he wanted, but he just said to me: "I can see the lads have a lot of respect for you. I want you to be my captain." He said what things he wanted from me as a captain. On the training pitch and around the place, he wanted me to be a speaker and [told me] that, out there in the game, he wanted me to get his words across to the players. Then he asked what I would prefer to win. He asked if I wanted the Premiership, the Champions League, the Carling Cup or the FA Cup. I told him the Premiership because it's a special one for everyone and it's what I've dreamed of for a very long time. And he just nodded.'

John Terry had originally been apprehensive about the new manager, Jose Mourinho, following his appointment as Claudio Ranieri's successor, but by the time the

Portuguese named him Chelsea captain, the young defender was already well on his way to becoming one of the coach's biggest fans.

Jose Mario Santos Mourinho Felix arrived in west London fresh from winning the Champions League in May 2004, a miraculous achievement by a club as small as FC Porto, but it was the natural conclusion to two-and-a-half years of spectacular progress for the Oporto club. Having served a coaching apprenticeship under Bobby Robson at Sporting Lisbon, Porto and Barcelona in the early 1990s, Mourinho developed into a world-class coach in his own right after taking over at Porto in January 2002.

The club was mid-table when he took over, but he had guided them to third place by the end of the season, and the following year the trophies began to arrive. Porto won a treble of domestic league and cup competitions plus the UEFA Cup in 2003. The following season Mourinho became the youngest manager to win the Champions League, while Porto again won the Portuguese league but lost the cup final to Benfica in extra-time. Mourinho had achieved all he could in his homeland and he was looking for a new challenge. Chelsea were looking for a new coach and the confident young Portuguese was the perfect candidate for the job.

The first time Terry met his new manager was when the man from Setubal visited the England team hotel in Manchester before the squad headed out to Portugal.

Mourinho sat down with his new players – Terry, Frank Lampard, Joe Cole and Wayne Bridge – and told them what he thought of them and where he was going to take them. He told the young centre-back that he believed he was one of the best defenders in the world, but he hadn't won anything yet. He added that he, Jose Mourinho, was going to change all that.

There was no need for the new coach to travel so far to make his introductions. He could have waited until the start of pre-season training to meet Terry but he went the extra mile and that meant a lot to the Chelsea boys. 'Pre-season, before we met Jose, we were scared, to be honest,' Terry said. 'We didn't know that much about him and we weren't quite sure what to expect. But once we met the man, we realised how good he was and how much he wanted to win. He wants to win everything; even in training you can see that. He doesn't settle for second best and, once that's instilled in you, you start believing and you don't even want to concede goals in training.'

Terry had been one of Ranieri's most loyal followers and it was important that the new coach got him onside as soon as possible. Luckily, he had made an ideal first impression. As part of the England contingent at Euro 2004, Terry was allowed to miss the first five days of pre-season training and, for the second summer running, there were plenty of changes to the squad ahead of the new season.

A number of players had been released as surplus to requirements at Stamford Bridge: Jimmy Floyd

Hasselbaink, Manu Petit, Mario Stanic, Jesper Gronkjaer, Boudewijn Zenden, Neil Sullivan, Marco Ambrosio, Mario Melchiot, Winston Bogarde and former club captain Marcel Desailly. As vice-captain under Desailly, Terry was desperate to succeed the Frenchman and Mourinho had already given an interview in which he made it clear that either Terry or Lampard would be the new skipper. The two good friends didn't talk about the vacancy but it was obvious how keen they both were for the role. It is alleged that initially Mourinho was leaning towards the midfielder for the captaincy, but after speaking to the other players it became clear how highly they rated Terry and, on the flight to America for the pre-season tour, Mourinho confirmed the defender would be the new club captain.

'It makes me very proud,' said Terry. 'I have been at the club since I was fourteen. The manager went round each player individually, as well as the staff who have been here a few years, and he just asked their opinions on who should be captain. Thankfully, he has listened to them. I spoke to the manager about what he wants from me. On the pitch, he wants me to be a leader, which I think I am anyway. He also wants me to get the lads together off the pitch, to be a bit of a social secretary as well. We have a very young bunch of lads who are gelling together well and I'll try to improve that.'

As well as all the players moving on, inevitably a new contingent was coming in, thanks to Roman Abramovich's billions. Ranieri had worked out deals to sign the Czech goalkeeper Petr Cech and Dutch winger Arjen Robben the previous season, and Mourinho added to these fresh faces by raiding his old club for two more players. Portuguese defenders Paulo Ferreira and Ricardo Carvalho joined Chelsea from Porto, and yet another of Mourinho's countrymen arrived from Benfica. Tiago Mendes would strengthen the midfield and PSV Eindhoven's Mateja Kezman as well as Marseille's Ivory Coast striker Didier Drogba were signed to bolster the attack.

The newcomers sent Abramovich's transfer spending past the £200m mark and, once Alexei Smertin came back from his loan at Portsmouth and Juan Sebastian Veron and Hernan Crespo had been loaned out to the Milan clubs Inter and AC respectively, the new squad was all set for the season.

Mourinho was confident he had the players to bring the title to Stamford Bridge for the first time in fifty years. 'Yes, I believe we will win the title, no question about that,' the manager said. 'I believe 100 per cent that we can win the title but I am not so stupid to say I can guarantee that we will win it... The spirit and ambition in this squad is good because they have never tasted winning the Premiership before.'

The new man's bold conviction was taken as arrogance by some and many didn't like it. Terry, however, had total trust in Mourinho. 'It is a good sign that he is confident and brash,' the defender said. 'He wants to win things and the players are exactly the same. He is a confident guy and, with his record, he has every right to be.

'There is no reason why we can't do it this year. In training he has installed that self-belief in us; we believe that we have a group of great players and that we can go out and win trophies. His man-management is great. He has sat down with every player and his training is spot on but there is no time to rest. He makes sure you are focused for every single second and there can be no loss of focus.'

Terry couldn't wait for the new season to start, and he was impressed by the new recruits. 'Overall the football in training is a lot sharper than it was last year. The standard has been raised. That is going to make myself and the other players even better. We've been doing a lot more defensive situations, which is obviously going to help me. But off the pitch as well, we go through set-plays, so it's good to go through things and touch up on them.'

But the defender refused to be complacent, and went on: 'I don't think being captain makes me an automatic choice at all. It's all down to me. I need to work hard and show the right things in training to get the right things at the end of the season. Hopefully, that's going to be trophies.'

Wary of Carvalho's imminent arrival, Terry added: 'Just because I am captain doesn't mean I'm going to be playing. With Marcel Desailly having left the club, we need another central defender. There will be a lot of games next season and, hopefully, we can go a long way in the Champions League, so maybe we need someone with a bit of experience who could step in. You never know what will happen with injuries.'

Chelsea started their season with a home game against Manchester United, a perfect way to check out their championship credentials. The Blues had finished above the Red Devils the previous season, but Alex Ferguson's side were still considered one of the teams to beat. Mourinho had got the better of the Scotsman on his way to Champions League glory in his time at Porto and the two were already developing something of a love-hate relationship.

But Mourinho insisted it was nothing personal. 'I respect every manager in the Premiership, but I have no problem with Sir Alex Ferguson. I am ready for my players to play against his – but I am not ready for individual fights with managers. It would be important to beat United because they will be fighting for the Premiership title like us – and it is good to take points off your direct competitors.'

Chelsea did just that, taking all three points thanks to Eidur Gudjohnsen's early goal. The visitors enjoyed the lion's share of possession, but Terry typified his team's resolve with a determined performance alongside Gallas. He was ecstatic after such a fine start to the season. 'It was a great one to get under way with,' the skipper said. 'To get off to a winning start was great. United are still a great side with great players and to win was a big boost.'

It was an ideal beginning to the season, and the Blues followed it up with two more wins and two more clean sheets. Mourinho was building his team from the back and, in their first eight games, they only conceded one goal. James Beattie scored in the first minute when Southampton came to the Bridge, but Chelsea came from behind for the first time to win 2–1, thanks to a Beattie own goal and a Lampard penalty.

After a fourth straight league win, Terry reported for England duty as the World Cup qualifying campaign got under way. As a vital part of such a tight defence at club level, it was difficult for him to comprehend England's capitulation in Vienna, when Eriksson's side threw away a 2–0 lead to draw 2–2 with Austria. 'It is bad play from our point of view,' the Chelsea man said. 'There was a real silence in the dressing room because it was two points lost and they could be vital at the end of the campaign. We're not keeping enough clean sheets and that is something we have got to look at in training. We need to tighten up because, if you don't concede goals, you don't lose games. It's as simple as that.'

England had led against France and Portugal in Euro 2004 before losing both games and it was embarrassing to see another lead disappear. 'After what happened in Portugal in the summer, we couldn't believe it had happened again,' Terry added.

England let another lead slip four days later, against Poland in Chorzow, but they recovered from being pulled back to win 2–1. With four points from their first two away games, England were second in Group Six on goal difference and thus well placed to qualify for the World

Cup. However, with a further eight games to play, they were taking nothing for granted. Terry started both England games in September alongside Ledley King and had also played with his former Senrab team-mate in the 3–0 defeat of the Ukraine in August. But with Rio Ferdinand's ban coming to an end and Sol Campbell returning to fitness, the Chelsea defender would have a battle on his hands to hang on to his shirt for the next England game.

Terry was still first choice at Chelsea though. He had been partnered alternately by Carvalho and Gallas since the season began. It didn't matter who stood alongside the captain, however, as the Blues backline was almost impenetrable and the clean sheets kept coming nearly every week. But Chelsea lost their one-hundred per cent start to the campaign at Villa Park immediately after the international break when Aston Villa held them to a 0–0 draw.

The game was marred by a horrendous refereeing decision when Ulises de la Cruz brought down Drogba in the penalty area ten minutes from time. No spot-kick was given and Rob Styles compounded his error by booking the Ivorian for diving. Terry was livid. 'The only thing De la Cruz could do was to pull him down,' the Chelsea captain said. 'And that is exactly what he did. It was a bad decision. It was a terrible booking.'

The next match was against Paris Saint Germain in Europe, and Terry was determined that the result in the Midlands wouldn't affect his team in Paris. 'Frustrated would be the word. I honestly believe we can win the Champions League. We realise what a great opportunity we had and we feel we are better placed to do well this time. The gaffer has won it, so he knows what it is all about. People go on about the big money in the game, the big transfer fees and the high wages players are on, but you would swap the lot for medals and trophies.'

Terry opened his account for the season in the game against PSG, heading Lampard's corner into an empty net after the keeper lost the ball in flight. It was an important goal, midway through the first half, since it allowed the Blues to relax and they went on to win the game 3–0. None of the Chelsea players could find a way past Tottenham keeper Paul Robinson in the next game, however, as Jacques Santini's side infamously 'left the bus in front of the goal' according to Mourinho.

After two league draws, the Blues got back on track with a 1–0 win at Middlesbrough's Riverside Stadium, and Chelsea's young skipper made it two goals from two Champions League ties in the next match against Porto.

The European draw had paired Mourinho's old employers with his current ones in Group H alongside PSG and CSKA Moscow, and the Portuguese coach knew exactly how to get the better of his previous club. Smertin and Drogba put Chelsea in control at Stamford Bridge, and Benni McCarthy pulled one back before Terry applied the coup de grace. Two minutes after the Porto goal, the Chelsea skipper dived full length to head Lampard's free-

Another match against an unpredictable and talented Balkans team – this time a friendly against Croatia at Portman Road in August 2003. Here Terry displays his agility and presence on the ball in a game which earned him well-deserved praise.

Above: Watched by manager Claudio Ranieri, Chelsea's Jimmy Floyd Hasselbaink and John Terry exercise in training, November 2003.

Below: John Terry looks on as Ranieri answers questions about his future in May 2004. Terry saw the Italian coach as the man who gave him his first chance.

Above: In the tense quarter final of Euro 2004, Sol Campbell heads into the net but the 'goal' was disallowed, as the referee ruled that John Terry had fouled the Portuguese goalkeeper. England lost on penalties.

Below: John Terry's partner Toni Poole (left) and Frank Lampard's Spanish girlfriend Ellen Rives watch the action.

John Terry lifts the Carling Cup, the club's first trophy under Jose Mourinho, following a hard-fought 3-2 victory over Liverpool in February 2005.

Above: John Terry jumps to score a valuable winning goal against Catalan giants Barcelona in the Champions League, March 2005. Chelsea won 5-4 on aggregate, and they were into the last eight.

Below: 2005 was not a year of unmitigated success for Terry. Here he battles for the ball against Denmark during a friendly in August which gave England their worst defeat since 1980, when they lost 4-1.

Another award – and this time it's personal. John Terry holds the PFA Players' Player of the Year trophy in April 2005.

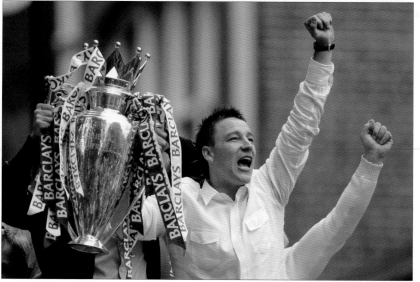

Above: John Terry, Roman Abramovich, Frank Lampard and Eidur Gudjohnsen celebrate winning the Premiership at Bolton. Chelsea's fifty-year wait was over.

© *John Ingledew*

Below: Chelsea's captain holds the FA Premiership trophy during the team's open-top bus parade near Stamford Bridge, May 2005.

Above: Déjà vu? John Terry celebrates winning back-to-back Premiership titles with team mates Frank Lampard and Eidur Gudjohnsen (now of Barcelona).

Below left: End of the world… A tearful Terry rues England's exit from the 2006 World Cup in Germany.

Below right: England's new captain wears the armband with pride against Greece at Old Trafford. He scored the first goal in the 4-0 victory, his first full game as captain, to leave England's international future looking bright with the Chelsea stopper at the helm.

kick into the back of the net. Terry completed a hat-trick of sorts when he scored a third Champions League goal against CSKA at the Bridge a month later, heading home a Smertin corner.

But before the game against the Russians, Terry again answered his country's call and joined an England squad containing Campbell and Ferdinand for the World Cup qualifiers against Wales and Azerbaijan. Chelsea had conceded just two goals in ten matches since the start of the season, and Terry had played every minute. He had also started England's last six internationals without letting anybody down.

Campbell and Ferdinand were Eriksson's first-choice partnership up until the latter's unfortunate missed drugs test. But the Manchester United defender was back for his club and was immediately called up by England. Campbell's season had been interrupted by injury and Terry was hopeful that his own excellent form at Chelsea would see him oust one of the more established players. He was careful, however, not to get ahead of himself.

'If Mr Eriksson believes that Rio and Sol are his best two, then he has to go for that,' the Chelsea captain said. 'I have got two of the best centre-halves in the world in front of me – and I do firmly believe that. Both of them are first class in different ways but they've both got fantastic qualities – they're great leaders, great on the ball and fantastic defenders. I believe I can learn from them and, if we are doing defending situations in training, they are the two I look up to. I'm going to look at it in a positive way that I'm going to learn from them whenever I'm in the squad.

'I've been watching Rio and I can learn from him. To come in after so long out he did brilliantly and I admire him for it. He's probably the best centre-half in the world... it's good for the country and good for football that he's playing again.'

Ferdinand's return forced Terry on to the sidelines as expected, but rather than dwell on it, the Chelsea defender focused on working hard until he was first choice. 'I think I'm in the best form of my career... But if Sol and Rio are the automatic first choices, then it's just something I'll have to deal with – and I'll deal with it in my own way. All I can do is work hard. It wasn't in my mind at Euro 2004 that Rio would be coming back. I was just enjoying every game I played for my country. I didn't worry about the situation until a couple of days ago but I'm still looking at the positives because we've got such a great squad and to be part of it is a fantastic achievement.'

Terry watched from the bench as England secured two wins to go to the top of the group with ten points from four games, putting them in pole position for a place in Germany in 2006. But upon returning to Chelsea, Terry found his team's great start had once again been disrupted by the international break, and Mourinho experienced defeat for the first time as a Premiership manager.

Playing Manchester City in the City of Manchester

Stadium, the Blues fell behind to a Nicolas Anelka penalty in the eleventh minute after Ferreira had brought down the French striker. It was only the third goal Chelsea had conceded but their troubles proved to be at the other end of the pitch and they were unable to beat David James to claim an equaliser. Adrian Mutu had been dropped after he tested positive for cocaine, Drogba was out injured and, up front were Gudjohnsen and Kezman who had scored only one goal between them after ten games. Such striking problems meant the Blues left Manchester with no points and fell further behind Arsenal at the top of the table.

'We want to win the title this season,' Terry said. 'But Arsenal are five points ahead of us now. A gap has started to form already and we simply cannot afford to let that gap get any bigger... Now it is imperative that we bounce back.'

Terry helped his side recover by scoring his third Champions League goal of the season when CSKA Moscow visited SW6. Coming after just nine minutes, the skipper's opener helped the Blues settle into their rhythm and they went on to win the game 2–0. The European victory rejuvenated Chelsea and they won their next seven games, a sequence which took them into the last sixteen of the Champions League, the last eight of the League Cup and to the top of the Premiership.

Chelsea's early-season form had been characterised by Drogba's goals, a solid midfield, a watertight defence and the impressive Petr Cech in goal. But in the absence of the big target man, Mourinho's men were struggling to unlock opposition defences from open play. All that changed with the introduction of Arjen Robben. The talented young Dutchman was a defender's worst nightmare, quick, strong, skilful and very direct. Terry was impressed.

'I tend to try and stay as far away as possible from Arjen in training,' the skipper said with a smile. 'That's the best way to do it. That way you don't get caught one on one against him. He's fantastic and, now he's back to full fitness, it's actually frightening. He's different class and him, Duffa and Eidur work really well together. Arjen can be as good as wants to be and he wants to be the best player in the world. He's so exciting when he gets the ball because he wants to beat his man and cross it and score goals.'

Chelsea had worked very hard to keep things tight at the back and, with Robben on one wing and Duff on the other, the Blues looked like they could score at will. Mourinho had previously gone on record as saying how difficult it would be to win the Premiership and the Champions League in the same season, but on this form, Terry insisted, they could win everything.

'I understand what the manager's saying but the belief that is running through the squad is that we can go all the way in every competition we're in,' said the inspirational captain. 'Some people might think Real Madrid and AC Milan are the best teams in Europe, but the way we're playing at the moment I'm sure we can match them if not better them. The win in Moscow was a great performance and four wins out of four is a fantastic start in the Champions League.

'We've got sixteen top players in the squad for every game, which means we sometimes have eight internationals travelling to games as spectators. Everyone is happy with their role and we're all in this together. We're joint top of the league and have won all of our European matches so we can cope with both competitions.'

Chelsea were going strong on all fronts and, except for the League Cup clash at Upton Park when former Senrab team-mate Bobby Zamora led the line for the Hammers, Terry had played in every minute of every match and was becoming more and more important to the Chelsea cause by the week. His significance at Stamford Bridge had been reflected in the award of the captaincy, but his value in financial terms was brought home by a new contract in early November.

His existing deal still had more than two years to run but it was renegotiated, taking his salary to £80,000 a week until 2009. 'It was a mutual decision,' Terry said. 'I only signed last year but I had a chat with Peter Kenyon at the end of last season and it has been ongoing since then. But finally it's all done and all sorted and I'm very happy.'

The twenty-three-year-old defender continued: 'Jose's been a key figure in it really. He's come in, he's made me the club captain this year, so on the pitch things are going well and off the pitch things are going really well too. I have been here since I was fourteen and I would love to stay at Chelsea for the rest of my career. Hopefully, I'll do that because I love playing for the club. I am just very, very pleased that it's another five years that I'm going to be here.'

His long-term future at the Bridge was secure, but Terry still wanted to force his way into the England side and he had another opportunity to do that in November. The squad travelled to Spain without Campbell, who was injured again, and Terry was hoping to deputise for the Arsenal stopper, as he revealed to the *Daily Telegraph*. 'I told Sven I was going to carry on working hard and fight for my place… I've had a good taste of England and I want to get my place back. I've not played as well when I've put on the England shirt as I've been doing for Chelsea. All I can do, should I get a chance on Wednesday, is try again to impress.'

Terry did start against Spain, but the only men to impress were wearing red shirts as the Three Lions were comprehensively outplayed. The England players stuck doggedly to their task and only Asier Del Horno found the target for the hosts, with the game finishing 1–0. Sadly an enjoyable match lit up by some sparkling Spanish attacking play was forgotten as the home crowd took football back to the Dark Ages with some abhorrent racial abuse directed at Shaun Wright-Phillips and Ashley Cole.

The international break again caused Chelsea's form to stutter, and Terry returned to club duty in a 2–2 draw against Bolton in west London. But the skipper again led by example and helped the Blues back to form with two goals against Charlton. Chelsea had lost 4–2 at The Valley in the last visit under Ranieri, but Mourinho's team was a far more dangerous creature.

Duff hit the opening goal after four minutes thanks to a brilliant pass from Gudjohnsen, but then Terry took control with a thumping header just after half-time and a precise side-footed finish a couple of minutes later to kill the game. Gudjohnsen added a fourth on the hour mark, but it was the captain who had made the biggest contribution to the game with another colossal defensive display and his first brace of goals.

'John Terry is an inspirational player for us in the way that he wants to be a winner,' Mourinho said. 'I only have good things to say about him. There are absolutely no problems. What he does outside the pitch is his private life but things must be very good for him. When you are so ready to work every day when you come into training, as he is, it can only be because your private life is in a good way.'

Terry had everything in place off the pitch to be able to concentrate one hundred per cent on his football when needed. 'I'm very happy at home,' the England defender said. 'I've got a wonderful girlfriend who looks after me and things are really going well at the minute. I've just signed a new five-year contract at Chelsea and I'm in the perfect position. It helps being skipper, not just because of the responsibility on the pitch but off it as well. I love it at Chelsea and want to stay here for the rest of my career.'

He was enjoying his football and his life and, in his position as captain, Terry was keen to help Chelsea's youth-team players out as well. 'I like trying to help out the young lads at the club,' he added. 'I do a few different things. It might be helping to pay for their driving lessons because I know what it's like to be on their wages. There's a good spirit throughout the team and the first-team lads get on well with the young lads. I think that's important.'

Chelsea racked up a second successive 4–0 Premiership win, this time against Newcastle United, and then the Blues turned their attentions to Arsenal. Five points separated the two teams at the top, but unlike the previous season, it was the Blues who were in first place. Terry was keen for that to continue at least until the end of May. 'The club is one hundred years old at the end of the season and our only league title came when we were fifty years old,' the defender said in the *Sun*. 'We want to be champions in this special year. To do that, we'll have to overcome Arsenal. But having beaten them in the Champions League last season, we believe we can show we are better than them in the league. Remembering Wayne Bridge's winning goal at Highbury last season will be crucial in our mental approach to challenging Arsenal.'

Having finally got a win against the Gunners at the end of the previous season, Terry hoped his team could repeat the trick in north London to stretch their lead at the top to eight points, but that wasn't to be as Thierry Henry stole the show in a 2–2 draw. The Frenchman opened the scoring with a sublime strike after barely two minutes, but Terry equalised a quarter of an hour later when he lost his marker, England colleague Campbell, at a corner. Henry struck again on the half hour, with a highly debatable quick free-kick that caught Cech napping, but Gudjohnsen headed a second equaliser just after half-time and the match finished all square despite several more chances for each side. Chelsea approached Christmas with a very healthy five-point lead at the top of the table.

'We have an edge over Arsenal now,' Terry said. 'We showed that when we were 2–1 down against a side who have been so great for so many years. But we managed to come back again. We are top of the league for a reason – because we are playing the better football and we are getting better results.

'It's a great team spirit and a great will to win. I've been too close to winning something too often and I'm fed up with it now. I desperately want to win something this year. We have to keep our nerve.'

Certainly one of the reasons Chelsea were top of the league was their impermeable defence. Henry's Highbury brace were only the seventh and eighth goals respectively to get past the Blues defence in sixteen league games and Mourinho was certain of the reason – he had the world's best defender in his team. 'I know Sir Alex would say Rio Ferdinand. I know Carlo Ancelotti will say Alessandro Nesta – but for me it's John Terry,' the

257

manager said. 'Since the first minute I arrived here, he's played at the same level. Not up and down, no mistakes. Not more committed against Man United and less concentration against West Bromwich.

'It's not like he prefers to play against tall and strong strikers or he finds it difficult against fast ones. For him, every game is the same, every opponent is the same, the level of his performance is the same. He leads the team. He is an important voice on the pitch, where I'm not... So for me he's the most complete one and the best.'

The admiration and respect was mutual. 'Jose has been fantastic and I can't speak highly enough of him for what he's done for me,' Terry said. 'He has given me a lot of confidence... the lads have got so much respect for him. Training and tactically, he's got it spot on and has a great staff around him. He's very clever at what he does and takes the pressure away from the players.'

The players were certainly doing their bit and, after dropping two points against their nearest rivals, Chelsea put together another incredible run of victories. Norwich City, Aston Villa, Portsmouth (twice), Liverpool, Middlesbrough and Tottenham were all brushed aside without even scoring a goal between them as the Premiership dream started to become more and more tangible. Minnows Scunthorpe provided little resistance in the FA Cup, even without Terry as Mourinho took the opportunity to rest his skipper for only the third time in thirty-two matches.

Having made it through to the fourth round, the Blues were still in with a chance of winning the famous old trophy. Yet to be knocked out of any of the cups, Chelsea were looking at a very hectic schedule, but Terry was happy with that. 'We're still in four competitions and we want to win them all,' he said to assembled media. 'People go on about Arsenal and say that, even when they're not playing well, they have star players who can turn a game around with a moment of magic. But we've got just as many players who can do that, if not more. Just look at players like Duffa and Didier, Arjen, Joe and Lamps.'

It took some brilliance from Lampard and a bit of luck from Duff to see Chelsea past Manchester United in the semi-final of the League Cup. After a 0–0 first leg at Stamford Bridge, Terry took his side to Old Trafford on Mourinho's forty-second birthday and came away with a 2–1 win, courtesy of Lampard and Duff's goals. The Irishman scored with a free-kick that was meant as a cross but eluded everyone and bounced up into the net, securing a first cup final of the new regime.

In their next game, the Blues maintained their four-pronged attack on silverware with a 2–0 win over Birmingham City in the FA Cup. Terry scored his seventh goal of the season but he made more headlines for his part in Robert Huth's opening goal in the sixth minute. As Duff's corner curled in from the right, Terry body-checked Huth's marker and the German centre-back rose unchallenged to head home. The captain got one for himself ten minutes from time when Lampard picked him out with a perfectly flighted cross.

Terry was happy to be in the fifth round of the FA Cup, but of the four trophies still on offer there was no mistaking the one he wanted most. 'There's no bigger Chelsea fan than me, so the title is the one I want more than anything,' he said in the *Sun*. 'Give me that and I'll die happy. As for all this stuff about Chelsea buying the Premiership and how unfair it all is – rubbish… Yes, we're fortunate that Roman Abramovich has come in to enable us to build a bigger and better squad. But I didn't hear people kicking up a fuss and saying how unfair it was when Manchester United signed Rio Ferdinand and Wayne Rooney for £30 million each. And what about Real Madrid?

'There's no bigger patriot than me and, yes, we do have a lot of foreign players. But if you look at this club in five or ten years' time, we will be providing a whole load of home-grown players for England.'

He added: 'Hopefully, this is our year… We hope that four trophies is still on but all we can do is take each competition as it comes.'

Entering February, the Premiership was the main concern and Manchester United's 4–2 win at Highbury meant that Chelsea could go eleven points clear at the top of the table with a win against Blackburn Rovers.

The Blues got off to the perfect start at Ewood Park as Robben drilled the ball under goalkeeper Brad Friedel after five minutes, but the home side's roughhouse tactics forced the Dutch winger out of the game six minutes later. Rovers continued with their aggressive approach and the game became something of a battle. Things threatened to get out of hand around the hour mark when Robbie Savage fell in the area under a challenge from Ferreira. Although Cech pulled off a fantastic save to deny Paul Dickov from the penalty spot, the Scottish striker caught the Czech keeper with his follow-up and the Chelsea players weren't happy.

But in the face of such hostility, Terry and his team-mates dug deep and, despite not playing well, they held out for a 1–0 win to claim another vital three points. Eleven points clear with thirteen games left – and having won eight league games in a row without conceding a single goal – Chelsea were looking increasingly worthy of the title they now seemed certain to claim. But Mourinho warned his men against complacency, and the captain insisted there be no let-up. 'Manchester United will fight all the way – but if we keep winning then eventually they're going to die off,' Terry said to the press. 'To go eleven points clear at the top of the Premiership was important. Rovers showed they can fight but we matched them all the way. There is still a million miles to go in the title race and we've got to keep playing like that.'

February was full of tough games for the Blues. Their winning streak came to an end four days later when they drew 0–0 with Manchester City, but they still managed to maintain their run of clean sheets and even added one more with a 1–0 win at Goodison Park. A week later, they suffered their third defeat of the season up at St James' Park.

Having only lost in the league to Manchester City back in October, as well as to Porto in a Champions League tie when qualification was already safe, it came as a shock to the system when Chelsea's Quadruple dream came crashing to an end with a 1–0 reverse against Newcastle in the FA Cup.

Terry was out suspended and could only watch from the sidelines as Chelsea started poorly; Patrick Kluivert opened the scoring after four minutes. Possibly with one eye on the upcoming Champions League clash with Barcelona, the Blues weren't up to scratch in the first half and Mourinho responded by making three changes at half-time. Unfortunately for the league leaders, Bridge was stretchered off with a broken ankle two minutes into the second half and, having used all their substitutes, Chelsea were reduced to ten men. Things got worse for the visitors as Duff picked up a knock and took to limping around the pitch. Unable to find a way past goalkeeper Given, the Blues' misery was compounded by Cudicini's 90th-minute red card.

This wasn't the ideal way to get ready for a trip to the Nou Camp and, with only three trophies left to fight for, the Chelsea players headed for Spain seeking a return to winning ways. Bad luck continued to dog them, however. Drogba received a second booking for an innocuous challenge on the Barcelona keeper and was sent off. Chelsea were leading the game 1–0 thanks to Juliano Belletti's own goal but, down to ten men, they eventually lost 2–1.

Having suffered two defeats in one week, Chelsea headed to Cardiff for the League Cup final. With a trophy to win, the players had no time to feel sorry for themselves. 'It's down to us to pick ourselves up after two defeats and this is a great chance to do it,' Terry said. 'Losing those two games has been a new experience for the team. Myself and Lamps have had to pick the players up in training. We've just told everyone that they have to forget about the Barcelona match and focus on the big game on Sunday.

'We have been to a lot of tough places and made some long journeys; we've got our reward now because we're in the final. But it will be worth nothing if we go there and lose, so we have to go there, forget about the last two games and just concentrate on one thing – winning.'

That's exactly what Chelsea did, although it took them two hours to finish their opponents off. Liverpool went ahead after 45 seconds, courtesy of a John Arne Riise volley, but Steven Gerrard scored an own goal after 79 minutes to take the game into extra-time. Jose Mourinho was banished from the sidelines for the way he celebrated the equaliser, but the Blues prevailed without 'The Special One'. Goals from Drogba and Kezman in the added 30 minutes won the trophy for Chelsea despite Antonio Nunez's consolation strike for the Reds.

At last, Terry had won his first piece of silverware, the perfect response to all the critics who had been knocking Chelsea after their successive defeats. 'We shut a lot of people up today,' the England defender said to the press. 'They were talking about us bottling it, but we showed what spirit we've got. This trophy means the world to us – the players, the management and the fans, everybody involved with the club. It is a great achievement and a great starting point for us. We hope it is the first of many. Now it's up to us…'

After victory in Cardiff, the Blues notched up a straightforward win over Norwich. The Canaries did become the first team to put a Premiership goal past Petr Cech since before Christmas but they were still beaten 3–1. Then came the visit of Barcelona.

In one of the greatest games in Chelsea history, the Blues were roared on by possibly the loudest Bridge crowd of all time and went 3–0 up inside 20 minutes, with goals from Gudjohnsen, Lampard and Duff. Chelsea were in complete control of the tie but they failed to press home their advantage and Barca came back strongly through Ronaldinho. Suddenly the score was 3–2.

The Brazilian-inspired comeback may have left the Chelsea players down, but they were certainly not out. They kept things tight until the break when they had a chance to regroup. Mourinho told his players they had nothing to fear and that the game was theirs for the taking. Thanks to Terry, his words rang true. Duff floated a corner across in the 76th minute and the Chelsea skipper shook off his marker to head home. Carvalho seemed to impede the Barca keeper but the referee didn't spot it and the goal stood.

It was his eighth of the season, his fourth in the Champions League, and by far the most valuable goal of his life. Chelsea held on to win 4–2 on the night, 5–4 on aggregate, and they were into the last eight. 'There's such a long way to go and there are some great teams still left in the competition,' Terry said in the *Sunday Mirror*. 'But I am sure there will be a few teams watching out there who are now afraid of us. Our ground is a lot tighter than the Nou Camp and we knew, if we put pressure on Barcelona, they wouldn't like it.

'Beating Barcelona was one of the best nights I have ever experienced at Stamford Bridge and the goal was arguably the most important one I've scored in my career. I'm not sure when I'm going to come down to earth… And to think I'm captain of this magnificent side. Life doesn't get much better than that.'

Things really were going well for Terry. He was in the middle of another one of those runs of victories that had typified Chelsea's season: they were top of the league, into the quarter-finals in Europe and they already had a first pot in the trophy cabinet. The Blues captain had also played his part in helping England edge towards the World Cup finals, starting alongside Ferdinand against Northern Ireland and Azerbaijan. In Campbell's absence, the Chelsea defender had helped the Three Lions to six points and two clean sheets as they took another big step down the road to Germany.

'If Rio and Sol were Mr Eriksson's first-choice pair, then I hope I've put a few doubts in his mind,' Terry said after the games. 'Things have gone really well this season for Chelsea, but on the international stage I don't feel that I've made that step up yet and proved myself. I feel I still need to do that. I've got my chance and, hopefully, I can keep my shirt, keep working hard and playing well for Chelsea, especially when Mr Eriksson is at the game.'

Terry's next big test with Chelsea came with the visit of the 2006 World Cup hosts' most famous club side, Bayern Munich. Mourinho was banned from the touchline for the game against the Bavarians following comments he made after the game at the Nou Camp. Even without the Portuguese in the dugout, the Blues still had too much quality for the opposition and they won 4–2 at Stamford Bridge.

The gloss was taken off the victory by the late penalty won, and converted, by Michael Ballack. The German midfield superstar tumbled under the faintest of touches from Carvalho, and the goal gave Bayern hope for the second leg. 'It was a harsh decision,' Terry said of the 90th-minute incident. 'I have seen it again four or five times and it was not a penalty. We had worked our socks off to get that three-goal lead, so we are disappointed it was thrown away by a terrible decision from the referee.

'It wasn't just Ballack; there were a few of their players diving and that's disappointing to see. That's not what we're about in England and it's annoying to see teams come over here and do that... There is taking the mickey and there is taking the mickey... It takes the shine not only off their performance but also off a big night. It was still a great result for us to win 4–2 and we will go there with confidence.'

The captain then spoke about Jose Mourinho's absence from the bench. 'The manager said it was down to us. We are all big enough personalities to have our say before the game. The lads rallied round and we got ourselves together. We are fully behind the manager and support everything he does. We get the same back from him – everything we do, he supports. We need to stay united as a squad.'

The Chelsea players stuck together in the return leg in Munich and took control of the game through Lampard's deflected drive on the half hour. The Germans struck back, but Drogba settled any nerves with a glancing header ten minutes from time. Bayern won on the night, thanks to a couple of late, late goals, but it was of little consolation as Chelsea advanced to the semi-finals to face Liverpool.

Two English sides playing each other in the last four of the competition meant that the Premiership would have a team in the final for the first time since 1999, and only the second time since English football returned to European competition in 1990. But before turning their attentions to Liverpool, Terry and his team-mates had an appointment with Arsenal in the league.

The Gunners were holding on to second place in the Premiership, but they were a massive eleven points behind the leaders. A thrilling game at the Bridge somehow remained goalless and, with only five league games left, Chelsea needed just five points to finally claim the title they craved so desperately. 'This club has not seen enough trophies over the years. The ultimate for players and fans is to win the title again fifty years on. If I'm the man to lift that trophy, I will be in tears,' Terry said.

Fifty years to the day since Chelsea won their only previous title, the Blues returned to winning ways with a 3–1 score-line at home to Fulham, which opened up a fourteen-point gap over Arsenal. The day got even better for Terry when he was named PFA Player of the Year at an awards ceremony later that evening.

There was a strong Chelsea flavour to proceedings at the Grosvenor House Hotel as Frank Lampard and Petr Cech joined the Blues captain on the six-man shortlist. But it was Terry who walked away with the trophy. 'It is unbelievable and the ultimate accolade to be voted for by your fellow professionals whom you play against week in and week out,' the winner said by way of acceptance. 'You just go out there and try to give it your best, and for them to show their appreciation and vote for me is fantastic. For Petr, Lamps and myself to be voted in, it was important that one of us won it. It has been a real special season with

Chelsea and this just adds to it. I want to thank all of my team-mates, because without them this would not have happened. It is my first year as captain and they have helped me a lot, on and off the pitch.'

The Chelsea captain was the first defender to win the award since Paul McGrath in 1993, the first Englishman to win since Teddy Sheringham in 2001 and the first Blues player ever to collect the prestigious accolade. He was also named in the PFA Team of the Year for the second successive season, and was joined by Cech, Lampard, and Robben. But everyone agreed the most deserving man had won the top prize. PFA Chief Executive, Gordon Taylor, said: 'John has not only been recognised by his fellow professionals, but by the whole country and critics alike and I am delighted that he has done so well after experiencing a few problems early on in his career. He has learned from his mistakes, as all young players who transgress have the right to do, and I find him an absolutely first-class professional. He is a genuine lad who deserves the success he and Chelsea are enjoying at the moment.'

Liverpool's Steven Gerrard was also on the shortlist, but Terry got the better of him in the voting and he was hopeful of doing the same in Europe. 'I think it will be really special for the manager to win the Champions League, especially in two consecutive seasons,' the Blues skipper said to the *Sun*. 'He's done it with Porto and he's taken us to the semis, but we've still got a long way to go. We've got a chance, we're in the hat and that's the main thing. But Liverpool will not be easy. Stevie G is obviously one of their key men…They are all dangerous and very good. They will want to get revenge on us for the Carling Cup final. Hopefully, we won't allow that to happen.'

The first leg at Stamford Bridge was a game dominated by defenders and, while Terry snuffed out the threat at one end, Carragher did the same at the other: 0–0 was the inevitable score-line. The tie would have to be settled at Anfield, but before Chelsea's date with their European destiny they had the opportunity to win the league.

Mourinho's side headed for Bolton knowing that a victory would give them an unassailable fourteen-point lead at the top of the table. It was finally time to turn the inevitable into the indisputable. Chelsea had long looked like champions and at the Reebok Stadium on Saturday, 30 April 2005 they confirmed it.

The Blues started badly and, considering what was at stake, it was an appalling time not to be at the races. Bolton were in typically muscular mood and they dominated the first half with their aggression and physical presence. Terry was even caught by an unintentional elbow from Kevin Davies just before half-time and played the remainder of the game with impaired vision. But this was not a time to be without the inspirational captain and, after a rollicking at the interval, Chelsea came out and played the quality of football that had brought them so far, and which would eventually result in their claiming the title.

The midfield started to compete and soon managed to

gain control. Appropriately enough, it was Lampard who scored the goals that gave Chelsea a 2–0 win, three points and the Premiership trophy. The former West Ham midfielder was Terry's vice-captain and the champions' leading scorer; he had lost out to his skipper in the voting for PFA Player of the Year, but was rewarded by the journalists when he won the Football Writers' Association Footballer of the Year award, finishing just ahead of Terry in a reverse of the PFA voting. From the start of the season, the two Londoners had been incredible and, as the season drew to a close, they got the prizes their performances deserved, including the league title.

'This is the best feeling ever,' Terry said after the game. 'We've worked so hard all season for it and to have done it with three games to spare allows us to go into Tuesday's semi-final fully focused on that.'

With the Champions League clash at Anfield looming large, the celebrations were somewhat subdued. 'The gaffer allowed us one glass of champagne each,' the captain continued. 'Now we're going back to the hotel, where we're staying until Tuesday, to have a quiet meal together. The beers will have to come later.'

The big European tie may have been responsible for Chelsea's poor first half at the Reebok, but whatever the reason, Mourinho sorted out the problem at the interval. 'He was fuming,' the skipper told the press. 'He was going: "Listen, give me the shirt, give Steve Clarke the shirt," and they would go out and work harder than we had done.

Sometimes you aren't going to play well; it doesn't matter as long as you give one-hundred per cent, but we didn't. Bolton were the first to headers, the first to tackles. Jose said he would put himself out there and do a lot better than we were doing. He told us to get out there and show how much we wanted to win the title. And we did.'

With the league title in the bag, Chelsea could concentrate on the match at Anfield. 'People thought we would beat Liverpool at home and I think it will be the same now, with people expecting us to win 1–0 or 2–0,' Terry said. 'But it won't be that easy. They've got great support, their fans will be behind them and their players will be up for it. It's a chance to win the best competition in Europe, so they'll be as hungry as we are.

'Last year we got knocked out at this stage of the competition. It's one of the worst feelings I've ever experienced and I don't want to go through that again... When we get to Anfield and see our fans and their fans, any little bit of tiredness we feel will go out of the window. It's such a big night, such a big occasion.'

Liverpool were equally fired up for the big night, however, and with two of the best defences in Europe squaring up, it would take something special to break the deadlock. Sadly for the Blues, that something special came from Luis Garcia with plenty of help from the linesman.

There were only four minutes on the clock when Steven Gerrard played Milan Baros in on goal. The Czech striker lifted the ball over his compatriot Petr Cech, but fell under the goalkeeper's challenge. The ball dropped to Garcia in the area and he struck it towards the goal. William Gallas was back covering and appeared to clear the effort before it crossed the line, but after consulting his linesman, the referee made his decision in Liverpool's favour and the Reds were ahead.

Terry tried valiantly to lead his troops forward, but lacking the wing wizardry of Duff and Robben, they could find no way through the home side's powerful rearguard and the game finished 1–0. Looking back at Liverpool's European campaign, it seemed their name was on the trophy from day one, and they eventually claimed the big prize on a memorable night in Istanbul, but that would do little to console the Chelsea players. 'William Gallas was in the way of the ball from where the linesman was, but he gave it, which was a bad decision,' Terry said of the controversial incident. 'If you're not sure, then don't give a goal.'

He continued: 'It's going to put a downer on things for the next couple of days but it's still been a great season for Chelsea. It is just a huge disappointment to lose in the European Cup semi-final for the second year running. It's not really acceptable. We came to Anfield hoping to win the game and we're devastated.

'We have to do it next season because it's something all the lads want desperately. We've stepped up the ladder again this season – we've won the Carling Cup and, more importantly, the Premiership, so it's been a good season. No one can take away the fact that we're champions and we've played well all season, home and away, but hopefully we'll get to the Champions League final next season.'

Chelsea picked themselves up for the last home game of the season and, after beating Charlton 1–0 with Makelele scoring his only goal of the season in the last minute, John Terry was presented with the Premiership trophy. It was his final contribution for the season. Chelsea beat Manchester United 3–1 and drew 1–1 with Newcastle in the captain's absence, as Terry had an operation on his toe. He would also have to miss England's summer tour of America. 'I've spoken to Mr Eriksson and he said it is OK for me not to go,' the Chelsea man told the *News of the World*. 'I am disappointed by that because I wanted to cement my place in the England team but something has to be done. Mr Eriksson said: "Just make sure you are ready to come back next season."'

Terry had been contending with a painful foot, as he revealed to the press: 'Bits of bone were growing on either side between two toes. Every time I put my boot on, they were rubbing against each other, bone on bone, making it very painful. I had surgery where both bits of bone were shaved away. I've still got a bit of pain, but I think that's just down to the surgery. I've had the problem for five or six years and it got to the stage where only a quarter of the way through the season I was having injections every day just to train. It was a numbing injection and then, going into games, I had an extra one as well. So once we'd won the title at the end of the season, I just got it done as soon as possible… Touch wood, it hasn't flared up again so I'm really looking forward to the new season.'

The 2004/05 season was one of many records for Chelsea – most wins in a Premiership season, most points, fewest goals conceded, most clean sheets, most consecutive minutes without conceding a league goal – but Terry was already looking forward to defending the title and bringing more silverware to SW6.

'Everybody says the hardest thing of all is winning the title in back-to-back seasons and we know that United are the only side who've done that since the Premiership started,' he said to the press. 'The challenge for us is to make sure we can do it as well.

'Our aim next season has to be to go through the season without losing in the league at all. Arsenal showed last season that it can be done. They did it, so why can't we?

'Winning the Premiership and the Carling Cup is a great achievement and a great starting point. But we must be thinking now that we can only build on what we have done and get better.'

With Terry at the heart of Chelsea's efforts, you wouldn't bet against it.

CHAPTER ELEVEN
CHAMPIONS AGAIN!

How did winning the title again feel for John Terry? 'Well, the champagne tastes just as good, it's fantastic, absolutely brilliant. What a season from the lads and to retain it is absolutely fantastic. We all dug in together, grafted and we came out of it again. That's been the best atmosphere I've ever seen at the Bridge here today – two years unbeaten in the League is fantastic.'

Terry was thrilled to have secured back-to-back Premiership titles with a win over Manchester United at home, and even picking up an early ankle injury didn't stop the Blues' skipper from enjoying his success against the team he had supported as a boy. 'I think I'd have had to have my foot amputated before I came off this pitch. I've got a bit of blood down there but there was no way I was going off.'

He needed ten stitches in the gash after the game, but

Terry's pain was easily soothed by the capture of the coveted trophy and the latest addition to his medal collection. The defender had ended the previous season in rehabilitation following surgery on his toe injury, but he was fit and raring to go by the time the champions returned to training for the 2005-06 season. 'There is a little bit of scar tissue which needs to be broken down, but the masseurs are going to do that and I am ready to go,' he said.

As well as having his skipper fully fit, Jose Mourinho had made other moves to significantly strengthen his squad in the summer of 2005. Asier Del Horno, Shaun Wright-Phillips and Michael Essien joined the club for a combined fee of over £50m, and with the backing of one of the richest men on the planet the best team in the land were looking to stay ahead of the chasing pack.

'The new lads look good and I think we've now got a better squad,' Terry told a press conference. 'We have set ourselves high standards. Arsenal were unbeaten the season before last, while last season we only lost one. Four or five years ago you could afford to lose five or six games and get away with it. Not any more.

'People accuse us of spending millions to buy the Premiership,' he said to the *Daily Mirror*. 'But it took something else to make it happen and that was the manager. Last year we spent a lot of money and brought in a lot of big players but there was one thing missing. We've got him now, and that's the gaffer. I would die for the man both on and off the pitch.'

Before the season got under way Mourinho told his players to concentrate on retaining the title rather than worrying about the following summer's World Cup. Terry agreed with him. 'Without Chelsea we wouldn't get the chance to play for our countries,' he said. 'We can start thinking about the World Cup at the end of the season.'

It was that focus which had allowed the Blues to race into an early lead at the top of the Premiership, and also saw them start strongly in Europe. Chelsea began the defence of their title in breathtaking form as they won their first nine league games, scoring 23 goals and only conceding three as they kept six clean-sheets. They began the campaign by beating Arsenal 2-1 in the FA Community Shield. It was the first time Terry had been on the winning side against the Gunners in domestic competition, and it served to further enforce the psychological advantage the champions held over their London rivals.

Having finally broken the domestic hoodoo Arsenal had held over the Blues throughout almost all of Claudio Ranieri's reign, Mourinho's team were yet to lose to their London rivals, and made it two from two in the new season when they beat the north London club 1-0 in their second league game. Chelsea had dug deep to beat Wigan Athletic 1-0 on the opening day of the season, and Terry had already played an international in August as he sought to cement his place in the England defence.

The captain of the champions still faced tough competition from Rio Ferdinand and Sol Campbell in the fight for first-team action, but Terry was adamant he could make the step up. 'I know I need to improve at international level and hopefully my success with Chelsea will help me,' Terry told the *Mirror*. 'I think the Turkey game in the Euro 2004 qualifiers has probably been the high point for me at England level. I've performed consistently well for Chelsea so far but I still need to prove myself for England. I don't feel as if I've been at my best for England at all and I need to prove to people that I'm ready to take that place and take the shirt.'

Terry did nothing spectacular in his 45 minute run out against Denmark, but after his substitution England fell apart on their way to a shocking 4-1 defeat in Copenhagen. After such a dismal performance there was inevitable criticism from the press and most of it was directed at the coach. 'The players still believe in Sven. He is still the man in charge. He picks the squad and the team,' Terry said in the *Evening Standard*. 'The players respect him and we have a great squad of players. No matter who is picking the team, once the players are on the pitch it is down to us and it is our responsibility to do our jobs, which we certainly didn't do against Denmark. I was disappointed and a little bit embarrassed by the performance. We all needed to come away from that game with one thing in our minds and that was to totally forget that game as quickly as possible. The players have come back and responded very well. We play Wales and Northern Ireland now and we have to get the six points.'

Terry missed the games against England's UK rivals due to a knee injury, but in his absence Joe Cole's goal secured a 1-0 win in Cardiff. Four days later Eriksson's troops succumbed to a David Healy strike to lose in Belfast, as Terry's importance to the team was becoming increasingly obvious. The uncompromising defender's significance to his club side's fortunes had long been felt and it was a relief when Terry was in fact fit to play in Chelsea's next match, despite an initial prognosis ruling him out for ten games.

With their skipper available the Blues continued to pick up maximum points as they won the next three games without conceding a goal, and maintained their flying start to the season. Chelsea then transferred their good form to Europe as they opened their Group G campaign with a 1-0 win over Belgian side Anderlecht.

After a routine 2-0 win over Charlton at The Valley, Aston Villa put a blemish on Chelsea's perfect record by being so brazen as to score a goal against them at the Bridge. Luke Moore was the man responsible for finally breaking through the impressive Blues' defence, but Frank Lampard's free-kick levelled the scores two minutes later, and the midfielder secured a 2-1 win with a second half penalty.

Villa received plenty of praise for their gutsy performance, but after the game their manager was full of admiration for the Chelsea captain. 'Terry would die for Chelsea and he epitomises everything about them. He's the real winner here,' David O'Leary told the press.

Terry's next game was away to Liverpool in the Champions League. Facing the European Cup holders at the site of the previous year's disappointment, Chelsea were out for revenge. 'I know I'm going to go cold when I first walk back into that changing room at Anfield,' said Terry in the *Mirror*. 'I've got a lot of bad memories from that night but I haven't got any hard feelings towards Liverpool. When we lost at the semi-final stage to Monaco the year before, I thought there couldn't be any worse feeling in football. But when Liverpool beat us at Anfield, it was ten times as bad. I'm desperate never to experience that kind of pain again. We're determined it's going to be third time lucky for us at Chelsea this season. We want to get all the way to the final and win it.'

The Blues only managed a draw at Anfield, but their next league game was at the same venue four days later, and this time they turned on the style to beat Liverpool 4–1. After a week on Merseyside Terry once again left his club to play for England, and in the World Cup qualifier against Austria the Chelsea skipper found himself lining up alongside Sol Campbell in the England defence; Rio Ferdinand was the odd-man out.

Sven Goran Eriksson was fortunate to have his three best centre-backs available for the game at Old Trafford, and Terry's fine start to the season had earned him his place in the starting XI. England weren't at their best but they still secured the three points necessary to take them to the World Cup in Germany thanks to a 1-0 win.

David Beckham was sent off after 59 minutes, and although the armband went to Michael Owen, the Chelsea captain helped to rally the troops and hold on for victory. Terry was in talkative mood after the game. 'We weren't great but did enough to win the game and get the three points,' he told the *Daily Star*. 'We are there now at the World Cup. We created so many chances and we could have been 3-0 up at half time but so many things went against us. It was a game where things didn't click.

'I am not too sure what needs to click. We have got a good few months ahead of us to prepare. The main thing is that we have qualified. Obviously we want to be top of the group. We realise we need to play well and want to beat Poland on Wednesday. I think we are playing well enough to go on and win the group.'

Ferdinand replaced Campbell when the Arsenal defender picked up an injury against Austria, and there was a place up for grabs alongside Terry for the Poland game. 'Myself and Rio get on really well,' the Chelsea man went on. 'I've played quite a few games with Rio. I'm looking forward to playing with him again. If it was me who had been dropped, I would have been disappointed and he was exactly the same. I think the boss has come out and said he wants his players to be disappointed if they are dropped. But Rio has got his chance and, with him coming on and doing well, it looks like he is going to be in again on Wednesday.'

With Terry and Ferdinand at the heart of the defence,

England claimed top spot in Group Six with a 2-1 win. As Beckham was suspended, Terry took the armband off Michael Owen for the last 20 minutes against Poland and it felt good. 'John Terry captain of England sounds very nice to me,' the Chelsea man said in the *News of the World*. 'It's obviously a dream of mine, to get the armband against Poland for the last 15 or 20 minutes was a fantastic achievement for me. I did hear the crowd cheering when I put the armband on, which was obviously very nice. I've kept the armband and I'm going to stick it in a frame with my England shirt from the game. It will take pride of place in my house – a few shirts are going to be moved out of the way.'

If Tony Adams had his way then there would be a few more armbands heading to the framers. 'John Terry has the ability not just to be a great player himself but to make other people great around him,' opined the former England skipper in the pages of the *Daily Star*. 'You can see the aura of the guy. He has an inbuilt leadership where he gives everything and the other players see that and it rubs off. It would be a tough call to replace David Beckham now but if it benefits the team then Sven has to do it.'

The Arsenal legend added: 'I think the players have to play with passion and that comes from a bit of leadership from your captain. John Terry has the right qualities. He makes other people around him play well. I'm not saying I wouldn't play Beckham. In fact, we need David in the team. His distribution is amazing, he's fantastic on that right side and there's not a crosser of the ball in the world like him. But the leadership is a different matter and that's why I'd love to see John Terry given a chance, and the sooner the better.'

It wasn't just defenders who thought Terry should take over from Beckham. The defender's former Chelsea team-mate, Gianfranco Zola, gave his opinion to the press. 'I am one-hundred per cent certain that John would be a great England captain,' said the Italian striker. 'He is a brilliant captain at Chelsea, one of those players who, when he is on the pitch, gives everything to the team. He leads by example and that is what other players want. Right now, Beckham is the right man to lead England, because he has the experience and the charisma. But John is the man for when Beckham is not there, and when he retires. I have no doubt about that.'

Beckham himself even sung Terry's praises and tipped the Chelsea man for the job that he had performed for more than fifty internationals. 'John is a potential England captain,' said the superstar midfielder. 'With a great manager like Jose Mourinho wanting him as captain, you can see that he is definitely a leader – a player with a lot of passion who leads from defence and can control the team.'

Having helped his country to the World Cup and further enhanced his increasingly secure position in the England team, Terry guided his club to twelve months unbeaten in the Premiership with a 5-1 victory over Bolton. And Chelsea kept their impressive form going with a 4-0 win over Real Betis to put them ahead of Liverpool on goal difference at the top of Group G in the Champions League.

The demolition of the Spanish side took the Blues to thirteen goals from three games, and buried their 'boring' tag after having to grind out a few results. 'We are very pleased because we hadn't scored for a few games and now we have,' said Terry in the *Daily Mail*. 'We started very well and it hasn't been a concern to us, not scoring. We know how good we are. We have a great team spirit and we feel we can go on from here.'

But after nine straight Premiership wins Chelsea suffered the first blip in what was fast appearing a title procession, drawing 1-1 away to Everton. Things got worse as the Blues lost to Charlton on penalties in the League Cup. Despite Terry claiming his first goal of the season, heading home an Arjen Robben corner to make it 1-0, the game finished 1-1 and went through extra-time to penalties, which Mourinho's team lost 5-4.

Although Chelsea rallied in their next game to beat Blackburn in the league, the manner of the win showed Mourinho's team weren't at their best, conceding two goals on their way to a 4-2 victory. And their sudden poor form was emphasised as they lost their next two games 1-0 – away to Real Betis and Manchester United.

Their first Premiership defeat of the season left Chelsea ten points clear at the top of the table, but before trying to turn around their fortunes at club level the Blues' players joined their countries, and Terry had a game against Argentina. With only seven months to go until the World Cup, a game against the South Americans gave Eriksson the chance to see how his side measured up against some world-class opposition.

England fought back from 1-0 and 2-1 down to win 3-2, and the result added to the belief that 2006 would be the year for the Three Lions to claim back the grandest prize in football.

The break from club action worked spectacularly to Chelsea's advantage as they returned from the internationals in the incredible form that had seen them build a thirteen-point lead at the top of the table, rather than the stuttering play that had brought just one win from the five games immediately preceding England's win over Argentina.

Terry was happy at the heart of a defence which kept six successive clean sheets in all competitions, but he also chipped in at the other end with the only goal of the game against both Middlesbrough and Wigan as the Blues won ten Premiership games on the trot. The highlight of Chelsea's incredible run was a 2-0 win over Arsenal at Highbury as Mourinho maintained a psychological edge over one of his closest domestic rivals.

In Europe Chelsea had qualified for the knock-out stages with a 2-0 win over Anderlecht in Belgium before a 0-0 draw with Liverpool which meant Terry's side finished second in the group. 'Of course it bothers us coming second in the group,' the defender told the press. 'We made it difficult for ourselves. We've beaten them comfortably in the league but the European games have been tight and difficult. It is up to us to break that up with something different. Sometimes it's just not meant to be. But it is hard to take. Even now the thought of Liverpool winning the trophy is still there in the back of our minds. I suppose it always will be for the rest of my career. I know we're a better team than them. The Premier League says it all, I think.'

Chelsea were totally dominant in the Premiership and had opened up an eleven point lead at the top of the table moving into the new year, and the Blues' skipper was excited by the twelve months that lay ahead. 'This could be my biggest year,' said Terry in the *Mirror*. 'It's a massive thing, a World Cup, and I'm certainly looking forward to it. But first thing's first. I want to stay fit and keep playing well for Chelsea. Hopefully, I will then be part of that World Cup squad. I'm playing against some fantastic players in the Champions League and obviously in the Premiership. Hopefully that gives Mr Eriksson enough chance to come and see me and give me the nod in front of some other players. But I must stay consistent with Chelsea.'

Terry was an immovable rock of consistency at the heart of the Blues' defence, helping to drive them towards what everyone in SW6 hoped would be a second successive title, but he watched from the sidelines as Mourinho chose to rest his skipper for the FA Cup tie with Huddersfield. It was the first game of the season which the England defender hadn't started, but his team-mates still saw their way past the Division One opposition in his absence, and Terry returned to the side the following week as Chelsea completed a tenth Premiership win in a row.

The victory over Sunderland at the Stadium of Light saw Chelsea's lead at the top of the table stretch to sixteen points. It may have been this monumental gap, and the cakewalk feel that the title defence had started to exude that led to complacency from the Blues' squad for the first time, or it may have just been bad luck and the absence of Essien (injured), and Didier Drogba, who was at the African Nations Cup, that saw Mourinho's men record three 1-1 draws on the trot, two in the league and one against Everton in the FA Cup.

There was further disappointment for Terry when Sven Goran Eriksson announced that he would be stepping down as England manager after the forthcoming World Cup, but the Barking-born centre-back was insistent his country's chances at the tournament wouldn't be adversely affected. 'If our rivals think that Sven leaving will unsettle our squad, or blunt our desire and commitment to win, they can think again,' said the Chelsea man in the *Sun*. 'We're all in it together. Sven is the manager and will be until the tournament is over so nothing has changed as far as the World Cup is concerned in my eyes. He picks the team but once you cross the touchline, it's the players who carry the hopes of the whole country. It's up to us. We understand and accept that. We play for Sven, but equally for the three lions on our shirts and our unflinching patriotic pride. We play for the fans and the dream to see England crowned world champions for the second time. Sven gave me my debut, just like a lot of those players who will travel to Germany. I have been behind him and will remain so, right to the end. I know the other lads feel the same. If I'm selected I will sweat blood and tears for the cause. Sven, like me, is a part of that cause.'

Terry remained vital to the Chelsea cause, and helped his team to a Merseyside double, beating Liverpool and then Everton at Stamford Bridge as the Blues returned to winning ways. Mourinho's captain scored his fourth goal of the season against the Toffees in a 4–1 win, securing safe passage to the fifth round of the FA Cup after a replay.

But rather than providing the springboard to launch another run of victories for Chelsea, the two wins were left in isolation as the Blues crashed to a humiliating 3–0 defeat away to Middlesbrough. On the final whistle the players disappeared down the tunnel, and their failure to thank the fans who had made the long trip to the Riverside Stadium left a sour taste in the mouths of many. Terry moved quickly to appease his loyal followers. 'I understand people are disappointed we didn't go over to them at the end; a couple of players clapped but we didn't go over,' said the skipper on Chelsea TV. 'But we just wanted to get off the pitch; we were more embarrassed than anything. But I'd like to apologise to the fans because they were great throughout the game. They kept singing throughout and we were delighted to hear them.'

Terry missed the opportunity to get the sorry defeat out of his system a week later as he was suspended for the FA Cup fifth round tie with Colchester, but Chelsea won without their inspirational captain, and he returned fresh and rested for the visit of Barcelona in the Champions League.

After falling at the semi-final stage in the previous two seasons Terry was desperate to lead his team to the 2006 final in Paris. 'We are hungrier to go that one step further,' he said. 'We have been unlucky though. Look at the teams we beat on the way to the semi-finals last year – Bayern Munich, Barcelona – and not to go one step further was so disappointing. We are even hungrier this year to get back into the competition and go again.'

But they would have to see off the Catalan giants once again to do so. The skipper was happy to recall the match the previous year, where his headed goal proved decisive. 'I bought a few copies of the DVD and dished them out to the family,' Terry said. 'Obviously it was pleasing to score the winner against such a great team but the most important thing was to go through. We are really looking forward to playing them again.'

The whole of Europe was looking forward to seeing the two great sides face up to each other once again, but the game proved more than a little disappointing for Terry as he scored an own-goal in Barcelona's 2-1 win at Stamford

Bridge. Most pundits wrote Chelsea off for the second leg, but Terry's confidence was unwavering. Asier del Horno was controversially sent off after 37 minutes, and the skipper was certain that with eleven men for the whole match the Blues could beat Barça. 'We played most of the first leg with ten men against supposedly the best team in the world and I believe we still matched them,' said Terry in the *News of the World*. 'In fact I think we showed we can beat them. We were a man down but even against a great side like that, we gave them a real run for their money. We started the second half really well and it didn't feel as though we had a man less. We still looked good and it's certainly going to be a different story over there when it's 11 against 11 – I'm sure about that.'

Terry had a busy fortnight before his trip to Catalonia, and he won all three games, two with Chelsea and one with England, where he was once again selected alongside Ferdinand. He couldn't make it four in a row at the Nou Camp however, as a 1–1 draw ended the Blues' European dream for another season.

Ronaldinho brushed the Chelsea skipper aside to open the scoring, and Lampard's late penalty was merely a consolation goal, but Terry was determined not to let the massive disappointment against Barça undermine their domestic campaign. 'Now we will have to go again,' he said in the *Evening Standard*. 'We will pick ourselves up, and our main priorities are the League and the FA Cup. We desperately want to win the Cup, we said that right from the start, and we need to keep winning to maintain our lead in the league.

'It is the worst feeling ever to lose a game, but a big one such as last night's on such a great stage leaves you gutted. We say it year after year and I'm getting déjà vu, but I don't want to feel this way again next season. Everyone at Chelsea wants to win the European Cup and we will happily play Barcelona again next term and go for it again. You want to compete against the best sides in the world and whether we got them in the first round or the semi-final, we would take that.' Only time would tell whether the two clubs would continue their increasingly fierce rivalry the following season.

Terry and his team-mates returned to London for two big derby matches, where the Blues continued their domination of Tottenham with a 2-1 win, stretching their unbeaten run against the Lilywhites to thirty-two league games since 1990. Williams Gallas's last minute strike brought a poignant victory on the day that Stamford Bridge paid homage to England and Chelsea legend Peter Osgood, who had recently died, aged 59, after a heart attack. 'He was a fantastic player and an even better man,' said Terry at 'Ossie's' funeral.

The win helped to lift the players' spirits after their Champions League exit, but a week later they lost west London bragging rights as they fell 1-0 to Fulham at Craven Cottage. The Blues remained at the top of the table, and they kept their hopes of a domestic double alive three days later when they saw off Newcastle at the Bridge in the FA Cup quarter-final.

Terry volleyed home Duff's corner after just four minutes, and his goal proved enough to put Chelsea into the last four and gain revenge for the previous season's Cup defeat at St James' Park. 'It was important to get a good early start and we did that straight from the kick-off,' Terry said after the match. 'We turned them around and squeezed them and that set the tone for the whole game. They knocked us out last year but this wasn't about revenge. It was about getting Chelsea into the hat for the draw for the semi-finals after a very disappointing result at the weekend.'

The Chelsea captain's joy was in utter disparity to the feelings of the Magpies' skipper, Alan Shearer, whose Cup dream was over in his last season before retirement. 'He's probably been the best player in the Premiership over the years, an absolute legend,' said Terry in the *Mirror*. 'For such a great player to have won the Premiership and nothing else, it's a shame really. We didn't swap shirts at the end of the game. I just wished him luck for the rest of the season. But it makes you realise that you have to win as many trophies as you can and while you can. That's my aim and it's the same as the other lads.'

Terry and his team-mates continued their march towards a second Premiership trophy with four wins and a draw in their next five games, and the centre-back took his tally for the season to seven with a goal against West Ham and another against Bolton the following week.

The victory over the Hammers was all the more impressive as Chelsea recovered from being 1-0 down after ten minutes and reduced to ten men five minutes later, to win 4-1 at Stamford Bridge. The captain was especially proud of his troops, saying: 'It was awesome, especially as Maniche was sent off early on. It looked like being difficult for us but the lads all came together and it went for us. Didier was superb and all the lads put in a great performance. It was one of the best I've seen from any of the lads this year.'

After beating their London rivals, Chelsea headed to Bolton, the scene of their championship coronation twelve months previously, to try and extend their seven-point lead over Manchester United with only four more games to play. Terry headed home the opener in a 2-0 win at the Reebok Stadium, and the Blues stretched their advantage over the Red Devils to nine points.

A 3-0 home win over Everton brought the title within touching distance, but before they could retain their trophy Chelsea faced an FA Cup semi-final against Liverpool. It was the tenth time in two seasons that the clubs had faced each other, and the Blues had lost only one of those encounters: the Champions League semi-final second leg at Anfield. But Rafa Benitez's side edged their way into the final with a 2-1 win at Old Trafford, and for the second year running Terry would have to watch Liverpool win a trophy that he had hoped to lift.

There was little time for the England man to dwell on

the departure of the Double dream as Chelsea next entertained Manchester United, needing just a draw to secure the Premiership. Having claimed the league title and the League Cup in 2005, and staring at just one trophy in 2006, critics accused the Blues of taking a backwards step. Terry was having none of it. 'The standards we set ourselves were awesome last year and coming into this season and the Christmas period we were playing really well,' said the skipper at a press conference. 'Even when we weren't playing really well we were grinding out results and getting a few points. We had a couple of slips and everyone jumped on the bandwagon to say we weren't playing as well as last season. But once again we're in a great position to win the Premiership for the second year running.'

The Blues wrapped up their second Premiership in spectacular style, beating second-placed Manchester United 3-0. Terry was imperious at the back, and the only trouble he had from the visitors was when Wayne Rooney accidentally caught him on the shin after seven minutes, opening up a gash which later required ten stitches and kept the Blues' skipper out of the final two league games of the season. But Terry had been raised to never show his opponents any signs of weakness, and he endured the pain to guide his team to victory and the title.

'There was no way I was coming off,' the limping defender told Sky Sports. 'What a season! To retain the title is absolutely fantastic. We found it more difficult going to places and getting results but we dug in and did it again.

That's the best atmosphere I've ever seen at the Bridge. That's a great result against a great side.'

As well as wrapping up the Premiership, the game against the Red Devils completed a second season unbeaten at Stamford Bridge, meaning Mourinho had yet to suffer a home defeat in domestic competition as Chelsea boss. 'He's been very important,' Chelsea's captain said of his manager. 'The tactics, the study he brought in, finding out about the opposition, training techniques and methods, the way he man-manages: everything he does is great. The players have enormous respect for him.'

With Terry's season finished by the gash to his ankle, Chelsea lost their last two games, away to Blackburn and Newcastle, and ended the campaign on 91 points, eight clear of Manchester United. The Blues' skipper had scored seven goals as Chelsea built on their reputation and success at home and abroad, but he was already looking ahead to the next season and how they could improve. 'Other teams are closing the gap and it's going to get tougher each year,' Terry told the press. 'We've improved but other teams behind have strengthened and improved. I'm sure other teams will strengthen again, we'll strengthen again and everyone will try to catch us again.

'It's a great achievement,' he added on the second title-winning season. 'Being knocked out of the Champions League and losing in cups was disappointing at the time, but we had one thing in our minds and that was the Premiership. We've always bounced back and over the course of the season we've been the best side in the Premiership. I believe our time will come in Europe. We've got the right manager and right players to go on and do that, and that's my dream.'

But before adding to his medal haul at club level, Terry had the chance to claim the grandest prize in sport: to try and end forty years of hurt for England at the World Cup in Germany.

CHAPTER TWELVE
END OF THE WORLD

'I have never felt that bad before,' he revealed. 'I've been in big games and losing to Liverpool in the Champions League semi-final in 2005 was probably the biggest disappointment, but multiply that by about a hundred. After the Portugal game I just wanted to get away and be on my own. I didn't even want to speak to family or anyone. I was absolutely gutted knowing that we had four years to wait for the chance to rise again. That's the thing that really burns me up, because I really thought it was our time.'

John Terry was right to be upset. A squad filled to the brim with quality players had travelled to Germany to bring the World Cup home, but had fallen at the quarter-finals, beaten once again in the dreaded penalty shoot-out. It was also the third tournament in a row that had seen Sven Goran Eriksson's side lose to a team managed by Luiz Felipe Scolari.

England's World Cup preparations had yet again been undermined by injuries; the first choice forward pair of Michael Owen and Wayne Rooney were battling for fitness going into the tournament. Nine minutes from the end of Chelsea's title-winning game against Manchester United, Rooney was carried off on a stretcher after a perfectly fair tackle by Paulo Ferreira. It later emerged that Rooney had broken the base of the fourth metatarsal in his right foot, and coming just six weeks before England's first game in Germany the talismanic forward was a huge doubt for the World Cup.

Terry had enjoyed some personal joy since the end of the club season however, as his fiancée Toni Poole gave birth to twins on 18 May 2006. The Chelsea captain missed the arrival of Georgie John Terry and Summer Rose Terry as he flew home from England's training camp in Portugal. But his baby girl was born at 12.29pm weighing 3lb 9oz and the boy followed at 12.37pm weighing 5lb 7oz. When Terry had met his new children at the private Portland Hospital in west London he released a short statement: 'The babies are well. Toni is doing well and we are both absolutely delighted.'

The new dad commemorated fatherhood with England's second goal in the 3-1 win over Hungary and he broke out the baby rocking celebration made famous by Bebeto at the 1994 World Cup in America. Terry headed home after 51 minutes and was then joined by Rio Ferdinand and Frank Lampard in his homage to his new children. 'It has been at the back of my mind to celebrate like that since the twins were born,' Terry revealed. 'I'm over the moon.'

It was the Barking-born defender's first game for a month following his ankle injury, but he came back in fine form. Through nodding home David Beckham's free kick at Old Trafford Terry claimed his first goal for his country, and coming in his twenty-third appearance it was long overdue. 'I was disappointed I hadn't got off the mark already,' he told the *Sun*. 'I said on a TV programme the other day that Becks has mastered the art of crossing. There is certainly no one better in the world at this present time. In training, Beckham just produces and finds people right on their head every time. I had a header which just went over the bar in the first two minutes of Tuesday's game from one of David's crosses. He just kept picking me out all night. I had a feeling that I was eventually going to score so I was delighted when I finally got one on target.'

The goal gave Terry a boost with the World Cup drawing ever closer, and the win over Hungary was good for the spirits of all the England players, as was the 6-0 drubbing of Jamaica four days later. With Owen making a tentative return from injury and Rooney still on the sidelines, Peter Crouch advanced his claims for a place in the team with a hat-trick against the Caribbean side. Eriksson had started the game against Hungary with Owen up front on his own, and many felt the diminutive striker would fare better alongside the newly prolific beanpole-esque Crouch.

Terry was unconcerned by the different formations, insistent that the talent at England's disposal would see them go a long way no matter how they lined up, even if Rooney failed to recover in time. 'Fingers crossed that Wayne is going to be fine,' the Chelsea star told the *Daily Star*. 'But I think we showed today that we will do really well in Germany whoever is playing up front with Michael Owen. Crouchie proved he can do a great job up there. I thought he was different class today and well done to him for scoring his first England hat-trick. This was the best possible way to finish off our preparations for the finals. We've had two great games this week but today was especially good. We played some great stuff, we sprayed the ball around, we battled hard but we were sensible too. The good thing is that the goals are clearly there for us while defensively we look very solid too.'

Despite the Three Lions playing well, and the old idiom of not fixing what isn't broken, people in the press were still calling for Terry to take over from Beckham as the England captain, following his inspirational performances in blue. But the Chelsea skipper merely reiterated his faith in and support of the Real Madrid midfielder. 'It's absolutely ridiculous. So many times you see it being asked if he should be England captain,' Terry said on *ITV1*. 'We have got the right man in charge, whether it be for another four or five years. He's certainly an example to the other players. It's such a massive World Cup and for Becks to be the man leading us with such a great squad of players, we've got a real chance. He must feel that inside as well… that you know that it's a chance possibly for him to lift the World Cup.'

With the captains of the Premiership's top three clubs – Terry, Gary Neville at Manchester United and Steven Gerrard at Liverpool – in the team there were plenty of experienced and inspirational characters in the England squad, and that would always be at Beckham's disposal. 'I'm not captain of this England team but feel I can make a contribution in terms of leadership,' Terry stated in the press. 'The same goes for Gary Neville, Rio Ferdinand, Stevie G, Lamps, Michael Owen… We're all leaders and winners. The hunger has been instilled in the whole squad. We're all fighters and we're all England fans as well. I think we've got something special.

'I think I've really improved as a player since Euro 2004. The last couple of years have been very good for me both personally and at club level. I've won successive Premiership titles and had two more years in the Champions League, gaining experience against the best strikers in the world. I've grown in confidence and have certainly brought that into the England team with me. People ask if this World Cup will be England's time and I think it might be. If we get that little bit of luck, we've a great chance.'

It was a first World Cup for Terry. In the four years since

the last tournament he had come in from the 'court case enforced cold' to become one of the first names on the team-sheet, and he couldn't wait for the competition to begin. There was a threat to his World Cup dream when he limped out of the Jamaica match after 36 minutes, but it was merely a precautionary measure as Eriksson was loathe to pick up any more injuries with the game against Paraguay one week away. 'The knee is fine,' said Terry in the *Daily Star*. 'The manager told us beforehand that any little niggles and we were to come off immediately. I felt something and signalled to the bench that I was struggling a little, but it wasn't a sharp pain. There is a little bit of swelling but I will definitely be okay.'

Terry was true to his word and seven days later he lined up against the South Americans for the Group B opener. Ahead of the match he told *The Times* of the team's conviction not to sit on any lead they might have, after England's caution had proved their undoing at the previous two major tournaments. 'Maybe when we have scored in the past, we have sat back and tried to nick a 1-0 win,' said the Chelsea captain. 'We need to be bolder. That is a regret from Euro 2004. We are a very good side. We can pass as well as anyone, get behind teams but we need to start killing them off now. It is about front foot, getting a lead, building on it. I think that will come from the players as well as the staff. When we get a goal up with Chelsea, Man United or Liverpool, you can generally see them going to get that two-goal cushion. We need to do that with England, to get that lead so then we can start relaxing and passing the ball about a bit more.'

Unfortunately, England found it difficult to transform words into deeds and laboured to a 1-0 win over Paraguay. The game started brightly as Carlos Gamarra headed a Beckham free-kick past his own keeper after just three minutes, but there was no second goal. As the game went on the players wilted in the 30-degree heat, and by the end Eriksson's side were left clinging to their lead. But with Terry at the centre of a back four alongside Gary Neville, Rio Ferdinand and Ashley Cole, they just about managed to keep Paul Robinson's goal in tact.

'Three points is three points and we have to take credit for our first-half performance because it was always going to take us time to adjust to that kind of heat,' Terry said after the game. 'The lads were all complaining about their feet hurting and mine felt like they were on fire in the second half but we had to battle on. This was an encouraging win. Three points is a good start in conditions like that. The pitch was a bit dry and all the lads were complaining about blisters and their feet being sore.'

Despite the poor performance the win left England in a strong position at the top of the group, as Sweden drew with Trinidad and Tobago in the other match. Eriksson was still awaiting the return of Rooney from injury, but apart from his absence it was a strong team with Beckham, Frank Lampard, Steven Gerrard and Joe Cole completing a midfield quartet behind Owen and Crouch.

The Swedish coach made just one change, bringing in Jamie Carragher for the injured Neville at right back to face Trinidad five days later, and with an evening kick-off the weather could provide no excuses. The World Cup first-timers proved a resilient bunch and England didn't manage a breakthrough until seven minutes from time, when Crouch headed home from Beckham's cross. Joe Cole added a second in the last minute and the win guaranteed a place in the knock-out stages for the Three Lions.

Terry was realistic about England's first two matches. 'We have to be encouraged about the fact we have six points but let's be honest about it, we aren't playing too well,' the Chelsea man said. 'Things can only get better on the performance side of it.'

The return of Rooney for the match against Sweden raised hopes that the England boys could start playing to the level expected of such talented individuals. There were questions raised about the fitness and readiness of the Manchester United attacker, but Terry was confident Rooney was ready. 'I think he'd tell you he's got 160 minutes in him,' the defender told the press. 'Marking him is a nightmare so obviously it's looking good. He's looking very sharp and very ready to go.'

Needing a draw to top Group B, and looking for a first win over Sweden for 38 years, Terry was hoping to maintain England's untarnished defensive record. 'As a back five we're going into games desperate not to concede goals. If we come off that pitch having kept a clean sheet it's like grabbing a goal for a midfielder or a striker,' the Barking-born defender said to reporters. 'We hope to get another one against Sweden. It would be nice to go through the World Cup without conceding a goal but obviously there are some world-class strikers who are always going to get opportunities.'

One of England's world-class players was finally available for selection and Crouch made way as Rooney returned to the starting XI against the Scandinavians. Owen Hargreaves came into midfield for Gerrard who was rested, as he was one booking away from suspension.

Eriksson's team started the game well, and during the first half they played their best football of the tournament, taking a 1-0 lead into the break thanks to Joe Cole's wonder goal. Unfortunately, England lost Michael Owen to knee ligament damage after just three minutes. After finally getting Rooney fit the irony of losing his other world-class striker would not have been lost on Eriksson. Worse was to come. Despite dominating the first 45 minutes the England team faded after the interval for the third match in succession, and twice conceded the lead. Marcus Allback equalised after 51 minutes and Gerrard restored advantage five minutes from time.

The defence wasn't helped by Ferdinand's withdrawal after 56 minutes due to a calf strain, but there was no excuse for the last minute equaliser. Terry misjudged the flight of a long throw, allowing the ball to fly over his head before bouncing in the six-yard box and being poked home by Henrik Larsson as the rest of the defence dithered. Sweden's first goal had come from a corner, and the defence was understandably disappointed with the loss of their unblemished record. 'Steve McClaren told us beforehand that about 35 per cent of goals at World Cups are conceded at set-plays,' Terry said. 'The fact we were made so aware makes it so disappointing. Normally we are so strong there but hopefully the sloppy goals are now out of the way. Set pieces are the bread and butter for central defenders. We should be organised to deal with them. From a defensive point of view, we are disappointed.'

It was a shambolic end to the game, but the point secured England's place at the top of the group and meant that they would meet Ecuador in the next round, whilst Sweden would face the hosts, Germany.

The England defenders let themselves down against the Scandinavians, and after the game Terry faced members of the press, one of whom voiced his thoughts that the Chelsea defender's performances at the World Cup had been in marked contrast to his imperious form at Stamford Bridge. The England centre-back fixed the journalist with a piercing stare and paused to compose himself before issuing his response. 'I wouldn't say that,' the 25-year-old said. 'When I sat down after the first two games I thought I did well. After every game I assess the things I've done well and things I haven't, and it was the same after Sweden. I'm my own worst critic. I know I could have done better. I had one bad game and you say that – it surprises me, but I take it on the chin. I don't agree with you.'

Terry gave the perfect response to his critics in the next game as his man-of-the-match display helped England into the quarter-finals. Still underperforming as a team, Eriksson's side won 1-0 with much of the credit for the 'nil' belonging to the Chelsea captain. The England goal again came from a set piece as Beckham curled home a trademark free kick after an hour. The sweltering lunchtime heat was responsible for the England skipper being sick briefly after scoring, and when Beckham was substituted four minutes from time the armband moved to Terry, who was already turning in a captain's performance.

After such a fine display everybody wanted to speak to the man-of-the-match. 'We all know that deep down we can play a lot better but we're encouraged by the fact that we're through to the quarter-finals and things can still improve,' Terry said to the press. 'We got through the group not playing so well, we improved again and we need to keep doing that to go even further. Speaking on behalf of not just the players but the fans as well, I think they'd settle for us not playing that well but going all of the way. We realise that we've got a lot more in the tank to give but other teams watching realise that as well from the players and the squad that we've got. But it's very encouraging and positive to get to the quarter-finals of the World Cup. We are not firing on all cylinders yet so that's pleasing that we have come through without being at our best.'

Eriksson was blamed in most quarters for the consistently poor performances on the pitch. The Swede's tactics and judgement had been under ever-increasing scrutiny since the early days of his England career, but the condemnation reached a new high in 2006. The selection of the inexperienced youngsters Theo Walcott and Aaron Lennon in the 23-man World Cup squad seemed bizarre, and whilst Lennon's brief appearances justified his inclusion, Walcott had spent his entire tournament on the bench.

With only four strikers in the squad, two of whom were returning from long-term injuries, the presence of the 17-year-old speedster seemed an ill-advised luxury. And when Owen then suffered his knee injury it left Eriksson with only Crouch, Rooney and Walcott. The coach then blunted the effectiveness of the supremely gifted Rooney by playing him up front on his own for the game against Ecuador, and again for the quarter-final clash with Portugal.

Hargreaves had replaced Carragher at right-back for the game against Ecuador, with Michael Carrick playing the 'holding role' and Gerrard returning to a five-man midfield. Eriksson retained this 4–5–1 formation against Portugal but shuffled his personnel as Neville was restored at full-back and Hargreaves moved into the defensive midfield position at the expense of Carrick.

The belief was that the new formation would enable the team to get the best out of Gerrard and Lampard, but it merely caused Rooney to get frustrated upfront on his own, leading to England's downfall as the fiery Manchester

United forward was sent off in the quarter-final for stamping on Ricardo Carvalho after 62 minutes.

Playing the remainder of the game with ten men, the Three Lions failed to break down Scolari's side, and with Terry remaining immovable at the back the scoreless game drifted towards penalties. A dismal tournament was rounded off as Lampard, Gerrard and Carragher all had their spot kicks saved, Portugal won the shoot-out 3-1 and England's World Cup was over. 'It's just the worst feeling I've experienced,' Terry said in the *People*. 'I've only cried a couple of times after matches, but this was one of those moments. Deep down, I believed we could win it and that's why the tears were there. We truly believed this was our time and you could say it was our best performance of the World Cup. We showed a lot of guts and we didn't sit back when we were down to ten men, but it wasn't enough.'

Terry had impressed for the most part, and deserved his place in the FIFA World Cup squad of the tournament. But the blood and guts approach once again proved fruitless at a major tournament, and the Chelsea defender would have to wait another two years for his next chance for international glory. Things would be different in 2008, as England would have a new coach in Steve McClaren, and a new captain.

CHAPTER THIRTEEN
ENGLAND'S CAPTAIN MARVEL

'It was about 1pm. I had finished training and was having a massage when the call came,' he recalled. 'I just froze and didn't know what to say. I am just so excited to be given this great responsibility and it hasn't sunk in yet. I want to do things my way. I'll learn bits off the great captains I've played with and hopefully I can make a great captain for England. I want to win things for our country. We have the most passionate fans in the world and the players are passionate about winning something.'

John Terry was fully focused on making his reign as England captain a successful one, and if his time as Chelsea captain is anything to go by the Barking-born defender could follow another Essex lad into football folklore. Terry grew up a stone's throw from Bobby Moore's childhood home and dreamt of emulating the West Ham legend. 'I hope I can do even a quarter of the things that man did,' said Terry in the *Daily Express*. 'They tell me he was never quick. I wouldn't say I'm slow but I'm not lightning. I like to think I read the game really well, and they say he was the same.

'My dad used to say if you can be two yards in front of people in your head, even lacking a yard of pace, you will get to the ball before them. That is where I feel we relate a little. Bobby's mum still lived on the road at the top of mine and one of my best friends lived there too. So basically we grew up on the same estate, and he is an absolute legend back there. It is not a great part of the world, but we are proud of where we come from and always want to better ourselves. We do that by working hard. Whether it is football, snooker, swimming or golf, I want to be the best and I hate losing.'

The 25-year-old defender was a popular choice as captain, taking over from David Beckham whose abdication came after the World Cup failure, and the old skipper was quick to congratulate his successor. 'Becks was the first person to call me after I found out the news, which was amazing,' Terry said. 'He wished me good luck and told me to enjoy my time as captain. He said he was always at the end of the phone for me if I needed anything. It was really nice, really special.

'It is the ultimate honour to be the captain of your country and I am very proud to be given this great opportunity. It is an incredible challenge and one I am looking forward to very much.'

The Chelsea man had edged out Steven Gerrard as the choice for the captaincy came down to a choice between the inspirational leaders of Chelsea and Liverpool. The Scouser displayed his attributes as a team player by getting over his personal disappointment and behind Terry. 'I would like to congratulate John on being appointed England captain,' Gerrard said. 'I'm sure he'll do a great job. He's a tremendous leader for Chelsea and has all the qualities required for the role. I'm also pleased to have been appointed vice-captain by Steve McClaren. I am grateful that Steve took the time to call me and inform me of his decision. There are a number of captains in the England squad and I know we will all be giving one hundred per cent support to Steve and John.'

McClaren had spent long enough with the England set-up to see Terry's qualities in depth, and he was confident that he'd picked the right man for the job. 'Choosing a captain is one of the most important decisions a coach has to make,' the new England manager told a press conference. 'I'm certain I've got the right man in John Terry. I'm convinced he will prove to be one of the best captains England has ever had. John has all the attributes an international captain needs: leadership, authority, courage, ability, tactical awareness and a total refusal to accept second-best. He has been an inspiration for Chelsea and is at his best in adversity. Over the five years I've been involved with the England coaching set-up I've seen first hand the respect that John has among his fellow players.

There are a number of strong leaders in the squad and he will not lack support on and off the pitch.'

There was plenty of support for the new skipper off the pitch, and many former players went on record to declare their belief in Terry. Former England captains Bryan Robson, David Platt and Ray Wilkins were all delighted with the appointment, as was World Cup-winner Jack Charlton. It was no surprise when Terry's club manager joined the ranks of supporters for the new England captain. 'JT deserves it. England deserves a captain like him,' Jose Mourinho said. 'He loves to work, loves to win, loves to make people happy and confident. He is a captain. I am really happy and on this occasion I also want to wish Steve success in the England job and tell him that at Chelsea we are here to help him.'

The new skipper got off to a great start when he scored in his first game as England captain, a 4-0 win over Greece at Old Trafford on 16 August 2006. His was the opening goal after 14 minutes, nodding in a flick-on from Stewart Downing. 'I had a lot of text messages before the game from people at Chelsea and I had one from Becks wishing me good luck in my first game as captain,' Terry said. 'It was the perfect start for me. It has been a dream come true for me, especially scoring the goal. I felt so proud leading the team out and then singing the national anthem as captain. I am more than happy with the result and with the performance.'

England went one better in their first competitive match

of the McClaren/Terry reign when they beat Andorra 5-0 at Old Trafford. Although Terry didn't score he helped keep another clean sheet as England got their European Championship qualifying campaign off to the perfect start. The Three Lions further cemented their place at the top of Group E with a 1-0 win in Macedonia, and the coach was singing the defender's praises after the game. 'You have just seen exactly why I gave the armband to John Terry,' McClaren said. 'This was his kind of game. Just think of the responsibility of being England captain. For a start you have to be an exceptional character and John is demonstrating that. He is more delighted at winning this game 1-0 than beating Andorra by five at home. When you have to dig deep and grind out results he is your man. You have to be mentally tough and his kind of desire is something you are born with. It's in there. Year in, year out he has been doing it for Chelsea and it is why he is England captain.'

England struggled in their next two games, as Macedonia held on for a draw at Old Trafford, and Croatia won 2-0 in Zagreb four days later. After such a faultless start to life as captain of his country Terry knew the honeymoon couldn't last, but the toothless display in the Balkans came as a shock to everyone.

McClaren's side still had plenty of room for improvement and the skipper definitely wouldn't be resting on his laurels. 'I've still a long, long way to go before I'm world class,' Terry said. 'Other people have different opinions, but I listen to my own opinion and I need to work on my game and keep improving. And if I can do that over the course of my career – and hopefully that's going to be with Chelsea – in four or five years I should be a very good player.'

Modest almost to a fault, the England captain was keen to keep growing and learning at Stamford Bridge to help his club to bring in more silverware. 'I set myself targets each year and I assess myself at the end of each season,' he said. 'I need to improve on everything I've done. I need to up my consistency, my concentration, and I need to score more goals. You look at Paolo Maldini, Alessandro Nesta, Rio Ferdinand and Marcel Desailly, players like that – I love those kinds of players.

'I look at Jamie Carragher, Sol Campbell, different players in the Premiership and I take little bits from everybody's game and try and improve myself and, hopefully, build myself up to be that great player in the end. But I've still got a very long way to go. I'm working on my sharpness, my quickness, my passing, my heading, my reading of the game, set-plays – just about everything.

'Each season I now look at every single match. It might take two weeks sometimes but I study each one to see how I can do better. I have now developed a strong concentration on the pitch, which is weird because off it I cannot do it for five minutes. I look back at games from when I first came in the team and some of the things I did make me cringe. I still make mistakes but then I was making mistakes and being destroyed for them. I am my own biggest critic, watching games and rewinding them.'

Always his own toughest evaluator, Terry got to the top through no small amount of hard work and application. 'I'm respected at Chelsea because I am English, I know the club well and I've seen the ups and downs here,' the captain said in the *Daily Mirror*. 'They know I am not passing through. I am here for the long term. I accept I might annoy team-mates because you need to tell players off if they are doing something wrong. Likewise, if someone wants to have a go at me, I have to take it too. But they know I would do anything for them. It's my job to be Jose's voice on the pitch. I have to be the link between the players and the manager.'

With no intention of moving on or relinquishing the captaincy, Terry has his sights set on a Blues record. 'I would love to stay with Chelsea for the rest of my career,' he promised. 'My target is to play as many times as I can and play more games for the club than any other player. I used to look up to Dennis Wise and Graeme Le Saux who were on 200-300 games at the time and I would love to be where they are.'

Terry is now moving out of that bracket, but he still has a very long way to go if he wants to break Chelsea legend Ron Harris's appearance record of 795 games. 'Chopper' racked up his incredible haul across 19 seasons from 1962 to 1980 and, for the current skipper to better that, he would need to keep playing at Stamford Bridge for another nine or ten years without serious injury, taking him to 2016.

As a player who relies on his ability to read the game and who uses his great sense of timing, rather than his pace, to get him out of trouble, Terry could conceivably carry on at the top level to the age of thirty-six. The biggest obstacle for the Blues' skipper in his record-breaking quest is how to stay fighting-fit for another decade. There is no question of him moving on and, in this age of multi-millionaire footballers, his loyalty to the club is exceptional and truly praiseworthy.

But his zealous allegiance to the Chelsea cause stands in stark contrast to newspaper stories alleging his lack of fidelity to his fiancée. Throughout his fledgling career, Terry has found himself the subject of countless kiss-and-tell allegations in the tabloids, while dating, living with and eventually getting engaged to long-term lover Toni Poole, the mother of his children.

The couple have been together since 1998, when Terry met beautician Toni in Essex, and the heroic defender was happy to have met someone special before he became a multi-millionaire, so he could be sure their attraction had nothing to do with fame or wealth. 'I'm engaged to my girlfriend Toni, she's been with me since I was a YTS,' said Terry in the *Independent*. 'She's good for me. She's been there from the start. When I was earning £46 a week she was earning £250 – she took me out to restaurants. It's nice she's there for the right reasons – me.'

They now live together in a five-bedroom house on the edge of Cobham, Surrey, as Toni is happy to take on the role of full-time mother and housewife. But it is the stories concerning the footballer's alleged performances away from home that have attracted so much publicity.

In September 2005, the Chelsea captain confessed to the *News of the World* that he had been 'naughty' with some other women. 'I really regret what I've done to Toni.' Terry said. 'I've misbehaved and slept with girls behind her back and that's not right. She knows about it all now – I've told her everything – and we're moving on. I'm not going to cheat on her ever again and I want to marry her more than anything else in the world.'

After forcing his way past Frank Leboeuf and into the Chelsea team, Terry had become a household name, and at least eight different women had sold stories about their dalliances with the defender since 2003. 'The last few years have been really hard for me and Toni,' he said. 'But I am determined to do my best to clean up my act now. I want to lift the World Cup with England one day. And I want to make Toni happy because she deserves it. I really am in love with her.'

'When these girls come up to me in a club and start chatting to me, I don't want to be rude so I stop and talk to them and buy them a drink. Unfortunately sometimes they take that the wrong way.' But he threatened legal action against any fabrications, maintaining that anyone who lied about him would be seeing him in court.

Seven weeks later Terry was in the papers again: 'TERRY AT IT AGAIN' read the headline in the *Sun*. The first paragraph alleged: 'Soccer hero John Terry couldn't wait to romp in his £100,000 Bentley, a busty teenager claimed yesterday. The England defender – a Champions League bonker – scored with sexy fan Jenny Barker just hours after she asked for his autograph in a car park.' A spokesman for Terry refused to comment and no further stories have emerged since he became a father to twins.

Terry already has high hopes for his son Georgie. 'Obviously I'm not going to push him because it's his decision, but I would love for him to be a professional footballer just like his daddy,' said the proud parent in *London Lite*. 'I would love to manage Chelsea; I could manage my son then. It's bit too far ahead to start planning but it would be great, wouldn't it?

'I want to change the twins' nappies and spend any time with them as I can. If that means getting up in the middle of the night, then so be it. I can catch up with my sleep in the afternoons, I can sleep after training. The great part about being a dad is waking up in the middle of the night and things like that. Obviously close to the game, like one or two nights before a match, my girlfriend deals with it because I am going to need the rest.

'I have already bought them kits with my number 26 and "Daddy" on the back. It makes me so happy to know that they are watching me. There is little more in life that could make me happier.'

Terry seems to be enjoying fatherhood, and he has always been very committed to his family. One of the first things he did when he started earning big money was to make sure that they benefited from his good fortune. His older brother Paul's footballing career only really picked up when Terry was earning enough to allow his then amateur sibling to focus on his football rather than his day job and, given the financial freedom to take time off work and train more than his rivals in the conference, he was soon picked up by League One club Yeovil Town. The Chelsea captain also bought property for his parents and stashes away most of his money into a pension, ensuring his future is financially secure.

That security is in no danger from any of Terry's occasional bets, despite media speculation that the England captain was gambling away £5,000-a-week. 'The figures that have started to be bandied about concerning my gambling are a joke,' Terry said in the *Mirror*. 'I haven't got a gambling problem. I had a couple of tips at Cheltenham this year and I had two winners at 11-1 and 8-1. I ended up being a few hundred quid up and yet suddenly there are stories that I bet £50,000. Then I got 20 or 30 letters from fans who were upset at the idea of me treating money like that. It even got to the point where the manager asked some of us about the figures that were being talked about and we put him right straight away.'

The story was of no concern to Mourinho. 'He is English, I can do nothing,' the Chelsea boss said. 'An

Englishman going to the bookmaker is normal. In every street I find a minimum of three bookmakers. That's your country. It's what you love, that's what you do. For me, John Terry betting is normal.'

Mourinho has never had anything less than one hundred per cent confidence in his captain, and even let Terry take over a day's training during the 2006 title run-in. 'The manager took me by surprise when he asked me,' the new 'coach' said at the time. 'I prepared myself that night, thinking, "Will the lads be happy with this, will they want to do that?" I think it went down all right, but I was stressed. I got everyone involved in seven-a-side teams, the backroom staff as managers and so on. We'd had a couple of draws and it was all about team bonding. I wouldn't want to do it every week, but one day I wouldn't mind stepping into that role.'

When he eventually finishes playing, Terry thinks he will stay involved in the game and coaching is definitely an option. But for the moment he is happy doing everything possible to make sure Chelsea win more trophies, and that includes embracing some bizarre superstitions.

Like many sportsmen, the Blues' defender will stick with whatever brings results, however irrational. So after a good performance he will try and remember anything special that he might have done in the build-up to the game and will then stick with that routine until a bad result necessitates change.

Before the first title-winning season, Terry already had some fairly unusual rituals he felt compelled to observe, but with all the following success came an inevitable glut of new quirks. 'I started off with a couple of superstitions and, because we did so well, kept winning and winning, I ended up with about fifty of them,' the defender said. 'Then it was a case of remembering them for every game! I am so superstitious. I've got to have the same seat on the bus, tie the tapes round my socks three times and cut my tubular grip for my shin-pads the same size every game. I even drive to games listening to the same CD.'

He has to have the same players sitting next to him on the coach to away games; he also has a specific seat for team talks and admits its position is crucial – it must be in the correct place. On top of that, he only uses one particular urinal in the Stamford Bridge dressing rooms, counts all the lampposts on his way to home games and he even has a lucky parking space. With such a strict routine, there will inevitably be problems.

'I always have to park my car in the same spot in the car park and when I drove in at lunchtime before the game, the space was taken and I was unsettled,' Terry revealed in the *Daily Mirror*, recalling an emergency before the Barcelona match at Stamford Bridge in March 2005. 'Every hour I went back to the car park to see whether the space was taken and eventually I got one of the kitmen to move it. Two hours to move my car – he thought I was mad!'

The tie with the Catalan giants also caused Terry to

upgrade his lucky shin-pads after he misplaced his old ones at the Nou Camp. 'Those shin-pads had got me to where I was in the game,' he added in the *Daily Mirror*, remembering one particular trauma. 'And I'd lost them. I really felt terrible because they were a big part of my routine. Before the Carling Cup final, I was having a go at the kitman even though it wasn't his fault. I was thinking: "F*cking hell, I've had those shin-pads for so long and now this is it, all over." But Lamps gave me a pair of his and luckily we won, so they've stuck with me. Now they have become my lucky ones.'

From the outside, it's easy to laugh at such absurd behaviour, but Terry's tried and tested preparations for every game allow him to relax on the pitch and give the composed and commanding performances that epitomise his game. They have also enabled the centre-back to become England captain at the age of twenty-five, and to have lifted the Premiership trophy twice.

With the recruitment of Germany captain Michael Ballack; 2004 European Footballer of the Year Andriy Shevchenko; England left-back Ashley Cole and promising youngsters like John Obi Mikel, Salomon Kalou and Khalid Boulahrouz it would be unwise to bet against Terry lifting more silverware in the coming seasons.

There was no question as to what trophy the England man was after next. 'I would look on it as a failure if I never won the Champions League in my career,' Terry said in the *Daily Express*. 'We are all very much aware here that if we won it, it would be something we'd be remembered for, for many years to come. Every player in the squad is desperate for that. We all have the necessary hunger and desire to win the competition. And the players who have been brought in this summer underline the ambition of the club, the owner and the manager. We've got the backbone now and there are not many weaknesses in the side at all, if any. When you look at the experience of players like Shevchenko and Ballack it can only help us. They have been very successful in their careers, they know what it takes because they have won it before.'

CHAPTER FOURTEEN

CUP DOUBLE AND INJURY TROUBLE

'To walk out with the armband on such a special occasion in front of my family and friends was enough,' he said. 'To score the first England goal at the stadium was the ultimate dream.'

John Terry had endured a tough start to life as England captain with some mixed results, but in the first game at the newly redeveloped Wembley Stadium the Chelsea defender put the Three Lions ahead against Brazil. It had been an arduous season for Terry as he saw his hopes of a third successive Premiership title with Chelsea scuppered by a troublesome back injury, and was forced to settle for two domestic cups.

The season began brightly for Terry as he aimed to put his World Cup disappointment behind him and add to his already bountiful medal haul. Despite losing the FA Community Shield to Liverpool in Cardiff and falling 2-

1 to Middlesbrough at the Riverside, Chelsea put together a run of six successive victories through August and September putting them at the top of the Premiership tree and in control of their European future.

Terry followed up his goal for England – against Greece in his first game as captain – with the Blues' first competitive goal of the season, heading home Arjen Robben's free-kick after eleven minutes on the way to a 3-0 win over Manchester City at the Bridge. It was a great way to respond to the defeat in Cardiff, as Terry told reporters: 'After the Community Shield, maybe a few people said Chelsea are beatable. Any team is beatable but we bounced back and showed the character we have shown the last two years. If we get that character, get the football and get the team spirit we have had the last couple of years, we have a very good chance of achieving something special.'

However, Jose Mourinho's footballing juggernaut clearly wasn't up to top speed yet, as a second defeat of the young season came at the hands of Boro three days later; but this reversal merely galvanised the Chelsea spirit as they won eleven and drew one of their next twelve matches. The run of fine form started against Blackburn where Terry helped his team on the way to a 2-0 victory, winning a penalty five minutes into the second half. 'We showed last year that when we are not playing at our best we can still come away with three points,' said the Blues' skipper after the game at Ewood Park. 'This is a tough place to come. After throwing it away in the last ten minutes against Boro we were really pumped up and ready to go.'

Terry was proving himself a Captain Marvel for both club and country, as he led England to victories over Andorra and Macedonia before returning to the blue shirt of Chelsea. Winning can become a habit, and so it proved for Terry and his team-mates as they put aside Charlton and Werder Bremen, before delivering a potential death blow to one of their title rivals, beating Liverpool 1-0 in SW6 to leave the Reds eight points adrift of joint Premiership leaders Chelsea and Manchester United.

The skipper was missing as the Blues overcame their West London rivals Fulham at Craven Cottage, but he returned to the side for the trip to Sofia where Levski were beaten 3-1 to keep Terry on course for some European silverware. But after the game in Bulgaria the Barking-born defender experienced his first blip of the season as September drew to a close. Chelsea dropped their first home points of the campaign as they drew 1-1 with Aston Villa, before Terry saw his faultless start to life as England captain come crashing down with two poor displays.

The Three Lions began their international week in Manchester, where they failed to break down Macedonia, drawing 0-0 at Old Trafford, before heading out to Zagreb for a tricky midweek match with Croatia. The Balkan side had yet to lose a game on home soil since emerging as an independent state from the bloodstained ruins of the old

Yugoslavia in 1991, and Terry was all too aware of the enormity of the task ahead of him and his team. 'This is the biggest away test since Turkey three years ago,' the captain said to the press, 'but you relish these sort of games.

'Croatia have got an amazing home record, many years without getting beaten which is a great achievement, but it is a great place for us to come and bounce back after Saturday. We feel we can do that. Everyone is very up for the game and looking forward to it. I think this sort of game brings the best out of English players. When it comes down to the nitty gritty, like the game in Turkey before, I think we can match anyone. It is an extra incentive to become the first side to beat Croatia at home for so long but they are a very good side.'

Slaven Bilic's team showed just how good they were as they dispatched an inept England team 2-0. Many excuses were put forward, such as the decision to try out a 3-5-2 formation that was supposed to allow McClaren's men to match the home side's creative talents in midfield, but merely resulted in positional confusion among the players; the injuries to Joe Cole, Owen Hargreaves, and Aaron Lennon; Steven Gerrard's one match ban; David Beckham's international exclusion. But the fact is that England simply weren't good enough on the day. They would have to get back to winning ways to qualify for the European Championship finals in 2008.

But with no competitive games in the white shirt of his country until March, Terry had plenty of time to concentrate on his other team. Chelsea's next match was away to Reading, where two horrific injuries to Petr Cech and Carlo Cudicini meant that JT played out the final minutes of a 1-0 win in goal. Cech fractured his skull when Stephen Hunt's knee caught him on the temple in the first minute of the match, and Cudicini was later knocked unconscious in a collision with Ibrahima Sonko. After a long delay Terry took the gloves and retreated between the sticks. The home side failed to test him in the closing minutes, and the part-time keeper insisted it was a scenario the ever-prepared Mourinho had considered. 'We had talked about what would happen if this ever arose, and I said I would go in goal,' Terry told the assembled media. 'We were disappointed with the first challenge on Petr. Of course, we were very concerned about both goalkeepers. Both were knocked out and concussed. We were disappointed, especially with the first one.'

Mourinho was more than disappointed with the challenge that left Cech sidelined for three months, and fearing for not just his footballing career but his life. 'To be angry doesn't help,' the Portuguese manager said of the Cech incident. 'I'm just waiting for the report of their injuries and what the FA will do about it. The first one is unbelievable – professional footballers should respect each other. It is one thing to break a leg or an arm but the head is another thing altogether. In terms of injuries in sport it is the one that scares you most.'

Fortunately the Czech international made a full

recovery and was back playing in the Chelsea goal by late January. But the scale of the injury meant that Cech needed delicate neurosurgery to relieve pressure on his skull. Missing arguably the world's best goalkeeper, the Blues took on the champions of Europe in the next match when Barcelona travelled to London. Before facing Frank Rijkaard's team, Terry made a trip to the John Radcliffe hospital in Oxford to check up on his fallen comrade. 'We went to show our support for Petr and his family,' the skipper told the *Evening Standard*, 'but he took his oxygen mask off and talked to the lads. Petr said go back to work and go and win the game.

'The main thing is Petr's okay and he's doing a lot better. I've spoken to his wife and family and they feel the same. We know he is on the mend so we can get fully focussed on the Barcelona game.'

Matches with the Catalan giants had taken on added significance and intensity in recent years, as the two sides were drawn together in three successive seasons in Europe's premier club competition. Terry was excited ahead of the big clash. 'It's a huge game,' the defender said in the *Sunday Express*. 'It's almost like a decider after we have won one each so far. It's an important one. It's a big group and probably one of the toughest but we have got off to a winning start and that's important. I think we're ready for Barcelona.'

Shrugging off the controversy of Cech's injury and the woeful England performance in Croatia, Terry led his men to a fine 1-0 win over Barça, followed by three wins in a week as Chelsea made light of their first choice keeper's absence. But the fine form couldn't last forever, and in the return game in Barcelona, Chelsea failed to win for the first time in six games as a scrappy affair ended 2-2.

After the game Terry was full of criticism for the cynical way in which the home side approached the contest, and he was disappointed with the referee, Stefano Farina, who fell for many of the Barcelona players' antics. 'Maybe they feel a little bit threatened by us,' the Chelsea captain said of Rijkaard's side in the *Evening Standard*. 'They were under pressure from their own fans going into the game after losing at Stamford Bridge two weeks ago. They are a great side but we are not too sure why they are so cynical.

'It is a shame when you see world-class players trying to get others booked. They tried all game. They were waving cards in the referee's face and it is disappointing when he falls for it. He gave everything their way, but the lads stuck together right to the end. The result says an awful lot about us. We have played well here in the last couple of years but last night, with the referee against us and everyone against us, we were the better side.'

The Blues showed a lot of character to twice come from behind and the result left them one point away from qualification for the knock out stages, while their opponents languished in third place in Group A. The match clearly took its toll on the Chelsea players however, as they slipped to their first defeat in fourteen games when they faced Tottenham five days later.

Unbeaten against the Lilywhites in the league since February 1990, Chelsea had history on their side at White Hart Lane, but luck was against them as Terry was sent off for the first time in his career in a 2-1 loss. Graham Poll was the man in black who showed Terry red after he picked up two cautions, but there was controversy surrounding the second card as the Blues' skipper revealed after the game. 'The first foul on Dimitar Berbatov was a yellow card, no doubt,' Terry said to reporters. 'The second one still baffles me. Ledley King and I fell to the floor, we got up, we had words, but I used to play Sunday football with him and it was just the pair of us shouting at each other. I walked away, Pascal Chimbonda pushed me in the back and I carried on running.'

Terry, no doubt affected by the emotion of the moment, overstepped the mark when he alleged, 'On the pitch, Poll said the card was for the barge on Hossam Ghaly when I just kept running. After the game, he said it was for the fall with King. He has obviously had a look at it or got people to look at it and decided that is the best option which covers every angle for him. I am just really disappointed that it is my first time sent off for Chelsea.'

Terry's accusation questioning the integrity of the official later landed him – as England captain – in a potentially embarrassing situation with the FA. But the initial result of the dismissal was a one match ban which saw Chelsea without their captain for Aston Villa's visit to Stamford Bridge, in the fourth round of the Carling Cup.

The Blues made light of his absence on their way to a 4-0 win, and the dominant centre-back returned for the next match where Watford were dispatched by the same score in SW6, as Chelsea extended their unbeaten run at home to 50 matches under Mourinho.

After notching up yet another impressive milestone at club level, Terry again turned his attentions to England and a trip to Amsterdam for a friendly against the Netherlands. As captain it was the Chelsea man's responsibility to face questions on the disappointment in Zagreb. 'I understand the anger,' the imposing defender said of the fans' backlash. 'It's been really disappointing, because when I look at our squad of players we really should be going to places like Croatia and getting a good result. We have a squad which is capable of getting a result anywhere. But I've seen the video of the match and there were times when we were sloppy at the back. It's pointless me saying before every match "we've got a great squad, we've got some great players" - it's time we started showing that with our results and performances.

'It's difficult to pinpoint exactly what went wrong,' he went on, but refused to blame tactics for their inadequacy. 'I think we've all agreed that the formation didn't work on the night but we have all played 3-5-2 for our clubs and nine times out of ten, if not every time, Chelsea have won when we have done it. We've all played that system at club level, so it's no excuse.'

The Three Lions put in a much-improved performance

against the Dutch in a 1–1 draw, only robbed of victory by Rafael van der Vaart's late strike at the Amsterdam Arena. But Chelsea still weren't back to their formidable best as they followed a workmanlike 1–0 win over West Ham by losing 1–0 to Werder Bremen.

The loss in Germany wasn't a complete disaster however, as it secured Chelsea's progress to the knock-out stages of the Champions League courtesy of their head-to-head results against Bremen. After the game Terry insisted that it was a game they had been focussed on, saying: 'We wanted to win and are disappointed we played so well and got nothing from the game. If we were happy to lose we would have sent our reserves.'

It was hardly the ideal preparation for The Blues' next match, as they travelled to Old Trafford to face their only real opposition for the Premiership title, but the captain declared the defeat in Germany would only spur them on. 'We always react well to defeats,' said Terry to reporters. 'We showed that when we lost at Tottenham and it seems miles away now. We bounced back and got ourselves on a run and we need to do that again. If we beat Manchester United and get on a run it could be a good few months for us coming up.'

Chelsea lay in second place, three points behind Manchester United, and Terry refused to underestimate the importance of the game. 'This is the biggest challenge we've faced since we became champions,' the England captain told the *Sunday Mirror*. 'We've shown over the last two years that we are a very good side. We have demonstrated that consistently, week in, week out. But Manchester United have put down the marker this season and they undoubtedly have the edge over us going into this game. I can assure you it's not nice looking at the table at the moment. I'm used to seeing Chelsea top, and there we are lying second to United.

'All credit to them, they are up for the challenge. This time last year we were around thirteen points in front of them but this season they have not let us pull away early on and they are the ones we're chasing. We're playing catch up and the only way we're going to do that is to beat them today. And believe me we are fired up and raring to go.' But on the day there was little to choose between the two teams as the match ended with honours even, 1-1.

Just as the Blues seemed to be recovering some of their Premiership winning form of previous seasons, they were dealt a heavy blow as Terry was ruled out for nearly two months, missing 13 games as Chelsea fell further behind Manchester United at the top of the table. Already without Cech, who had been in such fine form since joining the Blues, Mourinho's defence was further weakened when the England captain was sidelined with a back injury which needed an operation.

After the draw at Old Trafford, Terry helped Chelsea keep a clean sheet to win 1-0 in a tricky trip to Bolton's Reebok Stadium, and although he was missing as a 2-0 win over Levski Sofia guaranteed top spot in Group A of the Champions League, he returned for a 1-1 draw with Arsenal and a win over Newcastle at Stamford Bridge to keep the pressure on Alex Ferguson's team.

It was after the victory over the Magpies that Terry's problem came to light; his absence was felt immediately as Chelsea's previously miserly defence began to haemorrhage goals. Everton were beaten 3-2, and although Mourinho's team beat Newcastle 1-0 in the League Cup, they conceded six goals in the next three games, overcoming Wigan 3-2 before drawing successive home games 2-2 against Reading and Fulham.

Having conceded only eight goals in 16 league matches with Terry, the Blues had conceded the same number in four Premiership games without their talismanic leader, dropping four vital points in the process. The defence was struggling having lost Robert Huth and William Gallas in the summer, whilst Khalid Boulahrouz had fallen out of favour with Mourinho, leaving Ricardo Carvalho as the only fit and dependable centre-half in the expensively assembled squad.

The outlook was bleak, with some experts predicting the England defender could be out for three months after surgery in France to remove a 'sequestrated lumbar intervertebral disc', which in layman's terms equates to a slipped disc. But being the man that he is, Terry returned to Premiership action within five weeks of his operation.

'I can't believe how well I feel,' the centre back told the *Sunday Mirror* three days after the surgery. 'I had the operation on Thursday and the surgeon had me running down his corridor within hours.

'It was a last resort, I had tried everything else. I was struggling. I don't know how it happened but I could not sleep for weeks. I have really been uncomfortable. Basically part of a disc in my back had become dislodged and it was pressing on a nerve and making it impossible for me to play, kick… do anything. In the end something had to happen.'

Whilst the skipper was out he changed his plea in the case surrounding the quotes he made about Graham Poll, admitting improper conduct so he could put the business behind him and continue his rehabilitation without distraction. Chelsea recovered before their skipper however, putting together a run of three successive wins without conceding a goal just in time for Terry's return – but the damage had already been done.

Of the thirteen matches the Blues played without their captain they won eight, drew four and lost one. With four of those matches, three wins and a draw, coming in the domestic cups, Chelsea were through to the final of the League Cup, and the fourth round of the FA Cup, but they had picked up just 18 from a possible 27 points in the Premiership, leaving them six points behind Manchester United, and in danger of relinquishing the title they had fought so hard for in the previous two seasons.

Fortunately it was just the start of February when Terry finally returned, coming on for the last five minutes against Charlton Athletic, and there was still time to close the gap.

The defender said before the game at The Valley: 'We've got to make up six points on Manchester United in thirteen games. What that means is we've just got to go on winning because we can't afford to lose points. If we do go on winning games, they can't afford to lose points. The race is on.'

With Terry and Cech reunited on the pitch for the first time since October, the Blues continued their winning ways, beating the Addicks 1-0, before the defender was forced to miss his first England match since taking the armband for his country. Having only played five minutes of competitive football in the last eight weeks Terry wasn't up to the rigours of international football and Steven Gerrard stepped up as captain for the friendly at Old Trafford, where Andres Iniesta's second half strike secured a 1-0 win for Spain and England were booed off by disgruntled fans at the final whistle.

The Chelsea fans were happy their recently returned captain wasn't involved in the friendly as he approached full fitness, but he was finally ready for ninety minutes the following Saturday as Middlesbrough made the trip to West London. Gareth Southgate's team were no match for a Blues' side approaching full strength and were despatched 3-0. Norwich City offered even less resistance in the FA Cup, losing 4-0, and it looked like Mourinho's team were hitting form at just the right time as they entertained his old club Porto in the knockout stage of the Champions League.

A 1-1 draw in Portugal wasn't too bad a result as the away goal gave Chelsea the advantage heading into the home leg, but the bad news came as Terry ruptured an ankle ligament, was substituted and left the stadium on crutches. With the League Cup final only four days away nobody gave him a hope of facing Arsenal at the Millennium Stadium, but once again the imposing centre back surprised medical opinion and delighted his fans with a swift return to the pitch.

Having made a second remarkable return to fitness, Terry would have hoped his injury problems were behind him, but diving for a header on the Cardiff pitch he was knocked out by Abou Diaby's right foot as Arsenal's French midfielder attempted to clear a corner. The blow left the defensive colossus out cold, and with some memory loss. 'I remember walking out for the second half and nothing else until waking up in the ambulance on the way to the hospital,' said the skipper. 'I had the scan and they said it's OK. It was great to be back with the team, they were different class.' Terry's final was over and he was forced out of the next three matches, but ironically he was back playing before Diaby, who had injured his ankle in the collision.

Fortunately, the injury to the captain didn't stop the Blues adding to their trophy cabinet as two goals from Didier Drogba helped Chelsea back from a goal down to win 2-1, a great game that was sullied by a late brawl, which saw John Obi Mikel and two Arsenal players sent off. Drogba dedicated the winning strike to his team-mate. 'I pointed to my armband after the goal because that was for John,' said the Ivorian striker. 'I was scared when I saw him lying down and those are not very good images to see on the pitch. We are very happy for him now that we have won and he's OK. It's difficult to see that and I had ten minutes where I didn't find my game and my legs were shaking.'

Terry was taken to hospital for precautionary scans on his head, but once he was given the all-clear the defender was able to join in the celebrations at the Millennium Stadium and late into the night when the team got back to London. The Chelsea goalkeeper was impressed by the defender's quick return. 'It was emotional when John came into the dressing-room,' said Cech. 'And I told him, "If you have some trophy for Iron Man of the Year, you should get it." After the injury in Porto, he came back and played straightaway, he's almost indestructible.'

Almost indestructible but forced out for three games, Terry had to watch from the sidelines once again. Increasingly accustomed to playing without their captain, Mourinho's team beat Portsmouth in the league and Porto in Europe before Tottenham exploited some defensive frailty, going 3-1 up in an FA Cup tie at the Bridge, before drawing 3-3. After seeing such an inept performance at the back against their London rivals, the Chelsea fans gave Terry a hero's welcome when they travelled to Manchester for the game against City.

Sitting nine points behind Manchester United, Chelsea were under immense pressure, but with Terry returned to the heart of the defence there was a renewed confidence that the Premiership title, and possibly even the Champions League and FA Cup, could still be added to the League Cup in the Blues' trophy cabinet. 'The belief is there that we can win all four,' Terry said to the press after a 1-0 victory. 'The most important thing was to get that gap from Manchester United back to six points. We're taking each game as it comes and there are so many matches coming up in the next month. We're not thinking about the Champions League in a month's time or the FA Cup in a few weeks. For now, it's just great to be back and involved in a win.'

With Terry back in the side the wins kept coming for Chelsea. Sheffield United were brushed aside in the league and Tottenham were shown the true resolve of Mourinho's side in the FA Cup replay, as superb goals from Andriy Shevchenko and Shaun Wright-Phillips guided the Blues to a 2-1 win and a place in the semi-finals.

With games arriving thick and fast it was time again for Terry to join up with England as they tried to rescue their teetering Euro 2008 qualifying campaign. Two away games against Israel and Andorra presented the perfect opportunity to turn things around in Group E. 'There's no other option than for us to win the game,' said Terry in his pre-match press conference. 'After Croatia, we basically need to win our next four or five games. There are no excuses. Looking at the group, the position we are in is definitely not good enough. I know it's early days but it isn't good enough and all the players feel exactly the same. It is time for us as players to stand up and be counted.'

Tel Aviv is a tough place to go and the Three Lions couldn't bring away three points as they laboured to a 0-0 draw. It meant that England had scored just one goal in their last five winless games, representing their worst run of form in front of goal since the spring of 1981, when Ron Greenwood was still manager. Steve McClaren was suitably unimpressed with his charges and let them know what he was thinking after the game. 'The dressing room was dead after the game and the manager was right to have a rant and rave,' Terry revealed to the *Sun*. 'What happened in the dressing room stays there. That's between us and we'll talk about it more in the coming days. But it was just silence among the lads on Saturday, just a sense of frustration we hadn't won the game.

'I said leading up to the match that a draw wouldn't be good enough and with the chances we created we should have come away with all three points. Right now it's all about results. Performances don't really matter. If we don't start winning our games we're not going to qualify, it's as simple as that. But I believe we will get there and I'm sure all the lads think the same.'

Things were much easier in the next game as Terry and his compatriots took on European minnows Andorra in Barcelona, where a Steven Gerrard brace and a goal from David Nugent secured a 3-0 win. After helping his country to four valuable points Terry returned to the blue of Chelsea as they continued their own quest for silverware. The Blues had to fight right up to the death to beat Watford with Salomon Kalou's last minute winner, and having kicked off after Manchester United it meant that they closed the gap at the top back to six points. 'It was a massive result,' the skipper said in the *Daily Star*. 'They made it difficult for us and we're just pleased to pick up the three points. We're fighting right to the death. We obviously knew about Man United's result before the game and, coming here, we knew we had to win. It wasn't the prettiest of games but we got the three points.'

With eight games in 24 days in April, Terry and his team-mates had no time to rest on their laurels, and were soon back in action in the Champions League quarter-final against Valencia. A 1-1 draw at Stamford Bridge handed the advantage to the Spanish side, but after overcoming Tottenham in the league, Chelsea won 2-1 in the Mestella to secure a place in the last four, where they would once again face Liverpool.

Terry was delighted to have an opportunity to exorcise the demons from the same round two years previously. 'It's going to be interesting, us versus them again,' the centre-half said to reporters. 'It's a chance to wash those memories away. The semi-final left some hurtful memories and we're in the semi-final again and in the same situation.'

Before continuing their European adventure, Chelsea maintained their bid for domestic honours, gaining revenge for the league defeat at White Hart Lane with a 1-0 win over Tottenham and then booking a place in the FA Cup final after beating Blackburn 2-1 at Old Trafford.

The Blues made it nine consecutive Premiership wins when they beat West Ham 4-1 away, but that fine run came to an end at St James' Park where Newcastle held the champions to a 0-0 draw. Chelsea's hectic schedule continued unabated.

Terry led his side to a 1-0 win in the first leg of the Champions League semi-final at home, setting them up perfectly for the game a week later in Liverpool. 'We are confident we can take this lead to Anfield and hold it,' the skipper told the *Sunday Star*. 'But when we walked out there last time and heard the noise, I think we took it in too much and it affected us. I'm not saying we were frightened but it's an intimidating atmosphere and, of course, Liverpool rely on that. What we have to drill into everyone is that the crowd won't be playing. It's just us against Liverpool, eleven versus eleven, two teams battling to get to a European Cup final. Of course you have to deal with everything going on around you, but it's important the focus is on playing our natural game and not being distracted by anything else.'

Whether they were distracted or not is academic, but the Blues were forced to settle for a penalty shoot-out after losing 1-0 on the night. Frank Lampard was the only Chelsea player to score as Liverpool ran out 4-1 winners in the spot-kick lottery.

The disappointing European campaign had also taken its toll on Chelsea's title aspirations, as they followed up the draw against Newcastle with a 2-2 draw at home to Bolton in between the two legs of the Champions League semi-final, before a 1-1 draw away to Arsenal handed the title to Manchester United. In their next game the Red Devils headed to Stamford Bridge as champions.

In a reversal that was hard to bear for all Blues, Chelsea were to give Manchester United a guard of honour, similar to that which they had received in the northwest twelve months previously. 'They did it for us and showed us respect up at Old Trafford last season,' Terry told the *Daily Star*. 'Looking at some faces, it could not have been nice. We have to go through that and we fully respect them as players, and individuals. We'll do that holding our heads up high.

'No-one can take anything away from Man United. They have been awesome and some of their players have been fantastic this year. We pushed them as far as we can push them, despite injuries or whatever. We did not go away this year, we pushed them really hard and they did not really manage to do that in the past couple of years when we won it with a few games to spare. We take pride in pushing them this far with what has gone on.'

The injuries that decimated the title winning team from the two previous seasons were to blame for the title slipping away, but ever the gentleman Terry brushed over them. It is arguable, however, that without Cech's horrific head injury, Joe Cole missing five months of the season and Terry's own problems, Manchester United would not have won the title with two games to spare.

Having relinquished their title, the Blues were in no mood to surrender their two-year unbeaten run at home and held Manchester United to a 0-0 draw. The much-anticipated match between the league's top two no longer had anything resting on the result, and both sides seemed content to save themselves for their next meeting ten days later at the newly refurbished Wembley Stadium.

Terry was distraught at losing the Premiership and was determined to inflict some retribution on the Red Devils in the FA Cup final. 'It's the last game of the season and if we can win the FA Cup then we can go off and enjoy the summer while Man United would maybe have the kind of feeling that we had after losing the Premiership,' the skipper told the *Sunday Telegraph*. 'It would mean them having to wait until next season to get that winning feeling back again.'

The England captain was all too aware of the ability in the opposing ranks, as he would be lining up against one of his closest friends from international duty, the prodigiously gifted Wayne Rooney. But a cup final is no place for small talk, as Terry told the *Mirror*. 'If I do see Wazza there might be a quick hello in the tunnel but that will be about it. The time for joking is over. Normally we might be in touch but all the texts and stuff quieten down before a game like this because of the professionalism. It's the same for them, as Rio Ferdinand has said about not getting in touch with Lamps and that's how we treat it.'

The 2007 FA Cup final was special for many people, being the first at Wembley since 2000, but for Terry it was his first time in the starting eleven for the prestigious event. Having been involved on two previous occasions, in 2000 and 2002, it was of added significance to the defender as he led his side out and then – after nearly two hours of a finely poised match – lifted the oldest cup in the football.

The form of Didier Drogba throughout the campaign maintained Chelsea's challenge on four fronts, even when some of the biggest players were missing, and it was apt that he should score the winner in the FA Cup final, slotting past Edwin van der Sar after a delightful one-two with Frank Lampard four minutes from the end of extra time. It was the Ivorian striker's 33rd goal of an incredible season, and meant that the Blues picked up the last piece of domestic silverware.

'This makes up for it,' Terry said, referring to the loss of the title. 'It's not nice losing but it's nice coming here to Wembley and winning. It's absolutely unbelievable. It's one of the best feelings I have ever experienced. The way we hung right on to the death; the way Didier took his goal; it was first class. Both teams were tired, both gave the ball away and made mistakes. But we kept going – and it paid off.'

So Chelsea finished the season with an FA Cup and

League Cup double, to go with the more impressive trophy hauls of previous seasons, and stood second in the final Premiership table, with an impressive 83 points, but still six points behind the champions. It had been a difficult year for Terry as he suffered with injuries and ill-fortune, but he still had international commitments as he led England out for their first game at the new Wembley.

The defender made history once again as he scored his country's first goal at the incredible new stadium, when McClaren's team drew 1-1 with Brazil. 'To walk out with the armband on such a special occasion in front of my family and friends was enough,' Terry told the press. 'To score the first England goal at the stadium was the ultimate dream.' The friendly with the *Seleção* was followed by a 3-0 win against Estonia in Tallinn, as England consolidated their position in Group E of their European Championships qualifying campaign.

The three points left McClaren's side in fourth place, but only three points off top spot; qualification was back in their own hands, allowing them the possibility of relaxing before the start of the next campaign. 'It makes a big difference to end the season with a win and that makes for a good summer,' the England captain told the *Sun*. 'The lads are feeling really high now. We go away and have a well-deserved break. It's been a tough year mentally and physically for us all. It is important we come back and start well and you can find the energy from somewhere for another game like Estonia. But to be honest I am looking forward to having a complete rest to the muscles and the legs. That's what I need and that's what I intend to do.'

The summer didn't provide a complete rest to the Chelsea hero however, as he finally married his long-term girlfriend Toni on Friday 15 June 2007, in a lavish ceremony at one of the country's finest stately homes, Blenheim Palace in Oxfordshire. Lionel Ritchie performed for the couple and their guests, and their two-week honeymoon was believed to be a Mediterranean cruise on Roman Abramovich's luxury yacht, a £72m floating palace.

Terry was also busy with his agent over the summer as he negotiated a new deal, allegedly worth £135k-a-week, making him the highest paid player in the history of English football. The five-year deal was worth more than £7m-a-year and had taken months to sort out, but everyone connected with Chelsea was delighted to get it signed. 'I'm really happy this has now been concluded,' said Terry to the press. 'There has been a lot of speculation but these things take time and I never had any doubts that I wanted to stay at Chelsea and that the club wanted me to stay. I hope that the fans can see that we are all trying to build something special here, both for now and for the future, and I want to be a part of that. I have been at Chelsea all my career and have the privilege of being captain. Now it's time to look forward to the new season, which we are all very confident about.'

As the new season loomed large, the most important

thing in Terry's eyes was to win back the title, snatched away by Manchester United. 'Just talking about it makes the blood boil,' Chelsea's Captain Marvel said. 'That makes me more determined to come back and get the trophy we feel is ours.'

You wouldn't bet against him.